# Praise for *Belonging*

MW00561209

"Bushong astutely builds on the existing TCK literature to weave together a foundational work for mental health therapists who seek to thoughtfully engage individuals from a globally mobile population that is growing in size and scope. Her primer considers key questions and common underlying reasons many TCKs seek therapy, makes practical recommendations for therapists, and invites practitioners to more deeply cultivate the imaginative space that is so crucial in our work."

Josh Sandoz, MA
Licensed Mental Health Counselor
Founder, International Therapist Directory
http://internationaltherapistdirectory.com

"Lois grew up as a TCK and is a TCK therapist whose authentic voice arrests our attention to unique TCK characteristics that, if overlooked, lead to misdiagnosis. Drawing on a wealth of personal and professional experience, she expands our knowledge and increases our skills out of a commitment to best practice. This is a must-read for mental health professionals and anyone who cares for TCKs."

Duncan P. Westwood, Ph.D.
Clinical Director of Expatriate Care and Development
International Health Management
Toronto, Canada

"Finally, we have a book that explains, in clear and professional terms, how counselors can recognize and address the emotional needs of the globally mobile. Lois Bushong's authority and experience with Third Culture Kids shine through on every page. You will never do your intake interviews the same way again, and next time you discover you are sitting with a TCK, you will both be grateful for this treasure of a book."

Anne P. Copeland, Ph.D.
Clinical Psychologist
Executive Director, The Interchange Institute

"At long last, the book that has been missing from the global mobility shelf is here. Bound to be a bestseller. Bushong has produced the only resource of its kind—one that counselors, therapists, and expats alike can embrace on their way to understanding the issues of the globally mobile."

Tina L. Quick
Author, *The Global Nomad's Guide to University Transition*
Founder, International Family Transitions, www.internationalfamilytransitions.com

"Lois captures the essence of how to work with clients that have lost their sense of identity from moving around frequently and the feelings that accompany it. She uses helpful examples, informative theories, and powerful techniques to work with this population. There is no other book on the market like it. She captured the key concepts of working with global nomads."

Kristen Boice, LMFT
Pathway to Healing Counseling & Education
Noblesville, Indiana

"The first of its kind! Lois Bushong's book comprehensively delineates the essential building blocks for counseling Third Culture Kids and offers an opportunity for therapist self-awareness, knowledge of the unique TCK community/culture, and understanding of contextually relevant therapeutic interventions. It is indispensable reading for anyone who works with TCKs!"

Dr. Paulette M. Bethel
President of Land On Your Feet, LLC
Licensed Marriage & Family Therapist
TCA and mother of four military TCKs

"One of the best 'all-around' insights into counseling Third Culture Kids (TCKs) and Adult Third Culture Kids (ATCKs). It's worthwhile for anyone interested in understanding the challenges of global nomads (parents, TCKs, teachers) and a must-have step-by-step guide for counselors who are beginning to work with TCKs and ATCKs. Bushong shows you how to identify TCKs, listen for key insights into clients experiences to enable effective counseling, and make an accurate DSM diagnosis."

Dr. Donna Mischell Navarro
Psychologist, United States Air Force
Washington DC

"What a delight to finally to find a book that describes the world and experience of TCKs and how those experiences contribute to the struggles and challenges they face and which they bring to my counseling office!! As a TCK and psychotherapist myself, the insights and helps offered by Lois Bushong in her book, *Belonging Everywhere and Nowhere* have confirmed much what I have learned about myself as well as offering additional tools to help other MKs. In our increasingly multi-cultural world I would recommend this book to any professional counselor, TCK or not, as a much-needed, practical and helpful resource which should belong in every clinician's library."

David L. Wickstrom, Ph.D.
Clinical Psychologist and Missions Consultant
Columbia, South Carolina

"I am so excited about the potential benefit of *Belonging Everywhere and Nowhere* for therapists of global nomads and families worldwide! Lois' style is so practical, personable, and authoritative all at once, demonstrating how professionals can expand their skills to recognize and address the invisible and ambiguous losses that fuel the nuanced and hidden angst tied to identity and belonging in a globalizing world. This book and the practical wisdom it elaborates will help the international community—and its various sectors—more compassionately and competently care for those who struggle with the developmental challenges of a cross-cultural and/or internationally mobile upbringing. Thank you, Lois!"

Dr. Michèle Lewis O'Donnell
Consulting Psychologist
Member Care Associates, Inc.
Geneva, Switzerland

"This new book by Lois is fantastic. I am seeing more and more TCKs in my practice and this will be a beneficial resource full of practical and applicable information. This is a great book, filling a gap in therapeutic resources."

Felicia Snell, LMFT-A
Sunstone Counseling Center
Greenwood, Indiana

"Lois brings an acute cultural sensitivity to light in this book, as well as practical ways for therapists to discern and honor cultural mobility as a potential clinical issue. I appreciate her case studies, guidelines, and overall generosity and wisdom in sharing her unique perspective. I work in a culturally diverse area, and this book fills a gap for me in knowing how to explore clients' experiences."

Beth Spring
Licensed Marriage and Family Therapist
Herndon, Virginia

# Belonging

# EVERYWHERE

# & NOWHERE:

## Insights into Counseling

## the Globally Mobile

By

### Lois J. Bushong, M.S.

### Licensed Marriage & Family Therapist

MANGO TREE INTERCULTURAL SERVICES

First edition Sept./Oct. 2013

Published by Mango Tree Intercultural Services
Indianapolis, Indiana, U.S.A.

Cover Designed by Chuck Jarrell

Graphics by Chuck Jarrell and Barbara Knuckles

Edited by Sally Rushmore

Photography by Elizabeth Ewer

The term Third Culture Kid (TCK) is used throughout the book; however, the information in this book can be adapted for use with TCKs of all types and ages, including Adult Third Culture Kids (ATCKs), Cross-Cultural Kids (CCKs), and Third Culture Adults (TCAs).

Web addresses change frequently, so accuracy cannot be guaranteed.

ISBN   978-0-615-69606-5

Ebook ISBN   987-0-615-86689-5

Printed by CreateSpace, an Amazon.com company

# Dedication

To my parents, Burnis and Thelma Bushong,

and the wonderful legacy they gave me of growing up as a third culture kid.

And to my younger brothers, David and Bob,

who shared the journey with me.

I would not exchange my heritage for anyone else's.

# Table of Contents

# Foreword

Ruth E. Van Reken
Co-author, *Third Culture Kids: Growing Up Among Worlds*
Co-founder, Families in Global Transition

When Lois asked me to write this foreword, I was thrilled. Over the years I have seen how important it is that a therapist working with globally mobile clients understands their story. What are the often hidden realities of this lifestyle that might have brought them in to see you? How might you need to think the same or differently about them than clients who have essentially lived in one place their entire lives? This book will help you in that process.

Why do I believe therapists need to understand the story of globally mobile people? To begin with, therapists who understand the issues and thinking of the globally mobile can differentiate between seemingly unusual behavior or feelings which are actually "normal" given this person's experience and behavior or feelings that indicate a need for therapeutic intervention. Also, as the therapist knows what beginning questions are most helpful to ask a client with a global background, it can move the therapeutic process along more efficiently.

For almost thirty years, I have spoken and written about issues relating to those who, like me, have grown up in more than one country and among many different cultural worlds. Sociologists call us *third culture kids* or TCKs. This is a profoundly rich and meaningful childhood for most of us. We have seen the world, we have friends from many different cultures and nations, and some of us may speak several languages learned during our global childhoods.

At the same time, the very richness of our lives adds particular challenges. The high mobility that takes us or our friends from one interesting place to the next also means we have frequent cycles of separation and loss. Each transition involves leaving people and places we love even though we gain much from the new place to which we go. The cross-cultural nature of our interactions can make it more challenging to decide by which set of cultural values or norms we will live. Or, as the title of this book says, how do we decide where we belong when the truth is we often feel like we belong in many places?

After so many years of interacting with those who have grown up or lived among many cultural worlds, I am convinced that the global experience *per se* isn't the main challenge. Most TCKs are very comfortable living in a world where they interact with different cultural worlds on not only a daily basis, but sometimes even hourly, basis. Such a life for most TCKs is fun. It is rich. It is just the way life is.

The challenges for TCKs often happen when those in their "home" culture expect these global sojourners to fit into traditional ways of defining belonging and identity. But most of these expectations of who a person "should' be developed in the days when most people in the world grew up in a basically mono-cultural environment. How do we define the same matters in today's fast changing world? How does a therapist avoid being caught in the old models as well?

The truth is that often as globally mobile people encounter ever-changing relationships and cultural patterns inherent to their very lifestyle, they often begin to realize there is no place where they quite "fit" in the way others would traditionally define them. At that point, they often begin to wonder, "What's wrong with me? Why can't I settle down? How do I figure out who I am from the many options it seems I have had?" This is often the point when a person seeks out professional help.

And that is why I am so glad Lois' book is here.

You see, this book isn't about teaching anyone how to do therapy, *per se*. You already know the different methods you like to use for different clients. But it teaches you what you need to know about these global wanderers—not only *what* some common presenting symptoms are, but *why* they are. In addition, you'll learn some of the techniques Lois has found to be helpful in working in this arena. As you learn the story of the TCK experience, you will also see how some of the principles there relate to people of *all* backgrounds in today's globalizing world.

So how do I know what Lois is saying works?

Because I have seen Lois be an amazingly effective therapist to so many globally mobile clients she has served. I have seen what happens when these people begin to realize that instead of belonging everywhere and nowhere as they have felt for so long, they finally feel they belong somewhere—with others of shared experience. As they find new ways of naming themselves and putting together the pieces of this puzzle they have called "life," the skills they have also developed are free to be used in much broader circles.

Thank you for taking the time to read this book. I know it has the potential to not only change the scope of your counseling practice, but to impact countless lives of globally mobile folks for the good. Thanks. What you do matters. A lot.

# Acknowledgements

This book would not have become a reality if it were not for several very key individuals. First of all, I want to thank Ruth Van Reken, a more seasoned author, for the countless hours she spent helping me put all of the pieces of this puzzle together in a format that makes sense to the reader. Words cannot express the depth of appreciation I have for Ruth and her encouragement as I stretched my skills into the unknown world of writing down what I do so automatically.

Second, I must thank my editor, Sally Rushmore, for her wonderful talent to take all my words, rambling stories, and strange sentence structures, and gently cut what needed cutting and put it all together into a fantastic book. Without Sally there would not have been a book. She came through with her promise to help me, the rookie writer, in this complex, long, hard project of producing a book—and making me look good.

Thank you to Chuck Jarrell for his skills at taking a concept and turning it into an attractive cover. He nailed it—clear down to the Honduran flag on the old suitcase. Chuck and Sally, you two make an awesome team.

Thanks to my niece, Elizabeth Ewer, for her help with the photography. Even though her dad, Bob, and her Uncle Dave are employed as photographers, she was the one who came through with the results. At least, with the advent of the digital camera I don't have to worry about film in her camera!

And thank you to Pam Davis and Keith Edwards for their excellent contribution of an appendix on doing Emotionally Focused Therapy for the globally mobile. I appreciate their many years of experience in working with this community as well as their professional training that have contributed to their expertise in this area.

There are so many others who have been in the background and whose names are not mentioned in my book, but they are there in the blank spaces between the rows of sentences. I want to thank those who helped me in my own journey as an adult TCK. I want to thank David Aycock, Annette Murray, and Dee Goar who cheered me on to leverage my skills to become a counselor and use what I already knew to help others. They have been my quiet mentors.

I need to thank Tina Quick, Robin Pascoe, and my supervisees (Rebecca Hager, Elizabeth White, Felicia Snell, and Kristen Boice) who were my cheerleaders through the course of this project. They celebrated with me each step of the way. I must thank my reviewers Dr. Anne Copeland, Dr. Duncan Westwood, Josh Sandoz, and Dr. Paulette Bethel. Even though they each have their own careers, they took the time to review my manuscript and add their good suggestions to the project. I want to thank all my current and past graduate counseling students at Indiana Wesleyan University. This book is for you. Now, after graduation when you have all of that free time you are sure is just around the corner, you can read in a book everything I told you!

I want to thank my parents Dr. and Mrs. Burnis Bushong for giving me a wonderful heritage, a solid foundation, an exciting life filled with great experiences in Latin America and across the United States. They gave me many fantastic opportunities to reach my full potential. I want to thank my brothers, David and Bob Bushong, for living the journey with me. We shared many practical jokes, pranks, laughter, and hikes, and spent many hours creating our own entertainment as TCKs. Together we learned how to use the media to produce a story.

I want to thank my nieces (Elizabeth Ewer and Rebecca Swartz) and nephews (Scott and Todd Bushong) who have always been "my kids" and been there for me. Even though Scott is the only one who is a true TCK, all of you share many characteristics of the TCK since you were raised in the Bushong tribe.

And in conclusion, I want to thank my God for gifting me unexpected blessings in my journey and unconditional love as I travel this world as an adult Third Culture Kid. "Mil gracias."

# Preface

## Why do we need a book on counseling the globally mobile?

All over the world, adults and children are living out a social experiment never conducted to this degree in the history of the world. No generation before now has had so many of its members simultaneously living in, between, and among countless cultural worlds as is happening today. A large number of people, including entire families, now move among countries and continents with great regularity. How can anyone keep up with the impact such cultural interactions and patterns of mobility have on those who are in the midst of living them out? What does such a lifestyle do to the developmental process of children when the rules of the surrounding world keep changing with every airplane ride and they face a relentless barrage of goodbyes?

We are only beginning to find out. In this book, you will look primarily through the prism of what this experience does to the children sociologists have named third culture kids (TCKs)—those who grow up outside their parents' culture for at least some period of their first eighteen years. I do that for a simple reason: This was my childhood experience and many of my clients have grown up in that milieu. But the principles I use for working with them as a therapist apply in large measure to globally mobile people of all backgrounds and ages. Rather than cloud the landscape with too many "for instances," I will leave you to make the broader applications.

## Why did I write "Belonging Everywhere and Nowhere"?

In reviewing the literature on counseling TCKs—those children who grow up outside of their parents' culture, usually because of a parent's career—I found a number of books on the characteristics of the TCKs and a growing wealth of books on research done on TCKs, but I was unable to find any book on how to work with TCKs in professional counseling. The number of TCKs, and other types of cross-cultural childhoods in our world, is growing rapidly as I discuss in Chapter 1 of this book. When you put this rapid growth together with the many TCK clients I have seen over the years, the young counselors whom I supervise and have trained in recognizing and working with TCKs, and young graduate counseling students wanting to work with TCKs who contact me, I keep having the same conversation over and over again. Thus, I decided to write what I know and what I do in my office and share it with you, the professional counselor.

## Why do I counsel globally mobile people?

Why do I have a passion for working with TCKs and other globally mobile people? Because I understand what it is like to grow up in a globally mobile world. I know what it is like to live and work overseas as an adult. I have seen that it matters to recognize an often-invisible world my clients have lived in, and affirm what they know and have seen and learned when they are sitting in front of me, trying to understand their own story.

But three stories in particular moved me to make a career change at the age of 40 to become a counselor who specializes in the needs I have seen in this community.

The first event that profoundly affected me was watching a young girl, about the age of 13 (the same age I was when I returned to the U.S.), struggle with adjusting to a group of peers at a conference. I cannot erase from my memory the scene of her sitting on a step in a puddle of tears trying to convince her mother that it was okay for her to stay with her rather than join a group of girls in their activities. I listened to her mother, also in tears, try to understand what was going on with her daughter, as she tried to reason with her, "But I thought you would love to finally play with a group of girls your age and get to know them." Her daughter, who had lived for most of her years not far from the area where I had grown up, could only picture rejection since she did not know how to relate to this strange world called "home."

The second event was my observation of a group of about 15 international workers who had been evacuated from Burundi due to the tribal warfare that took place in this small African country. Most of the group had spent their entire careers in Africa and now they had to quickly walk away from the place they and their families had called home. As I watched the small, bewildered group grapple with their strong feelings of confusion, grief, and shock, the question that whirled over and over in my mind was, "How can we help them in dealing with the grief of the loss of their homes and lives?" That scene continues to play in my mind whenever I do a debriefing with those who have spent most of their adult lives working outside of their home country and find when they try to repatriate back to a country that no longer feels like home.

The third event was not something I observed, but something I heard during the time I was contemplating a career change. I remember exactly where I was when I heard the news: I was sitting at my desk writing a story on life overseas for children when someone came and told me that a young college student who was a TCK had committed suicide in his dorm room. I knew the family and the organization with which they worked. I had friends in that agency. I knew the college well as I have had family members graduate from that institution. I did not personally know the young man. Like so many, I asked "why?" I still do not know why he took his own life. I often wondered if this young man had a therapist working with him—a therapist who understood the challenges of working with a TCK. I wondered if he felt he was the only one going through this period of adjustment to life in college in a strange culture and on a strange campus. His story compelled me to make a new career choice. I wanted to make a difference in others' lives before they got to this point.

**What is my dream for this book?**

My dream is that you, the therapist, read this book and have an "aha!" moment as you begin to understand some of your clients better.

My dream also includes seeing this as a reference book in every university's Graduate Counseling Department. It would fit nicely into a curriculum on Intercultural Counseling. I suggest that it be used in conjunction with the book *Third Culture Kids: Growing Up Among Worlds* by David C. Pollock and Ruth Van Reken. The books fit together since *Third Culture Kids* describes the characteristics of the TCK and this book talks about how to work with them in counseling. I know students need to understand the foundational concepts, as described by Pollock and Van Reken, in order to better understand how to recognize what is normal or not normal, what is pathology and is not pathology, and then learn how to work with TCKs in ways that help them feel the counselor understands their world, putting them at ease to explore the impacts of their global lifestyle on their current world.

## How will you best use this book?

I have set up the outline in a logical pattern that begins by helping you recognize TCKs when they come into your office, then teaches you how to get to know them—what might be some of the most common reasons they present for therapy, which of the possible diagnoses are acceptable to insurance providers, and how to work with them in some of the more common presenting problems—and then concludes with the termination process at the conclusion of your work with the TCK client. After each chapter, you will find a set of discussion questions or activities that can be used for further class discussion and reflection.

There is a *Resources* section at the back with information on further resources (books, websites, movies, and organizations) that also can be used in the classroom to enhance the learning experience or in the counselor's office with a client. The appendices also include a handout that can be used with clients who have been wounded by a broken system (family, school, or vocational) and feel trapped in trying to untangle themselves from the influences of the broken system and move forward with their life. Many TCKs have rooted their identity in a system, since they live so globally, and when that relationship goes wrong, the impact is much deeper and broader than that of the individual who has his roots in a place rather than a system.

At the end of each chapter you will find a short summary of the most important points covered in that chapter ("What You Should Now Know"). If you are using this book as a textbook for your graduate counseling class, the "Discussion Questions & Activities" at the end of each chapter can be used with your students.

Even though the book is written with counselors in mind, I know that TCKs and parents of TCKs will also pick it up and read it in hopes of learning something new about themselves or their loved ones. The book is written in a simple format and layman's language so that they will be able to understand most of it without a degree in higher education. And hopefully, it will bring some meaning to why they do what they do. I want you to see that you or your loved one is not abnormal, but in many beautiful ways that person is very normal and right in step with our shrinking world.

## What about the stories in this book?

All of the stories told in this book are either fictional or composites based on the many stories I have heard through the years. All the names, locations and details of the story have been changed hide the identity of the person. Any resemblance between these fictional characters and actual persons is coincidental.

I am a visual and aural learner, so stories give meaning to concepts for me. They help me visualize exactly what the writer is trying to communicate to me. I use a lot of stories and metaphors in my counseling, so it is natural to sprinkle stories all through my writings. I get caught up in the feelings of the big picture rather than the exact meanings of the small individual words. I write like I talk or present in workshops.

## Who are the globally mobile in this book?

When I use the term "globally mobile" in my subtitle, I am referring to Third Culture Kids (TCKs) of all ages including Adult Third Culture Kids (ATCKs), some other types of Cross-Cultural Kids (CCKs), Third Culture Adults (TCAs—those who make their first cross-cultural move as adults, not as children), and International Students. Even though I use the term "Third Culture Kid" (TCK) throughout the book, it can be adapted for use with TCKs of all ages, Cross-Cultural Kids, and Third Culture Adults. That is, it can be used in counseling with anyone who has spent much of their life living outside of their "home" culture. I did not want to continually have a string of letters (TCK, ATCK, CCK, TCA) throughout the book, so in order to simplify my writing I used TCK to refer to all categories of the globally mobile. I know that good therapists can skillfully adapt the contents of the book to the particular client they have in their office.

Above all else, I want you to hear me say that I feel so very fortunate to be an adult TCK. Whenever our family returned to our *passport country*, the United States, we kids filled up on junk food, spent hours in front of the television, and met all of the relatives, but when we got our new bikes to take back with us, we were ready to return *home* again to Latin America. We loved our life— living globally mobile.


Lois Bushong

# Chapter 1

# Considering Patterns of Global Mobility

# among Clients is Important

*"It is my fate to wander from place to place, and to adapt to new soils.*
*I believe I will be able to do that because handfuls of Chilean soil are caught in my roots;*
*I carry them with me always."*

Isabel Allende, TCK from Chile whose father was a diplomat
(Allende, 2003, p. 30)

## Sandra's Depression[1]

When I first met Sandra, I felt as if I already knew her. Her story sounded so familiar. I had heard various versions of it from young adults coming from around the world, either as they passed through Indiana or as long-term expatriots who were trying to plant their roots in this their "home" country. Sandra's story bore several similarities to my own. It may even sound like your story.

Sandra sat in the hotel coffee shop and her story began to slowly spill out with a tear sneaking down her cheek every so often. She was feeling despair in her search for a counselor who understood her. Were her problems just too complex for hope? She spoke in emotionally flat, quiet words. I sensed that she was giving in to her isolation and depression as she was telling me of her past counseling experiences.

"I was in college and getting along just fine, until slowly I began to experience problems getting out of bed, going to my classes, and doing my homework. After a couple of months of feeling this way, I realized I might be depressed and made the decision to see one of our counselors on campus. I remember

---

[1] All stories in the book represent common themes I hear from clients, but names and details are fictionalized in each situation.

1

going to the first counselor. Well, actually, I ended up seeing two different counselors, but I did not click with any of them.

"The first counselor went through a Depression Inventory with me. After we completed the Depression Inventory, she put down her pad and said, 'You are depressed.'

"'Well, yes,' I thought to myself, 'I could have told you that. Actually, I think I did tell you that. I need to know *how to deal with my depression.*'"

Sandra paused a moment and swallowed hard before she continued, "After a few more sessions, I left, since I was not getting any help dealing with my depression.

"I decided to go to a more experienced counselor, since the first one was so young. I chose a male counselor in his late 40s. He was unable to help me too. I still felt I did not learn any coping skills. Part of it was that the counselors did not know or understand what was going on with me."

## Don's Restlessness

Don had driven to my office from three states away. He and his wife of twenty years had moved from city to city throughout their marriage due to his repeated job changes—at least five times in the last 20 years. He finally landed in a job he loved. With this new job he got to travel regularly across the United States. This helped him with his feelings of being stuck in the same city year after year.

He lived a simple life and reacted in anger and frustration whenever he saw organizations, especially not-for-profits, use a large portion of their funds on their buildings and their leaders' lifestyles, rather than on the less fortunate they were set up to help. He was restless and felt as if even his wife did not understand his desire to travel and his irritation regarding many large organizations.

He had fallen into a deep depression and was stuck in a conflict with his wife regarding his values. When he began to work with me, he was contemplating whether to file for a divorce from his wife, whom he still loved, or continue to live in his world of depression and feeling misunderstood.

In one of our first sessions, he shared with me just one example of his restlessness and inner turmoil.

> "My wife and I cannot agree on a home church. We will try one for a few months and ultimately I just don't seem to fit in with the people. My wife can get along with anyone and she loves the church and hates it when, in time, I say we need to move on. This last time she told me this was it. She wasn't church hopping anymore. I'm afraid to tell her that I don't agree with how this new church is spending their money. They seem so materialistic and it feels very wrong."

## Lois' Lostness

As I heard Sandra's and Don's stories, and countless others, I wondered about my own. This could easily have been a therapist's write-up of me if I had gone to see a counselor during my young adult years.

> Lois, a 30-year-old white female, employed by an international agency, arrived in my office with feelings of general anxiety and depression. While she receives positive job reviews, she feels as if she can never fit in with her peers or completely agree with the policies of her agency. Outwardly, Lois is outgoing and others see her as a very creative, friendly hard worker. To her, however, this job seems meaningless. On her Intake Form, Lois claims she has had no particular trauma in her past, that her family was strong; she had a happy childhood and did very well in graduate school. But this nagging sense of not belonging quite anywhere doesn't leave her. When others are not around, her sense of quiet depression intensifies and she wonders what is wrong with her when her life seems so perfect in many other ways.

## The Rest of the Story

What are the common threads of these three stories? And what did the therapist miss in the cases of those who tried to find help? Why couldn't these therapists help Sandra, Don, and presumably me? Let's look at the rest of each person's story and then sort out some common threads that tell a much bigger story.

## Sandra's Childhood

Sandra's father worked for a major manufacturing company based in the United States. She had been born in the Midwest. Just when Sandra was about to start first grade, the company moved her family to the Netherlands where she attended a local school for three years. Her fourth school year began in Finland, but the family moved to Australia before the end of it. Sandra ended up living in three other countries before she reached her first year of college in the Chicago, Illinois area.

As I listened to her story, Sandra explained how every time she was just getting used to a new country and had formed a new group of friends, her father's employer transferred him to another location. She was constantly telling friends Goodbye and facing the unpleasant task of being the new kid in school. When I met Sandra, her parents and younger siblings were currently living in Germany in a town she had briefly visited as she and her mother stopped there on the way to take her to college.

Although her mother accompanied Sandra to the United States and tried to help her make a smooth transition to college, she could only stay for two weeks. The family was still house-hunting in Germany and she needed to get them moved and enroll Sandra's siblings into yet another new school system.

Meanwhile, back at college in the U.S., Sandra discovered an amazing reality. Although her passport declared that the United States was her "home" country, it was the most foreign country she had ever experienced. Until college she had had her family to root her and support her, but now they were halfway around the world in a country that she barely knew.

## Don's Background

Don is the man who had driven from out of state to get counseling. Although he appeared Caucasian, Don described his life of growing up in countries where he felt at home—even though he did not appear like most members of the dominant culture.

Don's father worked for the U.S. government and had frequent reassignments from one country to another. Although Don attended a private school in Nairobi for his first six years of education. After that his father was stationed in Peru for three years. Then the family moved to Chile for one year. Obviously, Don made all of these transitions with his family, changed schools many times, and learned to speak fluent Swahili and Spanish. Eventually, the family settled down in the Houston, Texas area where his father worked for a large oil company.

While living with his parents in Texas, Don graduated from a public high school and then went off to college in France. There he soon learned another language and met his wife, while she was studying art there one summer. Eventually he landed a job in the Midwest as the head of human resources in a large, international company. Don became quite animated when talking about his various relocations and travel, and I could see a happy twinkle in his eye as he reflected on these adventures.

## My History

Some of my first memories are as a child growing up in Latin America. I was born in Laredo, Texas, but when I was four years old, my parents, my two younger brothers and I boarded a small Standard Fruit Company banana boat and sailed from New Orleans to Honduras. We children happily wandered the dirt streets of our small town, Juticalpa, playing with local friends, because our parents knew that the locals would be most protective of us. After all, we were the only blonde, North American kids in town so anything that happened to us would be noticed.

My brothers and I learned Spanish quickly and it became the language that we used among ourselves. It wasn't until four years later when we were preparing to return to the United States for a year that our parents made us start to use English with one another. They said we needed to be able to talk to our cousins and grandparents. We did learn English, but had a very heavy Spanish accent and would slide into Spanish in our arguments with each other. Our cousins in Ohio found this most amusing.

For kindergarten, we attended the local Honduran school where all the classes were taught in Spanish. After that, my mother began using the Calvert Correspondence curriculum with us for the first grade. When I reached third grade, my brother Dave and I went to Las Americas Academy in Siguatepeque, Honduras. I was nine years old and he was eight. The boarding school was very small at that time, with only 30 children of missionaries.

Because Las Americas only had classes through eighth grade, I returned to the States for high school and went to Toccoa Falls Academy in northern Georgia. For me, high school in the United States was a much harder adjustment than going away to boarding school at the age of nine. Why? I had to adjust to an entirely new culture, a new educational system, new rules, new friends, and greater separation from my family.

As an adult, I returned to Honduras to work for 10 years. Then I returned to the United States to eventually become a therapist.

### The Common Thread

So what, in fact, is the common thread for each of these stories? The simple fact is that each person described here grew up as a *third culture kid* (TCK)—someone David Pollock has defined as *"a person who has spent a significant part of his or her developmental years outside the parents' culture."* Pollock added, *"The TCK builds relationships to all of the cultures, while not having full ownership in any. Although elements from each culture are assimilated into the TCK's life experience, the sense of belonging is in relationship to others of similar experience"* (Pollock & Van Reken, 2009, p. 13).

By the time Sandra, Don, and presumably I, went to therapy, we were *adult third culture kids* or ATCKs.

We will explore the common themes that frequently occur in a therapist's office when working with those who have grown up, or lived for many years as an adult, outside their passport country. For the purposes of this book, and to keep things simpler, I will focus primarily on what happens to those who are growing up among many cultural worlds as they move from place to place. Although I will mention at times how a specific issue applies or doesn't apply to those who began their global moves as adults, I will presume for the most part on your ability as a good therapist to make applications from studying and working with children who grow up globally to similar issues their parents and other globally mobile adults may also face.

## Why the TCK Topic Matters to Therapists

Sadly, through the years, I have discovered that when I, or others, present specifically about TCKs at conferences for therapists, the attendance in the session is often low. Is it because therapists and others think the impact of global mobility that occurred during childhood is invisible, or seems irrelevant, and therefore, is not critical? Do they presume if it's such a big deal, they should have already heard about it or met a TCK in their practice?

As a therapist, you might be surprised to discover how many families from all over the world are now living outside their passport country. For U.S. Americans alone, the growth in families living abroad has been almost astronomical in the last fifty plus years. The 1960 Census Report stated there were 922,819 United States citizens living abroad. In 1999, the U.S. State Department reported 4,163,810 were living overseas. By 2010 the number had jumped to 6,320,000 U.S. Americans living overseas. Some believe that by 2015 the number of U.S. Americans living overseas will be 9.3 million (Wennersten, 2008, p. 2).

Although we don't know detailed numbers worldwide, one thing we know for certain is that there are vast numbers of expatriates on the move from many countries as well as the United States. Let's look at just two countries: Australia and Japan. Australia in 2006 had over one million citizens living in other parts of the world. There were over one million Japanese living outside of Japan in 2007 (Pollock and Van Reken, 2009, p. 4). Extrapolating from just these two countries, one can easily comprehend the enormity of the pool of people living outside their passport or home countries. These expatriates move around and then most of them come home, so no matter where in the world you have your practice, it is likely you will encounter clients with global backgrounds, even if they do not talk about this aspect of their history as relevant to their presenting problems.

Another way to attempt to comprehend how large this pool of potential TCK clients is would be to look at the rapid growth of international schools around the world. Although not all of the students in the international school system are TCKs, a large percentage of them certainly fit into the category of the TCK. John Wennersten in his book *Leaving America: The New Expatriate Generation* (2008) states,

> Around three thousand international schools have proliferated around the world…. And according to the European Council of International Schools, in Europe alone there are 245,000 students enrolled in eighty-eight countries. (pp. 4–5)

## Famous TCKs

To make the point of how invisible this type of childhood often is, take a quiz. When you read the following list of names, what do you know of their backgrounds?

- Barack Obama – President of the United States

- General H. Norman Schwarzkopf – Commander-in-Chief of the U.S. Forces in Operation Desert Storm

- Isabel Allende – best-selling author

- Shannon Lucid – record-holding astronaut

- John McCain – U.S. senator, U.S. Presidential candidate

- Kobe Bryant – National Basketball Association professional player

- Ted Dekker – best-selling author

- Tom Cruise – actor, film writer, director, producer

- Major General Scott Graton – former Special Envoy to Dafur and former U.S. Ambassador

- Andrew Luck – National Football League professional player

- Sandra Bullock – award-winning actress

- Christiana Amanpour – Emmy award-winning international correspondent

Did you realize before this moment that all of these people are, in fact, adult TCKs (ATCKs)? Do you have any idea how they are ATCKs?

- *Barack Obama* spent four of his early years in Indonesia.

- *General H. Norman Schwarzkopf* grew up in a military family, and lived in Switzerland, Germany, and Italy.

- *Isabel Allende* is the child of diplomats, was born in Peru, and grew up in Chile, Bolivia, Lebanon, Turkey, and various countries in Europe.

- *Shannon Lucid* was raised in China by missionary parents who are U.S. citizens.

- *John McCain* was born in Panama and grew up on various military bases in the Pacific.

- *Kobe Bryant* was born in Pennsylvania but spent much of his childhood in Italy where his dad played professional basketball.

- *Ted Dekker's* parents were missionaries in Indonesia during his early years.

- *Tom Cruise* had attended 15 different schools in the United States and Canada by age fourteen.

- *Major General Scott Graton* was born to missionary parents serving in the Democratic Republic of the Congo.

- *Andrew Luck* went to school in Germany and England while his dad managed two World League of American Football teams.

- *Sandra Bullock* is both a bi-cultural child—U.S. American dad and German mother—and TCK who grew up in various European countries.

- *Christiana Amanpour* is the bi-cultural daughter of a British mother and an Iranian dad, so she spent time in both England and Iran during her developmental years.

The list of well-known ATCKs is long and impressive. They are in all professions, many using well the influences of their past to excel in their current work. But for those who wonder how common this type of childhood truly is, I say when you have ears to hear and eyes to see, you will find them everywhere—including in your office! (You may enjoy keeping a list of your own.)

## TCKs as Prototypes of the Global Citizens of the Future

The TCK story is about to become nearly everyone's story. Their numbers are increasing across all countries and all economic statuses. It is interesting to note the predictions that were made years ago about this phenomenon.

Dr.Ted Ward, a sociologist from Michigan State University, said that TCKs were "the prototype [citizens] of the future . . ." (Ward, 1989, p. 57). He was right on target with his prediction. What he meant was that in today's globalizing world, more and more people would grow up among many cultural worlds even if they didn't go overseas with their parents.

Even those who never moved very far geographically would see the world coming to them. Ultimately, a cross-cultural childhood is becoming the "new normal" across our globe for virtually everyone rather than something that only affects globally mobile kids. It is true that the degree of interactions across many cultural lines has never happened to this degree in all the history of humankind.

This is why in 2001 Ruth Van Reken, co-author of *Third Culture Kids: Growing Up Among Worlds,* coined the new term *Cross-Cultural Kid (CCK).* She defined a

CCK as "a person who is living or has lived in—or meaningfully interacted with—two or more cultural environments for a significant period of time during childhood (up to age 18)" (Pollock & Van Reken, 2009, p. 31).

Note that while this definition *does include traditional TCKs*, it describes a much wider group and is not dependent on geography per se. CCKs may be children of immigrants or refugees, minorities, mixed race, or those from bi-cultural parents. Some attend school in a language or culture other than the one they return home to each night. Others are international adoptees. Even children of divorce who move between parental cultures on a regular basis or those who live between a deaf and hearing world could potentially be included in this new classification of CCKs.

These people are among those Dr. Ward predicted would live lives that were similar to the TCK experience. In fact, Van Reken says studying TCKs is like a "petri dish"—a place where we can see the effects of a cross-cultural childhood and mobility so common in today's world in their most basic form and then begin to make applications to understanding the impact of other types of cultural complexities many of our clients now face (Pollock & Van Reken, 2009).

In a world where many children grow up not only as one type of CCK, but with many layers of cross-cultural interactions—similar to President Obama, who is a TCK from a bi-cultural marriage of mixed race, seen as a minority, and attended schools in a language and culture not his own—the basic TCK story gives us a window of understanding to a growing phenomenon and sharpens our capacity to be effective therapists to any and all who enter our doors.

Of course, global mobility also affects those who begin their cross-cultural sojourning as adults. Paulette Bethel, an adult CCK, family therapist, and former Air Force officer used the name Third Culture Adults. *Third culture adults* (TCAs) are those who make their first international moves as adults, after having been raised in the more traditional way of living in one country and primary culture. We will take a detailed look later at what the third culture itself is and why growing up in this environment during key developmental years shapes a person's life in ways that are critical for any therapist to understand. We will see how there can be similar, although not always, identical themes for those who didn't begin this pilgrimage until their adult years.

## Why I Like Counseling TCKs

Having said all of that, let's return to the main topic. Despite how this topic ultimately relates to others who grew up cross-culturally for other reasons or made their first international move as adults, the focus of this book is to help you identify and work well with TCKs when they present for therapy. I am writing primarily about doing effective therapy with traditional Third Culture Kids because this is the population with whom I am most familiar. It is not only my own story, but counseling TCKs has become one of my key areas of focus. One reason I love working with TCKs and adult TCKs[2] is simple: It is having the chance to see the "Aha!" moment as they realize for the first time that they have a name for their experience, and that they are not alone. The joy they experience, and the relief they express, when they discover that they are a part of a wonderful, growing tribe called Third Culture Kids is a wonderful thing to witness. With that discovery comes new opportunity to help these individuals find both growth in the areas where they have struggled and a way to recognize and use well the many strengths that have resulted from a cross-cultural childhood.

> The focus of this book is to help you identify and work well with TCKs when they present for therapy.

To illustrate, let me give you a one-way window to the conclusion of Don's first session:

> After Don finished telling me his story, I said, "Well, it sounds to me like you are such a TCK."
>
> "What on earth do you mean by that?" he asked.

---

[2] To simplify the writing, I will generally use the term TCK generically through this book to indicate anyone who is or who grew up as a TCK, even though many are technically adult TCKs (ATCKs) when they arrive in your office.

"You say you need to constantly move to a new location, and you like to change jobs. You have a value system that is different from many of your peers, even your wife. And you love to travel. Those are common characteristics of Adult Third Culture Kids (ATCKs), people who, like you, grew up in a country outside of the one their parents would call 'home.' You think outside the box in many areas of your life because you've seen some of the harsh realities of life others haven't seen. You've lived life on the move since the day of your birth. Your internal clock has no idea how to stay in one place more than a couple of years. For the life you've lived, I'd say you were pretty normal and experienced many things other ATCKs have. We need to look at these various responses you have made to growing up among many cultural worlds and see which ones are serving you well, which ones are not helping you now as an adult and which characteristics you want to enhance."

Don began to cry. I waited in silence. After a few moments he was able to control himself and began to tell me more of his story. "My wife and I have spent thousands of dollars with psychologists and psychiatrists, trying to resolve my restlessness and depression. I don't have any traumatic stories from my childhood to tell anyone. My parents and I have always had a good relationship. The therapists my wife and I have worked with have been unable to figure out what is going on with me." He paused to wipe the tears from his face. "You don't know how freeing it is to hear you say that I am normal and to hear that I am not a freak. Just knowing that I am like other TCKs is freeing. You don't know how much hope you have just given me."

Time and again I have seen a similar reaction: a relief that finally someone seems to understand and have language for what they have lived but never been able to put words around before. Sadly, some therapists may never know the joy of watching this "Aha!" moment because few educational or training programs prepare mental health workers to consider a variety of specific issues that often arise in hidden spaces for the TCK population.

## Who Should Read This Book

I hope the answer is: "Everyone who wants to be an effective therapist in today's globalizing world." Take a moment to consider: How would you have responded if Sandra had shown up in your office? I would guess that Sandra's therapists could not figure out how to help her because they missed the most important piece of her story—which is that she had grown up in a different pattern than most of her classmates. Hers was not a typical "homesick college student" story. Sandra's statement of needing help working through her depression was only the tip of the iceberg.

Neither Sandra nor her therapists had any real comprehension of the number of losses she had encountered during her frequent moves as she left behind so many places and people she loved. Overtly, her life was so privileged. What could she have to complain about? Even if the therapist realized there was some type of grief behind her depression, it seemed she had not been able to precisely name it for Sandra.

> Malia Morteimer surveyed 88 TCKs for her dissertation: "Of those who have been to therapy, 46% reported a bad experience because the therapist did not understand specific TCK issues. When those who had been in therapy were asked what would have been helpful, the majority (62%) agreed that the therapist should have been a TCK or been familiar with TCK issues." (Morteimer, 2010, p. 59)

Would you be prepared to help a person like Sandra? Would you have known what to ask or say? Would you have recognized this person as an adult Third Culture Kid if she had landed in your office? Many therapists would miss this point and never understand what they had missed. And, had Sandra dropped out of therapy with you as she did with the two therapists she described, would you have been glad she no longer needed therapy or assumed she had simply dropped out of school?

In Don's case, where did his therapists—who were not educated in how to help a Third Culture Kid—likely misunderstand his story? I would guess that they saw his different values, restlessness, and unusual background as a problem rather than a resource from which to draw in order to enrich Don's life. They may have diagnosed him as one of those individuals who will never fit into society.

These cases are not unique. This book is for both for the counselor who is not a TCK and the one who is. It is for any counselor who really has a heart for individuals who have spent the majority of their developmental years in another culture and for the therapist who wants to learn all about the TCK's lifestyle, thinking, feelings, values, and worldview. It is for the therapist who is open to learn and explore a relatively new field of

> "I just need to tell you that I appreciate the counseling you've given me. In a measure more than you know, you've helped me. . . . It is so good to hear validation of progress made in terms of being authentic and real—so hard for some ATCKs. You've had a part in this. Thanks, Don"

counseling. And it is for the therapist who has a strong drive to learn all he or she can about that world so he or she can effectively work with this underserved population in the counseling community.

I have every confidence that you can and will be extremely effective in working with TCKs once you understand some of the common reasons behind the feelings or behaviors that frequently bring them to therapy. As you read this book you will:

- Understand the context of this experience by learning what the third culture is;

- Look at some of the normal—but often paradoxical—characteristics of TCKs;

- Consider why some of the challenges may cause the TCK to seek therapy;

- View samples of assessment tools I have developed for identifying this often hidden history of clients;

- Evaluate the common misdiagnoses if therapists don't understand the potential etiology of certain "normal" TCK characteristics;

- Understand what the most common accurate diagnoses are and why they may occur with such regularity in this population;

- Learn strategies to differentiate between TCK responses and other matters related to non-TCK life experiences that can bring anyone in for therapy; and

- Look at ways the theories you already know and use in treatment plans can be adapted and used for specific TCK issues.

# Things You Should Know

1. There are several terms used in reference to the globally mobile. This book will be using David Pollock's definition of a Third Culture Kid: *"A Third Culture Kid (TCK) is a person who has spent a significant part of his or her developmental years outside the parents' culture. The TCK builds relationships to all of the cultures, while not having full ownership in any. Although elements from each culture are assimilated into the TCK's life experience, the sense of belonging is in relationship to others of similar background"* (Pollock & Van Reken, 2009, p.13).

2. By the year 2015, there will be an expected nine million expatriots from the United States alone (Wennersten, 2008, p. 2).

3. The number of expatriates in our world is growing rapidly. A cross-cultural childhood will eventually become the new normal.

4. At times, the TCK part of a person's story is not obvious when he or she shows up in your office.

5. The resources for counselors working with Third Culture Kids are very limited and there is very little in any training available for working with this population. This book attempts to fill the gap in literature and training and provide insights, resources, and guidance for the counselor.

# Discussion Questions & Activities

1. Can you think of any clients you have had with similar stories to Sandra, Don, or me? If so, what factors or issues brought them to therapy?

2. Why should the topic of "global mobility" matter to therapists?

3. Looking at the list of famous TCKs presented in this chapter, how do you think their global mobility affected their teen years and adult lives and their careers?

4.  Activity: How to recognize the impacts of repeated adjustments on TCKs:
    -   Stand up and pair with a partner.
    -   Look at each other's appearance carefully.
    -   Turn your backs to each other and make one change to your appearance—such as putting your watch on the other arm, unbuttoning your top button, or removing your glasses.
    -   Turn and face each other and try to figure out what change the other person made. (Give the participants about 30 seconds to figure this out.)
    -   Ask the participants:
        *   How many of you were able to figure out what changes were made by the other person?
        *   How did you feel if you were unable to figure out what changes were made?
        *   If you did figure it out, how did you feel about your success at this?
        *   Why do you think we did this exercise?
    -   After there has been some discussion, ask the participants: "How many of you have put back what you had changed?" Then ask: "Why?" Remind them: "This was not part of the instructions given to you." Ask: "How would it feel to not put those things back to the way they were before you made the change?"
    -   Talk about how TCKs have to adapt to many changes over and over again in their lifetime, resulting in accumulated stress due to the constancy of the changes that are taking place and their inability to return to what they perceive as "normal."

5.  Activity: Start a list of people you now or well-known people who are TCKs and note why they are TCKS and the countries where they lived during their developmental years. Note what they have done or are doing with their cross-cultural and mobile experiences. This could be a project for individuals, pairs, groups, or a class to work on for the semester or term.

# Chapter 2

# Defining Our Terms:

# Who We Are Discussing

### *Uniquely Me*

*I am*
*a confusion of cultures.*
*Uniquely me.*
*I think this is good*
*because I can*
*understand*
*the traveler, sojourner, foreigner,*
*the homesickness*
*that comes.*
*I think this is also bad*
*because I cannot be understood*
*by the ordinary, mono-cultural person.*
*They know not*
*the real meaning of homesickness*
*that hits me*
*now and then.*
*Sometimes I despair of*
*understanding them.*
*I am*
*an island*
*and*
*a United Nations.*
*Who can recognize either in me*
*but God?*

By Alex Graham, a TCK
(Dyer & Dyer, 1991, p. 234)

A new client who came to see me some months ago was dealing with a lot of anger because his girlfriend did not understand him. Fred had started to work with another therapist who is a friend of mine. My friend called me and said, "Lois, I have a client that I can't figure out. When he talks, he says things that sound like what I've heard you say and I think you can do a better job at helping him than I can. May I refer him to you?"

## Fred's Journey—Discovering He Was a TCK

When Fred showed up in my office, he was well dressed in a well-pressed suit and well-polished shoes. Yet, his face was that of a young man struggling with depression. Fred's story began with, "My parents are from Asia. My dad was in pharmaceuticals. We moved constantly." He proceeded to list all of his schools and the places he had lived in the world and across the United States. During his late teen years, his family settled down in New York. Upon law school graduation, Fred moved to Indiana for a job in a law firm and was making a valiant attempt at settling down in the Midwest. He fell in love with a young lady, packed up his stuff and put it into storage since she did not have room for all that he had collected from around the world, and moved in with her. All seemed to go well for a while and then they began to fight. Why?

He wanted to move to Colombia and his girlfriend thought he was crazy. So the fights began. His girlfriend had always lived in Indiana. Her big move was from a small farming community to the big city of Indianapolis with a population of about one million. He was depressed and feeling trapped. He could not figure out why every few years he had this strong urge to make a major move. There was a long string of broken romances behind him which all shared the common theme of his restlessness.

When I asked him about his support system, he responded that he hadn't lived long enough anywhere to form long-lasting friends. He stated that the friendships he did try to make always seemed to end badly because he kept moving.

Then he corrected himself, "Well, that's not completely true. I don't know why but I seem to be able to keep my international friends over the long haul, even though all of us are often moving!" I watched his face brighten up when he began talking about these friends and how much he loved to learn their languages and eat their foods.

When I run into anyone who has spent a considerable amount of time outside of their home culture, I always ask them if they have read David Pollock and Ruth Van Reken's *Third Culture Kids: Growing Up Among Worlds*. It is the most thorough book to date explaining the terms "Third Culture Kid," "Global Nomad," and "Cross Cultural Kid" as well as the unique characteristics of this population. Fred had never heard of it, or any of these terms, but seemed intrigued.

Fred bought the book and had read it all by the following week. He came in to the session with a glow on his face, book in hand, and tons of questions. I asked him, "Did you find yourself in that book?"

"Yes! Here is an entire book about me. I called my sister as soon as I finished reading it and told her she had to go out and buy this book!"

I would love to be able to say that I spent many months in helping Fred and his girlfriend iron out their differences and now they are happily married and traveling the world together. But as is so often the case, all within the space of three weeks, Fred broke up with his girlfriend and called me from the airport to let me know that he had found a job in South America and would not make that week's session—he was moving.

## Understanding the Terminology

### *What is the "third culture?"*

If there are third culture kids, then there must be a "third culture." We are not discussing "third world," which is a completely different concept. So hang on and see if you can follow this discussion closely as it sets the stage for all that follows.

So what in the world is this "third culture" idea? The *third culture* term dates back to the 1950s when social scientists **Drs. John and Ruth Hill Useem** from Michigan State University coined this phrase when they went from the United States to India to research how people from one culture would do business with those from another culture in these early post-World War II days of burgeoning international trade.

During this process, they discovered a previously unrecognized phenomenon: that people who had moved to another culture for the purposes of their *career* (often called "expatriates" or "expats") rather than as immigrants had formed a way of life that was like neither the home, or *first culture,* they had come from nor like the local host, or *second culture,* in which they were now living. It was, however, a way of life common to how other expatriates lived, despite the different "sectors" from which these expats came (sectors refers to sponsoring agencies such as military, corporate, diplomatic, and missionary communities).

The Useems called this *shared* lifestyle an interstitial, or *third culture,* and defined it as "a generic term to discuss the lifestyle 'created, shared, and learned' by those who are from one culture and in the process of relating to another one" (Brembeck & Hiler, 1973, p.122). That includes the third culture adults (TCAs) we mentioned in Chapter 1 and why the topics we will be discussing for TCKs relate to these globally mobile adults as well.

Please note that in today's world TCKs may ask, "Well, am I a fourth or fifth culture kid? My parents came from two countries, we lived in four more when I grew up, so I'm way past only three cultures." This is a fair question, but it also shows why understanding the third culture concept is important. While this language formed in a day when most expats came from one country and primarily worked in only one basic host country, in reality, the *third culture* is not related specifically to the number of different passport countries a family carries or how many host countries a person has lived in during childhood. Why? Because it is discussing a *particular lifestyle* expats have formed and live out no matter if this is their first or tenth global assignment. It is a way of life shared by others with similar internationally mobile experiences.

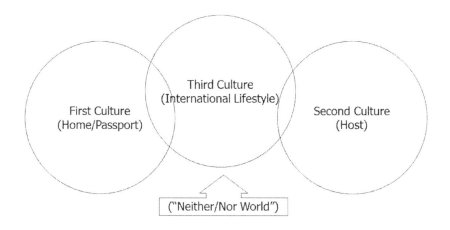

## Third Culture Model

### *Who are third culture kids?*

In time, Dr. Ruth Useem became very interested in studying the children who grew up in this expatriate experience—those she now called *third culture kids* (Cottrell, 2012). She gave them a simple definition: "Children who accompany their parents into another society" (Useem, 1993, p. 1), but all those she studied had parents who had gone to another country due to a career choice. Dr. Useem noticed there were some differences between, for example, the U.S. American students she met who were TCKs and those in her classrooms back at Michigan State who had never lived in another culture. She began studying this group of children but her results stayed mostly in academia.

David C. Pollock changed all of that. In 1975 Dave and his wife Betty Lou (who became good friends of mine in the 1990s), along with their four children, moved to the beautiful Rift Valley in Kenya, Africa. There he taught in a seminary and served as a dorm parent at Rift Valley Academy (RVA), a boarding school for missionary kids. During that time, as he listened to the kids' stories, he began to hear common themes that were different from those of the young people he had worked with back in the U.S. and wondered who was helping these children navigate some of the complexities of a global childhood. In the end, Dave returned to the United States to begin an organization called Interaction International with the mission "to provide and contribute to an on-going flow of care that meets the needs of Third Culture Kids (TCKs) and internationally mobile families." By 1986, Dave had developed this definition of TCKs we mentioned in chapter 1: "A *Third Culture Kid (TCK) is a person who has spent a significant part of his or her developmental years outside the parents' culture The TCK builds relationships to all of the cultures, while not having full ownership in any. Although elements from each culture are assimilated into the TCK's life experience, the sense of belonging is in relationship to others of similar background*" (Pollock & Van Reken, 2009, p. 13).

Dave felt strongly about keeping the words "developmental years" in his definition. As we know, it is during these critical childhood and teen years that children learn language, cultural mores, traditions, appropriate dress, and values from the world around them. While parents who grow up in one place or culture may have made the same global journeys with their TCK children, they have already established a sense of identity as "British" or "Korean" or "Liberian" or "U.S. American." Although a global career undoubtedly changes a parent's life in marked ways, too often parents mistakenly believe their child's experience is no different from their own since they have done it together.

Therapists, too, may underplay the importance of cultural switching during childhood if they have not done it themselves. Even some, who also have grown up globally, may overlook the impact of a cross-cultural childhood if they haven't discovered there is language for or research into this type of experience. On the other hand, Dave Pollock believed many of the challenges to identity and belonging that TCKs often face occur, at least in part, because of their switching cultural rules so completely, profoundly, and often repeatedly during the first 18 years of life. This interrupts the traditional developmental process of how children learn identity from the world around them and how they develop a sense of belonging to a place or national community.

I would like to make one more point. Sometimes people mistakenly read the TCK definition and believe that the phrase "elements from each culture are assimilated into the TCK's life experience" means some sort of joining of cultural pieces from two different cultures is what makes the "third" culture. A popular saying or metaphor among TCKs is the "I am green" idea. "I take pieces of my blue (home) culture, and other pieces from my yellow (host) culture and when I mix them together, I am green—that is the third culture." If this were true, I could not be writing this book because no individual would have anything to share with others who hadn't picked up the same two home and host cultures to mix and match into the same new experiences.

A critical distinction for you as a therapist to know is that if someone says to you that they *feel* "green," this phrase can be true to describe that a person feels he or she is not fitting perfectly into either the culture from which they came or the one where they now live. However, the *third culture* itself is not something green; the third culture is not a mixture of blue (first culture or home culture) and yellow (new culture or present host culture). It is *not* an *assimilation* into the new culture nor a blending of two different cultures— even though families may do things like eat both the local food and food similar to what others in their first or previous cultures eat—but the third culture itself is a *distinct way of life* different from either home or host cultures. Even learning to enjoy more than one type of ethnic food is an experience shared by others who live internationally, although the specifics of which type of food is enjoyed may differ. That is why Dave's definition ends with this reality: the sense of connection with others who have lived a like experience is strong among TCKs because *they share the life experiences of being mobile in a cross-cultural world.*

In the years that followed Dave's return from Kenya until his untimely death in 2004, he expanded his work beyond missionary families to include Foreign Service, military, and international business families. Based on his experience, he developed his now classic *The TCK Profile and The Transition Experience*— one of the first major looks at the psychological process of physical transition. Each year, Dave traveled to many countries and groups speaking to TCKs, parents, schools, organizational leaders, and caregivers, presenting his models and becoming recognized as the authority or spokesperson on the topic of TCKs. In 1984 he met Ruth Van Reken, herself an ATCK, and together they wrote the book I ask all my TCK clients to read: *Third Culture Kids: Growing Up Among Worlds.* (See the Wall of Fame in the appendices for more details.)

### Other Terms for TCKs

During the mid-1980s, Norma McCaig, herself an ATCK who grew up as a corporate kid in the Philippines, Sri Lanka, and India, coined another term for TCKs: *global nomads*. As an adult, she didn't like the appellation of "kid" on herself. Norma also believed Dr. Useem had not been clear enough in her definitions that TCKs had moved to another country because of a parent's career, not simply as immigrants or refugees. She believed if this difference in the reason for a globally mobile experience wasn't clearly differentiated, it would lead to problems later with further research. She defined global nomads as "*anyone raised abroad because of a parent's career choice*" (McCaig, 2008, p. 1) (You can read more about Norma in the Wall of Fame in the Appendices as well.)

Others have tried to define this cohort without knowing the terms TCK, Global Nomad, or CCK. One of them is Pico, Iyer, a journalist and author who also happens to be an Adult TCK. He coined the term *global soul* and defined that term as "*a person who had grown up in many cultures all at once—and so lived in the cracks between them*" (Iyer, 2000, p. 18).

TCK journalist Pico Iyer describes the Global Soul in his book *The Global Soul.* While pondering the globalization of our world, he stated, "I began to wonder whether a new kind of being might not be coming to light— a citizen of this International Empire—made up of fusions . . . a 'Global Soul'. . . . This creature could be a person who had grown up in many cultures all at once—and so lived in the cracks between them" (Iyer, 2000, p. 18). Iyer describes what it is like to be that Global Soul in the first chapter of his book. See if his ruminations sound familiar: "His sense of obligation would be different, if he felt himself part of no fixed community, and his sense of home, if it existed at all, would lie in the ties and talismans he carried round with him. Insofar as he felt a kinship with anyone, it would, most likely, be with other members of the Deracination-state....fellow in-betweener....'When I'm in England, there's a part of me that's not fulfilled; that's why I come here – to find the other part'" (Iyer, 2000, p.19).

## Shared Experiences of Third Culture Kids

So what is that "experiential something" that is shared by those who live and grow up in the third culture? What types of things fall into this experience?

Although the Useems did not specify exactly what it was those living in this third culture shared, editors asked that question when Dave and Ruth were writing *Third Culture Kids*. In answer, they noted several components that are realities for those growing up in the third culture (Pollock & Van Reken, 2009, pp. 17-18). Because the essence of the expat experience includes all its members—adults as well as children—interacting regularly with others from different cultural worlds and frequent migrations between at least home and host cultures, they contend that virtually all TCKs share the following experiences:

- *Growing up in a genuinely cross-cultural world.* TCKs don't simply study other cultures, they experience them by living in them.

- *Being raised in a highly mobile world.* With each flight from passport culture to host culture or vice versa, some family or friends are left behind while others are met. With the next move, those friends are left, but old friends they expected to see once more have often also moved while they were gone. And so it goes. In addition to personal mobility, they live in a community where virtually all members are also living a relatively transitory lifestyle. This blurs for them what is normal for a given culture, what is normal as a TCK, and what is not normal for either. Everyone has some mobility and associated losses in their lives, but for TCKs, the repeated cycles of separation and loss poses one of the biggest challenges they face.

- *Having distinct differences.* Often in the host culture, TCKs may not look like their peers, but even when they do, in both home and host culture, they often don't think like those around them. This reality creates sharp distinctions and forces TCKs to ultimately question their identity.

- *Expecting repatriation.* Unlike immigrants whose goal it is to permanently settle in a new land and assimilate into that culture, families in the third culture move to a new place with the expectation that "one day we will go 'home' again." This has profound ramifications for school choices (they need to be ready to return to school in their passport culture), a sense of roots, or even a refusal to become a part of the local culture.

For many, but not all TCKs, two other characteristics are common:

- **Living an privileged lifestyle.** While this is not universally true, even TCKs who are missionary kids (MKs) and whose families may not have as much money as other expat families or peers in their passport culture have often lived a lifestyle that appears more affluent than peers in their host culture (and those in their home culture). Many expat families of all sectors have local people working in their homes. For security or other reasons, embassy, military, or even corporate children may have drivers who chauffer them to school, shopping, and elsewhere.

- **Identifying with a system.** Again, while this is not universal, many TCKs feel very committed to or attached to the organization or corporation for which their parents work. Dr. Ruth Useem noted in her first studies that many TCKs had the feeling of being in a "representational role." They believed it was up to them not to let down the system for which their parents worked. In addition "people around them (including parents) expected the children's behavior to be consistent with the goals and values of the organizational system for which the parents worked" (Pollock & Van Reken, 2009, p. 15). The book, *Military Brats: Legacies of Childhood inside the Fortress* by Mary Edwards Wertsch (1991) is a good description of this pressure of "positive performance" on the children of military parents. Living up to the spoken and unspoken expectations of the system under which the parents go overseas can have an impact on some TCKs that is as great as or greater than the family system itself. Therapists must learn to understand that in this third culture environment, the community of fellow expats working with the same sending agency (such as military, religious mission, diplomatic mission, non-governmental agency like USAID, or corporation) often takes the power and place of extended biological family in a way that those in the homeland would not experience or understand. In Appendix A we explore in greater detail why the system itself can play such a major part in a TCK's life.

## Common Characteristics of TCKs

What is it that develops in many children when they grow up in the third culture? How does a cross-cultural, highly mobile lifestyle affect those who have such an experience?

A key word to remember when working with TCKs is PARADOX. While it is easy for all of us to think in *either-/or* concepts, with TCKs it is particularly important to remember that their lives are often about *both/and* realities. Often the reasons for their greatest gifts are also the roots of their main challenges.

For example, many TCKs have an expanded view of the world because they have seen much of it firsthand, but they may not be well versed in the cultural expectations and nuances of their own home or passport country. Researchers describe TCKs as "cultural chameleons" because they are usually skilled at adapting to and blending in to various cultures. Ironically, the greatest struggle often comes when TCKs return to their passport culture and can't seem to blend into the one place where they and others *expect* them to fit in perfectly.

Due to their global mobility, TCKs have a 3-dimensional view of the world. They have seen places and cultural events in person that many only view in *National Geographic* magazines. Ultimately, however, this same mobility creates chronic cycles of separation and loss, as they and their friends are frequently moving. Dealing with the chronicity of grief that each farewell engenders can become a major challenge for many.

Most TCKs have friends all over the world. I have heard it said, "TCKs sort their friends by continents." That is true. What richness they have in friendships of all sizes, colors, statuses, religions, ages, and history! But then, how do they keep up with all of these great relationships? Today's world of social media has helped enormously, but a new challenge facing some is to make "in-person" friends in the new place rather than spend all of their time on Facebook with friends from a previous location.

*truth.*

29

A great gift for many is that they are multi-lingual because of living in different language environments or having friends who speak other languages. Sadly, however, some TCKs lose their family's original language when immersed in another linguistic world. Shockingly, they discover they can't converse easily with grandparents or other relatives when they do repatriate one day. Even those who keep oral fluency but do not attend school in their original language may never be able to go to university back "home" because they are not fluent in reading and writing skills for that language.

Parents and therapists also become confused when they watch TCKs, particularly the college-aged TCKs, lag in their developmental skills. They seem so mature in their ability to deal with various worlds, yet they can be so immature in terms of how they relate to others in their presumed "home country." The truth is that learning a sense of being in cultural balance is a greater challenge and can take a bit longer than "normal" when the worlds around a child are always changing.

Could this create what Murray Bowen from Family Systems Therapy describes as "fusion"? Fusion is defined as "the merging of the intellectual and emotional aspects of a family member, paralleling the degree to which that person is caught up in, and loses a separate sense of self, in family relationships" (Goldberg & Goldberg, 1991, p. 325). Or when we look at Eric Erikson's Stages of Development, and he talks about getting stuck at one developmental stage, is this what happens with the TCK when they attempt to return to their "home country" in their early teens, right at the stage of resolving their identity? (Okun & Rappaport, 1980, pp.14-17)

Yes, it is often this paradoxical nature of the TCK lifestyle that creates such angst. Without understanding that reality, many TCKs begin to wonder at certain points, "What's wrong with me?" To say there is pain seems to deny the good. To affirm the good appears to say there was no struggle. This means many TCKs are left without the means to process their story if locked into an either/or decision about how it was to grow up globally rather than seeing it as a *both/and* story.

In the end, most ATCKs I have met believe that the benefits of growing up globally far outweigh the challenges they have faced. But many also admit to common struggles along the way to move into that full appreciation of their past. Here are the key issues many TCKs must process in order to use well the great strengths of their gifts:

- **Unresolved grief.** Why do I feel so sad when my life is so good? Why do I get angry so easily? *yes.*

- **Questions of identity.** Who am I? Which of my many selves am I? Where do I fit? *Yes.*

- **Questions of belonging.** Where am I from? Where is home? *Yes.*

- **Relationships.** Why can't I let anybody in? Why do I push my partner away whenever we start to feel close? Why does it seem as if others never understand me or I them? *yes.*

In upcoming chapters we will look more deeply into the reason these are common challenges, but for now, know that if you can help TCKs find answers to these questions, you will have done them a great service and unlocked opportunities for them to use the gifts of their experience as well.

We have now looked at the basic nature of what it means to grow up in this rather mysterious *third culture* and some of the common characteristics developed by many TCKs. Next we will begin a discussion of how you can work more effectively with this population using the skills you already have, learning to apply them more specifically to your clients who are TCKs.

*Are these also normal thoughts and struggles of all teens? What about all people? Does it ever end? Do I ever belong?*

# Things You Should Know

1. The term "third culture" dates back to the 1950s and two social scientists from Michigan State University, Drs. John and Ruth Hill Useem. They described the term "third culture" as *"a generic term to discuss the lifestyle 'created, shared, and learned' by those who are from one culture and in the process of relating to another one"* (Brembeck & Hiler, 1973 p.122).

2. Although a global career undoubtedly changes a parent's life in marked ways, too often parents mistakenly believe their child's experience is no different from their own since they have done it together.

3. Dave Pollock believed many of the challenges to identity and belonging that TCKs often face occur, at least in part, because of their switching cultural rules so *completely*, *profoundly*, and *repeatedly* during the first 18 years of life.

4. The sense of connection with others who have lived a like experience is strong among TCKs because *they share the life experiences of being mobile in a cross-cultural world.*

5. In the 1980s, Norma McCaig coined another term for TCKs—*global nomads*. A Global Nomad is *"anyone raised abroad because of a parent's career choice"(McCaig, 2008, p. 1).*

6. In the late 1990s Pico Iyer, a journalist and author, coined yet another term for the TCK—*Global Soul*—which he defined as *"a person who had grown up in many cultures all at once—and so lived in the cracks between them"* (Iyer, 2000, p. 18).

7. A key word to remember when working with TCKs is PARADOX. While it is easy for all of us to think in *either/or* concepts, with TCKs it is particularly important to remember that their lives are often about *both/and* realities. Often the reasons for their greatest gifts are also the roots of their main challenges.

8.  Virtually all TCKs share the following experiences:

    - Growing up in a genuinely cross-cultural world
    - Being raised in a highly mobile world
    - Having distinct differences in appearance compared to home or host cultures
    - Expecting repatriation

    For many, but not all TCKs, two other characteristics are common:

    - Living an privileged lifestyle
    - Identifying with a system

9.  The key issues many TCKs must process in order to use the great strengths of their gifts are:

    - Unresolved grief
    - Questions of identity
    - Questions of belonging
    - Relationships

## Discussion Questions & Activity

1.  What are the differences among the "first culture," the "second culture," and the "third culture"?

2.  Why does living in the world of paradoxes (*both/and* reality) cause so much conflict for the TCK?

3.  Draw a line down the center of a piece of paper, making two columns. List some of the benefits (on one side) and challenges (on the other side) resulting from the global lifestyle.

4.  What other groups or subcultures are defined by a shared experience rather than by a more typical way of defining culture? (Example: the Deaf community)

5. What other type of non-TCK experiences might result in children feeling as if they must hold up the reputation of some system that is greater than or encompasses themselves or their families?

6. Activity: If you are in graduate school, work together in groups of two to four to describe the culture of your university and the shared experiences you have with other in your graduate counseling program. Extend that to include the traditions and shared experiences with past classes. How do those experiences set you apart from your former undergraduate classmates? Talk about the culture of the graduate counseling program versus the undergraduate program.

# Chapter 3

# Starting When a TCK Walks

# Through Your Door

*Even in high school, Bryant could be a loner. Having grown up with his parents
and two older sisters in Europe, where his father played professional basketball
for an Italian team, Kobe had a difficult time adjusting to life in the United
States when he returned at the age of 14. "It was tough because I didn't know
English really well, and I really didn't know the different lingo that the black
culture had,"* Bryant told Newsweek Magazine *in a lengthy 1999 interview.
"So I had to learn two languages when I got back here, and that was tough. But
if I didn't do it, I would have never fit in. And kids are tough, you know? You
got to be just like them or else."*

(Samuels, 2003)

Samuel set up an appointment for himself and his wife, Deb, to see me.
When they showed up, they were still recovering from jetlag because of their
recent long flight from the Ivory Coast. They sat shivering in my air-
conditioned waiting room because their bodies were not yet used to the chill
of the air conditioner. Their clothes were wrinkled from being packed too
long in a suitcase and both wore dusty, open sandals.

I quickly forgot their attire as they began to tell me their story. Although he is
a United States citizen, Samuel grew up in the Ivory Coast where he had been
born. Deb was raised in North Carolina. They met in college in the U.S.
where he was studying how to set up micro-enterprise businesses to help
those struggling to get out of poverty in third world countries. Deb's degree
was in nursing which seemed to complement his desire to go back to the
Ivory Coast and help his parents in the organization for which they worked.

All went well for about three years after they moved to the Ivory Coast, until
for no apparent reason, Samuel began to slide into a deep depression. He
pulled away from Deb and their two little boys and began to hang out at a

local bar with a couple of his Ivorian childhood friends. He slowly slid into the world of drugs and affairs in an attempt to gain relief from his depression.

One eventful night, Samuel accidently overdosed and ended up in the hospital. Deb was frightened that he was going to die and she would be a widow at the young age of 28, left to raise their two little boys alone. He came out of that near-death experience and, in an attempt to try to put all of the pieces of his life back together, he told her about the affairs. Understandably, she was angry since she had given up a nice life in North Carolina to follow Samuel halfway around the world to *his* "homeland" and now he was the one who was sabotaging it all.

As soon as Samuel was able to travel, they landed in my office. She was angry and hurt; he was depressed and dealing with addictions; and their marriage was in shambles.

So how do you begin with a TCK client like Samuel?

## Meeting Your Client

As you know, the first session with all your clients is crucial. This is when new clients are making the mental decision of whether or not to enter into a relationship with you as the therapist. You will have about 55 minutes, the length of that intake session, to either make a positive impression and keep your clients in therapy or lose them as they find creative reasons for not scheduling another appointment at

> If your clients sense that you are interested in them as individuals, they will work with you in learning about their world.

this time. If your clients sense that you are interested in them as individuals, they will work with you in learning about their world. If they don't believe you care, they won't stay.

For TCKs, this first visit is particularly critical. When they are deciding what to tell you about their past worlds, many worry that you will see the international part of their story as a matter of geography, not as a dynamic which has shaped them profoundly. Some TCKs have convinced themselves that what happened "back then" is basically irrelevant to their present situation, yet intuitively they know something is "wrong." Even worse, a

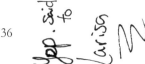

number of them really don't expect you to understand them since it seems no one has up to this point—especially if they have already tried other therapists. That means if you can ask even one question or offer one insight into the long-term effect of their fascinating childhood experiences, they will look up in surprise and begin to dare to hope.

"But wait," you say, "How can I do that so quickly? How would I ever know Samuel—or any other client—is, indeed, a TCK? If he or she is, how do I assess if that TCK experience relates in any particular way to the presenting symptoms? What are the steps you go through to begin to unlock the mysteries of this seemingly hidden world? How do you make a correct diagnosis? How do you help a client understand what are, in fact, normal responses for those of similar experience and what are places where therapeutic intervention is needed?"

These are great questions and that's what this chapter is all about. I'm going to take you through the process I use with all new clients that also helps me identify those who are TCKs while making my initial assessment. I will give you "talking points" that will help you develop a better understanding of the individual, as well as the corporate TCK story. These talking points will also allow opportunities for your clients to discuss events in their lives, the memories of which they have long since pushed aside as these events seemed irrelevant to the life they are living now. Even if they think these stories might have relevance, they can be reluctant to share them unless you ask because it seems no one has been particularly interested in this part of their life story for years. Why bother to talk, or think, about it?

After walking through the process of how you initially identify that you are dealing with a TCK, I'll show you how to make an accurate assessment and diagnosis. The most common presenting symptoms for this group are depression, relational problems, anxiety, or a general sense of, "What's wrong with me? I just can't seem to fit anywhere." Obviously, non-TCKs can present with similar symptoms for many different underlying reasons. But just as you must assess the reasons behind the non-TCKs' depression or anxiety to choose which type of therapeutic approach you will use, so it is for TCKs. The more you understand their basic third culture story as well as their specific background, the more you will understand their current behavior or feelings and be able to offer appropriate interventions.

## Expanded Intake Form

When clients walk through our doors—TCKs or not—the first thing we want to know is why they have come and a bit about who they are. I begin like I imagine most therapists do. I hand all my new clients a clipboard containing an "Intake Form."

I found out years ago, however, that most intake forms I have seen do not ask enough questions to help me pick up the whole story from those who are TCKs, or even be able to recognize they might be a TCK. Because of that, I have devised my own Intake Form. Let's look at it and see how it can help you discover and assess important pieces of the deeper story for potentially all of your clients. After that, I'll tell you how I used it to begin working with Samuel.

Here is the form I have developed. It is available for download as an 8.5" x 11" Word document so that you can put your own address on it. Just go to my website www.quietstreamscounseling.com

*Quiet Streams Counseling*
*14074 Trade Center Drive, Ste. 225*
*Fishers, IN 46038*
*317-523-5517*

## Client Confidential Information

### Client Information:

| Last Name | First Name | Middle Initial | Home Phone | Cell Phone |
|---|---|---|---|---|
| Address | City, State | | Zip | |
| Email Address | Date of Birth | Age | Sex | Marital Status | Communication Clearance Text___ Home___ Work___ Cell___ Email___ |
| Birth place | | Number of Moves | Countries Lived in Longer then 4 months | |
| Fluent in what language(s) | | Passport Country | Length of time in current home | |

### Employment:

| Occupation | Employer | Educational Level |
|---|---|---|
| Work Phone | Length of Time at Current Employment | Typical Work Hours |

### Family Information:

| Spouse/Partner Name | Do they know you are in therapy? Y___ N___ | Years Married |
|---|---|---|
| Spouse- Work Phone | Spouse- Cell Phone | Spouse - Employer |
| Children and Ages | | |

### Referral Source: *(Check all that apply)*

___ Telephone Book
___ Internet
___ Counseling Center Website
___ Insurance Company

___ Doctor (_____)
___ Employer (_____)
___ Client of Counseling Ctr. (_____)
___ Other (_____)

**Briefly Describe Your Presenting Problem:**

```
_____

_____

_____

_____
```

**Symptoms:** *(Check all that apply)*

| | | | |
|---|---|---|---|
| ___Anxiety | ___Depression | ___Thoughts of Suicide | ___Loss of Self Esteem |
| ___Nervous | ___Sleep Changes | ___Mood Swings | ___Impulsive Behavior |
| ___Palpitations | ___Weight Loss/Gain | ___Memory Lapses | ___Relationship Problems |
| ___Severe Stress | ___Appetite Changes | ___Sexual Problems | ___Parent/Child Problems |
| ___Panic Attacks | ___Problem Concentrating | ___Addiction Problems | ___Work Problems |
| ___Excessive Worry | ___Personality Changes | ___Increased Alcohol Use | ___Financial Problems |
| ___Restlessness | ___Loss of Identity | ___Grief | ___Transitional Challenges |

**By signing below I acknowledge the following:**

\* I have received a copy of the Notice of Privacy Policies.
\* I have received a copy of the Client Information & Policy Statement.
\* I have read and agreed to the payment/cancellation policy.

**CANCELLATIONS** If you find it necessary to cancel a scheduled appointment, 24 hours notice is required. **With less than 24 hours advance notice, you will be responsible for half of your total regular fee for a 50-minute session. Failure to appear with no prior notice will result in a penalty equal to your full charge.** Late cancellations and missed appointments are not covered under any insurance. In case of a serious emergency, school closings due to weather or illness, if you notify us immediately, we will reschedule your appointment without additional charge.

**Signature:** _____ **Date** _____

*(Guardian must sign if you are younger then 18 years old.)*

Note that most of the Intake Form is like other Intake Forms therapists use in our industry (at least in the United States). Some agencies have multiple pages for clients to complete that first session. I prefer to have my clients tell me their story in their own words, rather than reviewing sheets of information. The information asked for on the form is reflective of the country where your counseling center is located. In Latin America, there would certainly be a longer line for Last Name as the last names of both the mother and father would be written in this blank.

From the perspective of the United States, the differences on this particular form are the questions that would alert me to the fact that I probably have a TCK (or some other form of a cross-cultural kid) across from me, even though my new client may not be aware of the TCK term.

## Assessing the Information Given

Under Client Information, I make particular note of their responses to the following questions:

- Birth place
- Number of moves
- Countries lived in longer than 4 months
- Fluent in what languages
- Passport country
- Length of time in my current home

Each of these questions gives me clues to their rate of mobility in childhood plus some basic facts about their exposure to other cultures as well. As I compare the countries where they have lived to where my office is located in Fishers, Indiana, I consider the extent of differences among the cultural experiences they have known. In other words, the transition from Tokyo, Japan, to Fishers, Indiana, would be a major cultural shift. If, however, they have moved many times but don't list another country, I realize those *transition cycles* can be significant but the *cultural shifts* between, say, Minneapolis, Minnesota, and Fishers, Indiana, would be less severe. On the other hand, it is possible to move between vastly different cultural communities within the same country as a "domestic TCK" (Pollock & Van Reken, 2009, p. 32). Certainly it is important to ask the ages they were when they made these various intranational and international moves.

If they have lived in other countries but for a relatively short time in our local community, I ask where they lived before moving to their current location. If I see their "passport country" box says they are from the U.S. and realize that they have just repatriated from a country overseas, I ask how they are doing living in a place that others see as their "home" but they may not quite feel is home yet. Often there is a widening of the eyes with that simple question as in, "Oh, my goodness. How did she know?" and they begin to open up immediately.

By these few facts alone, I can make a good assessment of whether my client was raised in one basic cultural world with little mobility, is a traditional TCK, or is some other type of CCK. For Samuel, it wasn't hard to know he was a TCK because his passport said he was a U.S. American, but he was born and raised in Ivory Coast. I saw he had moved back to the U.S. for university, and then gone back to Ivory Coast after his marriage. For him, as for all my clients, right on this Intake Form, the important picture of the basic context in which they grew up had begun to form even before getting to the details related to family of origin or personal history.

After this initial checklist, I proceed to look at these next boxes and make further assessments about their history.

- *Employment.* I note their occupation and employer. The question that runs through my mind is, "Is this an international company?" If so, I ask what sector my client is currently working in—diplomatic, corporate, missions, or another international sector. Many TCKs who have grown up in the international community will continue to live and work in this community or one with extensive international roots. If I am already aware that this person is a TCK, I will also ask what organization or company the parents were associated with when they went overseas. This can be important information later on when dealing with systems and potential system identities.

- *Briefly describe your presenting problem.* I carefully review this section and note if they are discussing a challenge that sounds like grief and loss issues, depression or anxiety, identity struggles, or relationship challenges. I know that frequently other non-TCK clients deal with these same challenges, but these presenting issues seem to be the "ticket in the door" for many TCKs who seek counseling.

- *Symptoms.* Like most therapists, I look first to see if they checked the line "Thoughts of Suicide." When I see that this has been marked, I know that I need to put a safety plan into place for my client before we focus on anything else in counseling—TCKs or not. Next, as I review their various symptoms, if they have checked any of these lines—"Restlessness, Loss of Identity, Personality Changes, Grief, Relational Problems and Transitional Challenges"—along with earlier demographic information, I realize these may also be clues that at least some of their issues may have roots in the TCK experience. I make mental note of that and use the talking point I will describe below to explore this possibility later on.

---

### How I Began with Samuel and Deb

The fact that someone is a TCK or ATCK (adult TCK) does not protect him or her from things that many other human beings struggle with as well. While the TCK piece may be a strong undercurrent, when I looked at the Intake Form Samuel filled out and saw that he had checked "thoughts of suicide," "relationship problems," and "addiction problems," I did what I expect you as a therapist would do—I dealt with the most acute issues first.

First, I made sure that Samuel was safe and was not actively suicidal. Second, I got him involved in therapy with an addictions counselor (since I am not an addictions counselor) along with our sessions together. Third, I began to try and stabilize the marriage and help Samuel put into place some good coping skills for his depression before I began to focus on the TCK issues that I believed might be lurking behind some of this other behavior. In other words, I tried to stop the bleeding before attempting to deal with the cause of the wound.

On the other hand, in that first session I also offered him the hope that I might understand his story in a place he might not expect by asking him questions related to areas I know ATCKs have some typical reactions. As he told me his story and spoke of coming to the States for college, I asked, "How was it to come back to attend university in the U.S. after growing up in Africa? Did anything in particular surprise you about life here?" He seemed surprised by that question at first, but then said one thing that had frustrated him had been how much his peers cared about American football and the Super Bowl, but how few knew or cared who was playing in the World Soccer Cup games. When he talked about moving to the Ivory Coast, I asked how it was for them as a couple when Samuel had grown up there and I had seen on Deb's intake form that she had never been to Africa before. "Did anything surprise you about each other—a feeling you had just learned something about your partner or your marriage that you hadn't known before?"

Deb said, "I didn't have any idea how African Samuel was in his soul. He fit right in and I felt left out. I didn't know the culture or the language like he did." And Samuel said, "I couldn't believe how squeamish she was about the lizards running through our house. I thought she was tougher than that." In this way I let him know I "got it" even as we initially concentrated on these other areas.

## After the Client Intake Form

Whenever I realize that I am working with TCKs, I ask them if they have heard of the term *third culture kid*. If they haven't, I briefly describe the world of the TCK and give a definition of the term. For their first homework assignment I will ask them to purchase a copy of *Third Culture Kids* by David Pollock and Ruth Van Reken on Amazon.com and begin to read it before our next session. If the TCK is younger than 18 years old, I will ask the parents of the TCK to read the book so they can learn about their child and understand the formation of his or her identity as a TCK.

I also make this point for parents of younger TCKs (and for you as therapists). While it is easy to see how the profile described in the book is developing in most TCKs, even in their younger years, the full impact of this experience isn't always felt or acknowledged until adulthood. Besides, younger TCKs don't want to be labeled and often refuse to believe any of this even relates to growing up as a TCK. Usually in their opinions, any problems they have are simply someone else's fault!

During the second session after the adult TCKs or parents of younger TCKs have read the TCK book, I ask if they read anything that seemed important to them or simply ask, "Did you read anything that sounded like you (or your child)?" or "What didn't seem to fit or sound like your experience?"

## Questions to Guide Your Intake Interview

I have developed a talking guide to help you get to know the world of your TCK clients beginning with the first session and building over several sessions. These are not typical questions that we use with most of our clients unless we know they are a different nationality or ethnicity from ourselves. The trick for working with TCKs, of course, is that this cross-cultural experience is often invisible to us. Chapter 5, which is about identity, will cover that at great length.

For now, suffice it to say that once I am aware that I do have a TCK in my office, I realize that I am working with someone who grew up in cultures that may be quite different from my own or even the various Latin cultures I knew as a child. Some were raised in cultures where they communicated through the use of storytelling and this is how they will communicate with you, their therapist. Some grew up in cultures where it was not acceptable to speak negatively about someone who is older. And some may even struggle in communicating in your language.

You do not need to walk through all of these questions those first few sessions, but keep them in mind as you work with your client over the coming sessions. I am sure that you already learned the lesson well in your training, that as we learn more about the world of our clients, the more their actions or lack of actions make complete sense. Much like when an adoptee comes in, the therapist knows there are specific questions to ask that might not relate to a non-adoptee, so when a TCK or an ATCK is the client, there are some very specific issues to consider that might be behind the symptomatology being seen that may differ from working with a non-TCK.

# Talking Guide for Working with TCKs and ATCKs

(Available for download on www.quietstreamscounseling.com)

1. Where all did you grow up?
2. Did you have a caregiver, amah, or nanny in any location you lived?
3. What language did you speak in your home? Did you speak a different language with your friends? With your caregiver?

4. How many languages do you speak fluently?
5. How did you find out you were leaving each time?
   a. How long did you have before the move?
   b. Were you able to say Goodbye to people who were important to you?
   c. Were you able to say Goodbye to places, events, and animals that were important to you?
6. Where did you go to school in each of these countries?
   a. Types of schools
   b. Where were they?
   c. How many students were there?
   d. Boarding (stay there or with a family) or day or home?
   e. Who ran it?
   f. Language spoken in class? Language in textbooks? Language you spoke with your friends?
   g. How was it different from or the same as other schools you attended?
   h. How often did you return to your passport country for school? How did it differ or how was it the same as other schools you attended?
   i. Who were you closest to at school?
7. How did you feel about your school experiences?
   a. What did you love about them? Do you have a funny story or favorite story?
   b. What were your biggest challenges? Can you tell me about a particularly challenging experience?
8. What kind of work did your parents do overseas?
   a. What organization did they work with or for?
   b. What sector was it? (missionary, diplomat, military, etc.)
9. How would you describe your parents' relationship with their employer (the international agency that sent them overseas)?
   a. Did they talk about their company/agency much in your presence?
   b. What were their feelings about their employer?
10. How often was your parent (or were your parents) gone from home?
    a. How did the family roles change when your parent(s) left?
    b. How hard was this emotionally on each family member?
    c. Who was your caretaker when your parent(s) was/were gone?

11. Explain any ways in which your parents' work impacted you and your siblings.
    a. Were you or your parents ever in danger?
    b. Were you or your parents ever victims of a violent crime such as rape, kidnapping, or armed robbery?
12. Were you closer to your mother or to your father growing up? Why?
13. Do your parents still work overseas?
    a. If not, when and why did they return to their home country?
    b. Was this due to the client's (or sibling's) behavior or maladjustment?
14. How often did you return to your passport country?
    a. How long did you stay?
    b. Where did you stay in your "home country"?
    c. What schooling did you have in your "home country"?
15. If they are wearing something that is typical of another culture, ask:
    a. I love your bracelet/necklace. Does it have a story?
    b. Are you wearing anything from your favorite or "home" country?
16. What type of friends are you attracted to since you left your passport country?
17. What would you like to hire me to do for you? What would you hope I could do for you?

Listen for clues about what they are feeling, their value systems, or a glimpse of what they are processing deep within their souls. Drawing a timeline of the client's life will help you to not get lost or confused in their story.

Each question adds valuable information to understand more about their psychological make-up. For example, note the question, "Do your parents still work overseas? If not, when did they return to their home country and why?" Depending on the reason for the repatriation, some TCKs have internalized that it was their fault (misbehavior, special needs, lack of adjustment) that their parents are no longer following their dreams and working internationally. These clients struggle with trying to figure out if their own tremendous sense of guilt or shame for being responsible for ending a parent's career is realistic or unrealistic.

The bottom line is that the more you understand the TCK story, and the more clients you work with as you have this new awareness, the more these kinds of questions will become intuitive to you. You will find ways to adapt them to the situations your clients are facing, and probably add a few more to my list!

## Looking at the Factor of Age

Interestingly, those who have counseled many TCKs say that the average age for ATCKs they see is thirty-something. This is not to say that younger TCKs do not voluntarily see the therapist. There are many that do so during their adjustment to their passport country and college. Or the younger TCK may be brought in by a deeply concerned parent to work with you due to some behavior that is abnormal for their child. Those in their twenties, or past their thirties, often come in as well.

But the majority seems to show up a little later in life when life is supposed to have settled down for them. People ask me why this is.

First, as I said a bit earlier, younger people tend to blame the current situation. "If only.... would change, I would be fine." In earlier years while adjusting to new cultures, figuring out how to survive in them, going through educational pressures, making decisions regarding career and marriage—any sense of angst or restlessness or relational difficulties these ATCKs face—is attributed to the circumstances. Later they realize that while all these circumstances have changed, and often resolved favorably, this indefinable angst remains. That is when the questions and feelings seem to intensify. Why?

They wonder, "Wasn't life supposed to settle down into a more stabilized routine by now? Then why do I still have so many of the feelings of restlessness, grief, and depression? Why do I never seem to fit into the groups I should?" Their brains seem to have reached the conclusion that now is the time to understand the many memories and feelings which in the past were not "that big of a deal." It is very similar to what happens to victims of some forms of abuse.

Another reason ATCKs seek therapy in this time frame may be that many are now parents and, as they look into the face of their young child(ren), they remember some of their early years in faraway countries. They recall the not-so-good as well as the good. Those who went to boarding school at the age of six now wonder how in the world their parents could have sent them away because they can't imagine doing that with their own children. Or, conversely, some ATCKs who are now settled in one place feel grief that their children will not experience the international lifestyle they once knew. For whatever reasons, the need to process the past happens for ATCKs as it does for people of all backgrounds. But the invisibility of their world can add a particular stress they can't understand because they have "no apparent reason" to feel as they do. That's why they have come to see you!

## What Are the DSM Codes for "TCK Disorder"?

By now in this first session, however, you may be wondering about one other reality of your life as a therapist: Figuring out how to pay your bills. All of this theory is interesting and you want to help your clients, but how do you make an accurate diagnosis for both the client's sake as well as your own ability to collect from your client's health insurance if they are the ones picking up the tab for your work? What DSM code will you list on the bill since there isn't anything in the DSM akin to "TCK Disorder"?

First, let me reassure you that I am not reinventing the wheel for how you can be a good therapist. TCKs are first of all persons—like all other people. Their symptoms and potential diagnoses are not new; it is only that as you continue to work with them that you realize some of the *reasons* for their symptoms or the particular issues they face are new to you. This book is merely trying to expand your awareness of new considerations therapists need to take as they work in a globalizing world. You will use the DSM codes for them as you do for any client.

But I have also seen how the therapists who do not understand what is part of the "new normal" for TCKs can look at their behavior or presenting symptoms and come to wrong conclusions. Too often I have seen the normal responses that many TCKs have to a globally mobile childhood misdiagnosed and common characteristics for TCKs labeled in pathological terms. Here's one example.

## Common Misdiagnoses

Carmen, age nine, was taken to the therapist's office by her parents. Their family had lived and worked in the diplomatic service in Latin America for the last ten years. They had moved every few years and Carmen had attended two different schools by the time she got to the fourth grade. Now, they were trying to get settled into a small community on the west coast where her father had gotten a job as a professor in a large state university. The parents had been very careful in selecting a home that was located close to a good school system. They thought their three children would quickly settle into their new school and make new friends. Thus, all would be normal for once in many years.

For the two younger children, ages seven and three, life did settle down quickly as they made smooth adjustments to life in the United States. But for Carmen, it was a completely different story. The first morning of the new school year, Carmen woke up with a stomachache and cried and cried, declaring she did not want to go to school. Her parents let her stay home that day, noting that she seemed perfectly fine around ten that morning. The second day was just like the first day with complaints of a stomachache, many tears, and begging to stay home. This time her parents insisted that she go to school. Her mother walked her to the door of her new classroom and watched her quietly enter the room. When her mother called her daughter's teacher a couple weeks later, she was told that Carmen would not talk or interact with the other students. She just sat at her desk or on a far corner bench during recess and watched her classmates. She did not join in their recess activity, but just observed her classmates. Whenever the teacher would ask her questions in class, the only response she got was silence. Her parents and Carmen's teacher agreed they would just be patient and not force the situation, giving Carmen more time to adjust.

Now, it was six months down the road and Carmen and her parents were in a local therapist's office. Carmen was still throwing a fit in the mornings, begging to stay home from school. At school, she had begun to talk with her classmates. Only instead of the fun-loving, kind Carmen they had known in Latin America, she was acting like a bully. She got into trouble for fighting on the playground and the normally straight-A student was failing all of her classes in the fourth grade. At home, she constantly picked on her younger siblings and when her parents tried to correct her, she would run to her room, screaming hateful things, slam her door, and lock it. Her parents were completely befuddled. What had happened to their happy, well-adjusted little girl with good grades and many friends? They thought they had done everything right so that their children would thrive. The budget had been stretched in order to purchase a home in a good school system. Was Carmen just being a spoiled kid?

A therapist might think Carmen should be given the diagnosis of Oppositional Defiant Disorder due to her negative and defiant behavior. She certainly did fit some of the criteria of Oppositional Defiant Disorder, but was that it? Should the therapist see only the parents and give them some parenting skills on how to deal with their daughter's out-of-control behavior? Should they be encouraged to be unsympathetic to the behavior and adopt a stern approach with their daughter's emotional outbursts? What was the root cause for Carmen's behavior? The key point not to be missed in Carmen's story is *she was not displaying this type of behavior before their last move.*

> What a shame to give a TCK a label that may follow them through life instead of simply recognizing and naming an anxiety or grief issue. Anxiety and grief are socially accepted diagnoses while Oppositional Defiant Disorder is a serious label.

The correct diagnosis for Carmen was anxiety due to her loss of control over her own life. What a shame to give a TCK a label that may follow her (or him) through life instead of recognizing it as an anxiety or grief issue. Anxiety and grief are socially accepted while Oppositional Defiant Disorder is a serious label. Carmen had been carrying much unresolved grief due to all of the transitions she had already experienced in her young life.

What are other common misdiagnoses I have seen given to TCKs? And why do TCKs tend to get slapped with these in particular?

*Borderline Personality Disorder*

Because TCKs have had to repeatedly say Goodbye to family and friends, they often form close relationships quickly and have a sixth sense that quickly kicks in when there is any form of movement in their relationships. Their grief and/or panic may be so intense regarding the departure of yet another close relationship that it is easy to misdiagnosis them as Borderline Personality Disorder since the DSM describes the it as "a pervasive pattern of instability of interpersonal relationships . . . . frantic efforts to avoid real or imagined abandonment . . . a pattern of unstable and intense interpersonal relationships." (APA [DSM IV], 1994, p. 208). This is a good description of the relationships of many TCKs. But they don't fit the rest of the criteria in the DSM.

*Narcissistic Personality Disorder*

Narcissism is another diagnosis that often appears in the TCK's treatment plan. When they recount all of the countries they have visited or lived in, it sounds at times like bragging. It is natural for TCKs to talk about running around in Paris on spring break or mention going to New York City over their Christmas holiday. When they talk about their friend, the son of the President of Kenya, it is usually simply talking about their good friend and not with the intention to impress you.

My brothers and I learned to roller skate in front of the Presidential Palace, a block from our downtown apartment, in Honduras. Why did we skate there? It had the best sidewalk with a gentle downhill slope that made for a fast, thrilling ride. As a result, we got to meet several Central American presidents. Whenever I tell this story, I try to normalize this experience so as not to come across as arrogant with the statement, "Who could turn down three cute little blond-haired kids on roller skates?" Yes, if you don't know my dry humor, it still sounds narcissistic.

Tina Quick gives an example of TCKs coming across as narcissistic in her book, *The Global Nomad's Guide to University Transition* (Quick, 2010, p. 122). There she makes the suggestion to college-aged TCKs that they should just say they went to the beach and leave out which country. That works well unless the other person asks the TCK which beach. Then the TCK is busted and may be seen as arrogant. TCKs try very hard to make friendships wherever they live, only to be perceived as something they are not. This even happens in the therapist's office when a therapist might write "delusions of grandeur" on their chart.

*Schizophrenia*

I met Katie, a middle-aged woman, for lunch. She wanted to share her writings with me around the topic of transitions. Katie grew up as a TCK in Asia, the daughter of military parents, and talked about the severe depression she had gone through during her college years. Sadly, although Katie had recognized this problem and sought professional help, none of the many therapists she had seen were able to treat her effectively. She had gone from one therapist to another only to repeatedly get a misdiagnosis. One was Borderline, as mentioned above, or a form of Dissociative Disorder due to possible abuse. In her final attempt at seeking professional help, the therapist diagnosed her with schizophrenia. That's when she dropped out of counseling completely.

As I chatted with her, I quickly assessed that there was nothing schizophrenic about this young woman. Her thoughts were lucid—no scrambling of words, no paranoia. She was very much in touch with the real world and seemed quite normal to me. I was glad that she had not just crawled into a cave to die upon that most unfortunate misdiagnosis, but instead had fought her way up and out of the severe depression that had plagued her for years once she understood the normal stressors of any transition cycle and realized how many times she had gone through that experience as her family moved from base to base. She was now working hard to help other expatriate families deal well with these predictable patterns of transition so their TCKs didn't have to go through the despair she had known when no therapist seemed to understand this basic piece of her story.

These are some of the more common misdiagnoses that I have heard about in my work with TCKs. All therapists, myself included, have likely given clients a wrong diagnosis at some point in our career, but for most of the ones TCKs have told me about, I am sure if their therapists had known more about their invisible world and upbringing, a better label could have been given that would have led to faster healing rather than more false guilt and shame.

Having said all of this about how a TCK might be mistakenly mislabeled with a Personality Disorder or something more severe, let me be clear I do understand that there are times when such a diagnosis is justified. Because TCKs are first and foremost human beings, we know humans of all backgrounds can struggle with major mental health issues for reasons perhaps none of us will fully understand. TCKs can, in fact, struggle with any one of the above diagnoses just like others.

The trick is for therapists working with a globally mobile population to differentiate between those situations where we may be seeing true psychosis and the TCKs who come in exhibiting behavior that would be easy to classify in a dramatic way but, in reality, are showing quite common patterns or coping mechanisms for those who have shared similar globally mobile experiences. If we normalize the following three realities for our TCKs and ourselves as therapists, it will help us differentiate between what are coping methods for some of these experiences and may need to be addressed in that light and what behavior goes beyond "Normal for a TCK."

These are three realities we need to understand that are common for the TCK story:

- Cycles of transition give rise to multiple losses that result in grief that can come out in other ways.

- Changing cultural environments at critical stages of life interrupts the traditional process for learning a sense of cultural balance and belonging, so it will simply take a longer time for them to resolve these questions of how to define who they are and how they fit in the world.

- Changing cultural worlds, and the frequency with which they have lost close relationships due to the high mobility of the expat world, can lead to some difficulties in establishing or keeping relationships.

I will take the next chapters to discuss some of the diagnoses found in the DSM that you are likely to see as accurate diagnoses among your TCK clients and help you see how and why these symptoms develop when there are so many wonderful things about their life as well. The three most common presenting symptoms for TCKs relate to depression and anxiety, adjustment disorders, and signs of post-traumatic stress disorder (PTSD). Relational issues are also a big factor when TCKs arrive at therapy. While there is overlapping of why certain parts of this experience manifest in these ways, I will spend a chapter on explaining some of the common etiology I see behind each of these diagnoses.

# Things You Should Know

1.  The more you understand the TCKs' or ATCKs' basic third culture story as well as their specific background, the more you will understand their current behavior or feelings and be able to offer appropriate interventions.

2.  The first session with your TCK client is crucial because most are deciding what to tell you about their past worlds. They worry that you will see the international part of their story as a matter of geography, not as a dynamic which has shaped them profoundly.

3.  The majority of TCKs who voluntarily show up in your office are in their 30s because life is supposed to have settled down for them by that age and they are now in the emotional space where they can focus on their history.

4.  The common misdiagnoses are: Borderline Personality Disorder, Narcissistic Personality Disorder, and Schizophrenia.

5.  When working with a globally mobile population, it is important to differentiate between those situations of true psychosis and the common patterns or coping mechanisms for those who have shared similar globally mobile experiences.

6.  There are three realities that are common in the TCK story:
    a.  Cycles of transition that give rise to multiple losses and grief that can come out in other ways.
    b.  Changing cultural environments at critical stages of life which interrupt traditional processes for learning cultural balance and belonging.
    c.  Changing cultural worlds that result in broken relationships and difficulty or reluctance in establishing relationships.

# Discussion Questions & Activities

1. After having read this last chapter, how would you rate your intake interview and assessment process in terms of how it might help you discover if your client is or is not a TCK/ATCK? What factors would you now listen for that might be related to a globally mobile childhood?

2. What is something you learned from reading this chapter that will help you in a new way the next time someone with a similar story comes to your office?

3. What are some ways that you might learn about the world of the TCK or the Third Culture Adult (TCA)?

4. Are there other diagnoses that might mistakenly end up in the client chart of the TCK or ATCK? Why might they end up with that particular "label"? Why does it matter?

5. Activity: Get out your Intake Form. (If you are in training, use a standard Intake Form.) Start the process of changing it to allow you to recognize an adult TCK. Go to www.quietstreamscounseling.com to download Lois' Intake Form. Share with the class why you added to or deleted from the Standard Form or Lois' form.

6. Activity: Create your own talking guide or download the one at www.quietstreamscounseling.com and modify it to fit your personality and comfort level.

# Chapter 4

# Dealing with Depression and

# Anxiety Disorder: "Why Do I Feel

# So Sad When My Life is So Good?"

*"Mobility introduces tears into our story."*

Doug Ota, adult Cross-Cultural Kid (CCK) and Psychologist

---

From Ruth Van Reken's book, *Letters Never Sent*

This is a story about healing—not physical healing, but emotional. It took me a long time to recognize that I needed this healing; after all, compared to many other lives around me, my life was unquestionably good.

From my earliest days, I was taught of God's love for me, and I returned it. My parents' love was consistent. Their warm relationship to one another was a positive example. Despite the usual squabbles among my brothers and sisters, we maintained a deep commitment to each other. My husband, David, is a wonderful, loving man and an exemplary father to our three healthy, beautiful daughters. We had enjoyed our lives together, both in the States and overseas. With all of this going for me, how could I be anything but gloriously happy?

Yet the appearance of perfection hid a person given to depression, anger, and a spirit of criticism. No amount of praying made it better. Sometimes things improved for a while, but soon everything was as before. I couldn't understand why my soul, earnestly crying out for help, was unable to change. What was the key? (Van Reken, 2002, p. iv)

---

## Depression and Anxiety Disorder

Often TCKs show up for therapy because they are experiencing severe depression. They may not know why they are dealing with depression; they just know they are miserable. And as you walk through the symptoms of depression or give them the Beck Depression Inventory, they might certainly fit into that diagnosis. But rather than focusing only on what is currently taking place in their lives, such as what we do when we do Brief Therapy, here are some other areas you should explore.

Often a major problem in trying to understand what might be causing depression for those who have been globally mobile is one simple fact: Their lives are often so rich and filled with privilege, they and thosr around them don't see how they could have a reason to be depressed. For the TCKs, many don't have the usual markers that often seem to precipitate a depression. Ruth wrote the words that begin this chapter in her preface to *Letters Never Sent,* the journal she wrote as she tried to understand why she struggled with depression when she had "no reason."

Ruth had no history of terrible abuse in her home, or growing up with an alcoholic parent. She had enjoyed her life as a child growing up in Nigeria and was back in Africa doing what she loved. Yet there had been this place of silent depression off and on for years. Why?

As she did her journaling Ruth began to understand for the first time that the very goodness of her life was one of the reasons the grief of losing the world and land of her childhood had been so painful. The very joy she knew in her family meant that when her parents returned to Africa and left her in Chicago for her four years of high school, even though she had a great situation with her aunt and grandma, that separation created a loss.

With loss is grief and it had been greater than she recognized at the time. At age 39, Ruth had to do the grief work she should have done for these and other losses encountered but never acknowledged in her global childhood because, as she explained, "compared to many other lives around me, my life was unquestionably good." This is a common theme among many TCKs.

## Understanding High Mobility

A major reality for those who grow up as TCKs is that their lives are filled with chronic cycles of separation and loss. Obviously, such cycles are part of the human experience for everyone. Non-globally mobile folks go through this as well. But for the globally mobile, the cycles are chronic and often relatively sudden or severe. They not only lose a friend here or there, but often they lose a whole world when they take an airplane ride away from a place and people they have loved.

That's what we mean when we say that one of the characteristics of the third culture itself is that it is a lifestyle filled with high mobility. Not only do particular individuals frequently go back and forth between home and host culture themselves, but also so do most of their friends. Some international schools filled with TCKs have a 40% or more turnover rate in their student population every year. That's a lot of Goodbyes, even for those who stay. Think about it: Each time they say Goodbye, whether because they themselves are leaving or because friends are going, there is grief. The more they love their friends or feel connected to the place where they are living, the deeper the grief.

But what do they do with it? Life is going on and there are no rituals of mourning to name and process the loss. Often the excitement for the adventure of travel and all that lies ahead, including friends and relatives they want to see, masks the enormity of the loss so it gets tucked away and life continues.

## The Transition Cycle

These cycles of mobility affect all globally mobile people, not only the children. One helpful model for therapists to keep in mind as they work with families who have moved around the world together is that the members of a family do not process transitions at the same speed. David Pollock created his Transition Model to help show the clear stages in transition. He spoke primarily of physical transitions but also pointed out that this model works for life transitions as well. In short, these are the stages and the basic characteristic of each stage (Pollock & Van Reken, 2009).

David C. Pollock's Stages of Transition Cycle (as it relates to physical mobility):

- *Involvement*

  o You know where you fit, and others know where you fit.

  o You live mentally in the present.

- *Leaving (Change)*

  o News comes that you are leaving. You begin to think about the future instead of living in the present. You often look at the "bright side" of what is to be rather than the "dark side" of the losses that will also be.

  o You begin to "lean away" from those around you.

- *Transition*

  o You have left your former place but are not yet feeling at home or part of the new place. You may have arrived physically but you have not arrived emotionally. This is when the reality of the loss can often hit and you begin to wonder why on earth you made the decision to move.

  o Time is lived with a sense of remembering the past and wondering/hoping that the future will be better and more settled than the present.

  o Others in the community also don't yet know who you are or where you fit.

- *Entry*

  o Here you begin to make the decision to move towards the new place and situation.

  o Others are beginning to accept you and know how you function as well.

  o Time begins to return to a clearer focus on the present, with less frequent regrets for what you have lost.

- *Re-involvement*
    - Once again you are part of the community. They know you, you know them, and you have a sense of belonging.
    - The sense of time is once more the present.

One of the special challenges for families who are doing frequent transitions is that each member may be at a different stage at any particular time. While the parent whose career brought the family to this place is off and running to his or her new job, the accompanying spouse and children may still be struggling to figure out how to use the new public transportation system or long for familiar friends and food. Or one child may be happily settled in the new school and the other child can only cry for the friends left behind. For some TCKs the moves have been so frequent and so many that they never truly entered the re-involvement stage for any or most of their moves. This can be part of their depression as well—that they never got to the point of feeling as if they belonged anywhere. The same thing can take place with adults who relocate every two years; they never get to the stage where they belong in any locale.

wooy.

## Comparing the Transition Model to the Stages of Grief Model

One interesting fact you might notice about the transition cycle is that if you look closely you will notice a similarity in the emotional responses to each stage of the Transition Cycle and the emotions of Elisabeth Kübler-Ross's classic stages of grief.

Stages of grief by Elisabeth Kübler-Ross (Kübler-Ross & Kessler, 2005):

- Denial
- Anger
- Bargaining
- Depression/sadness
- Acceptance

This would make sense because, as noted earlier, globally mobile people experience chronic cycles of separation and loss simply because they and those around them are moving so frequently. But in comparing the two models, we can learn another lesson from Kübler-Ross's stages of grief that applies to those in stages of transition.

In past years this Stages of Grief Model was used with clients to show them they were not abnormal and to help them see that their various responses to loss could come out in these different ways. But the reality is the process is better depicted in a circle model drawn up by a professor of psychology, Pam Davis, in 2003. She uses this to depict how we can move from one stage of grief and back to another after any given loss.

Adapted from Pam Davis' Grief Wheel

## The Grief Wheel

© Pamela Davis, Ph.D.
Used by permission

Keren Humphrey, a retired professor of counseling from Texas A&M who wrote the book *Counseling Strategies for Loss and Grief* (2009), claims that clients get stuck in the idea of stages and think when they have finished the stages they are done—only to be disappointed later when they find themselves again in what they think is a previous stage. She makes the point that individuals walk through grief at their own pace and in their own unique style. It is not unusual for people to circle back through a stage, triggered by an event, person, or comment.

All of these are important principles when working with clients who are in the middle of physical transitions. They may believe they have said Goodbye well in the leaving stage, only to find that a longing for home in the former place suddenly overwhelms them six months down the road. Also, each family member goes through transition at their own pace. That means conflict can arise when one member—often the spouse who has moved for a career's sake—goes to the office instantly in this new land, makes a quick adjustment, and is soon re-involved while others in the family struggle mightily. The person in the stage of re-involvement can become quite impatient with the family member who seems to remain lost in the grief of leaving, and all of this adds to the daily stress of adjusting to a new culture.

The simple fact is that like the stages of grief, no one goes through the transition stages in absolute sequence either. Nor, as mentioned previously, will each member go through them at the same pace as others. When a family comes in, I have both the transition and grief models in mind, as they help me assess how the process of global mobility is impacting my clients, but I remember they are helpful tools, not absolute guidelines.

## Types of Expatriate Grief and Mourning

With just this quick look at the transitions inherent in any globally mobile experience, it's not hard to see why there is grief. Duncan Westwood is an expert on this subject of grief most commonly experienced by those who live and work internationally. He not only grew up cross-culturally himself, but also has worked extensively as a psychologist for International Health Management, a holisitic clinic in Toronto, Canada, which offers physical as well as emotional support for globally mobile individuals and families.

During Westwood's doctoral research, he discovered that there are eight types of grief commonly seen in this community (Westwood, 1998). He listed them as:

1. *Abbreviated Grief and Mourning.* This is genuine but very short-lived. It is due to the loss being minor, with little attachment to the loss, or recognition that the loss has already become a gain. And it often occurs when TCKs have no time, space, or permission to grieve.

2. *Anticipated Grief and Mourning.* Most of the grieving occurs before the loss has taken place. This is common among adolescent TCKs as they anticipate another transition when they have to say Goodbye to their friends/peers.

3. *Ambiguous Grief and Mourning.* This type occurs during, betwixt, and between times when losses and gains are not clear and/or final. Times of ambiguous grief and mourning are present throughout expatriate life.

4. *Delayed Grief and Mourning.* This is postponement of normal grief, long after the loss has occurred. It is common among expat parents during the years when kids are at home. For example, the mother delays her own grief and mourning in order to care for her kids.

5. *Exaggerated Grief and Mourning.* This type occurs when symptoms are intensified and/or prolonged. It can be associated with acute and/or accumulated losses.

6. *Inhibited Grief and Mourning.* When symptoms or manifestations of normal grief are masked or repressed and revealed later in psychosomatic complaints, it is referred to as inhibited grief and mourning.

7. *Normal Grief and Mourning.* This is the normal human response to, and recovery from, loss which can persist for a period of 3–24 months after the loss.

8. *Unresolved Grief and Mourning.* This involves a history of losses that haven't been processed, a common presenting concern for ATCKs.

I agree with Westwood that you will see all of these various types of grief in your globally mobile clients, and the skills you have learned for dealing with grief will be useful as you sort out which type of grief you may be seeing in your clients. Because, however, I also agree that the number one factor I see underlying many of the presenting symptoms of TCKs, ATCKs, and yes, even their parents and other TCAs, is **unresolved grief,** I want to look at this one type of grief in more detail. It's not hard to see how the high mobility most of these individuals experience can lead to grief, but the question then becomes, why is it so often unresolved? This is a key understanding for you to have as you work with the internationally mobile community.

One reason you will often see unresolved grief among your clients is simply that many TCKs (like so many of our clients who are non-TCK) are fearful of tapping into their grief. Some fear if they name the grief, they will deny the good in their experiences. They tend to polarize their feelings. Things are either all good or all bad. Yet, life is not quite that clear-cut.

Their thinking goes something like this: "If I tell you something bad about my international school, then you will think there is nothing good about my school." Or "If I tell you something bad about my school, then you will think my parents are bad for sending me there." It is easier to just say, "I loved my school" in order to avoid dealing with the complicated emotions of embracing both. True.

There are many other reasons our clients do not want to tap into their grief. Some of the reasons that are more commonly used are the following:

- "If I start to cry, I may not stop crying."

- "I will disappoint my parents if I cry."

- "We don't show emotions in our family; we are strong. I need to be strong."

- "I am so over that part of my life."

- "If I cry, then I will have to explain to you why I am crying. And I don't understand why I am crying." Yes. Yes. Yes. Yes Yes Yes Yes.

Pollock and Van Reken list four reasons they believe unresolved grief happens so often with TCKs (Pollock & Van Reken, 2009, pp. 76−83):

➢ Lack of awareness

➢ Lack of time

➢ Lack of permission

➢ Lack of comfort

Let's look at each of these in detail. These are some of the ways I see these played out with my TCK clients.

## *Lack of awareness*

One of the major reasons many globally mobile people have unresolved grief is that they simply do not recognize what they have lost. These are not the usual overt, concrete objects or visible losses such as death, divorce, injury, moving away from friends, having the box that contained all of your family picture albums stolen in the move, or some other catastrophic event. These are *hidden losses*—the often subtle, unnamed losses that are invisibly connected with the more visible losses of transition. Again, Humphrey has wisdom for us in this area. In her book on grief, she encourages therapists to focus not only on the "primary loss" such as the death of a loved one, but also on the "secondary losses," which are really the guts of the loss and should be the focus of therapy like the "loss of a companion, [with] expectations of a future together"(Humphrey, 2009, p. 29). It is those types of losses Pollock and Van Reken describe as "hidden."

This was my story. The first time I heard David Pollock speak was at the first Families in Global Transition (FIGT) conference in 1998. His entire section regarding grief and the many hidden losses TCKs experience particularly intrigued me and touched the core of my emotions. I felt and related to the deep grief of the TCKs whose stories he told that afternoon. His presentation made a powerful impact on me because I had been on my own long journey of realizing my various pieces of unresolved grief. Several years earlier I realized that when I returned to the U.S. for high school and my family stayed in Honduras, I not only lost their involvement in my life but I also lost the joy of the competition with quick puns with my brothers and the easy familiarity of switching between Spanish and English when we played together. On top of that, my parents never saw me play one basketball game for my high school, nor met any of my high school boyfriends. Through the years, my family and I realized all that we had lost as each of us kids went off to school. This is one reason my parents made the decision to return to their passport country so that we might be together once again as a family. My parents did not want to lose their own children. I admire them for making that hard decision. Yes, grief is painful.

Pollock listed examples of many hidden losses TCKs experience when they return to their home culture. TCKs experience the loss of such things as:

- Friends who already know their world,

- Use of second language,

- Easy access to favorite foods,

- The comfort of favorite objects that were too large to carry back,

- A sense of cultural balance—knowing how life works in this place,

- The loss of the past that was—the world as they knew it, and

- The loss of the past that wasn't—arriving "home" and realizing cousins and other relatives have shared many experiences as family that the TCK missed by being away. When others say, "Do you remember when…?" they don't.

The memory is still very clear in my mind of a missionary family's return from the jungles of Bolivia. They went through all types of paperwork to bring home "Teresita" their parrot, as she was a much-loved family member. My brothers and I were jealous, as we had to leave "Rosita," our parrot of many years, in El Hatillo, Honduras. Teresita became the surrogate pet of all Latin American TCKs who visited them.

The list of losses can go on and on. Many ATCKs did not have the language or rituals of mourning necessary to process the depth of their losses when they happened. And so life went on and the grief was buried.

## Lack of time *yep.*

As you well know, grief for any reason takes time to process, yet we live in a fast-paced world. In former days, when the early settlers in the U.S. moved to new places, they went by covered wagons pulled by horses. The pace was slow. The changes in surroundings happened bit by bit each day. There was time to consider both the past and the future. This same gift of time is offered to those who lose a loved one in death. In most cultures, they are excused from work to attend a parent's funeral. There is a time to sit with friends and remember the person who died, whether this takes place at a formal wake, a viewing and visitation, or just with friends coming to the house. The funeral takes place with formal times of remembering this person and facing the loss head on. The body is buried or cremated. Closure takes place in this way even though the grieving is not yet done. Everyone knows "it takes time."

But for those who lost their worlds with one cross-cultural transition, where was the funeral? Where was the process? A jet airplane landed in an entirely different world and culture in a matter of hours, not even days. After disembarking, the expectation was that those who were arriving would take a day or two to get over jetlag (maybe!) and then get going full force with settling into the new place. Where was the time to process what they had so recently lost—particularly when those in the new world often didn't want to hear their stories about the past? And so, life went on and the grief was buried.

→ *insert sobbing alone in bathrooms.*

## Lack of permission *yep.*

Another reason for unresolved grief is simply that, like the globally mobile adults and TCKs who see "no reason" for the depression they are experiencing, those around them also can't imagine how or why these folks who are living such a fabulously interesting life should feel grief. In particular, the human resources professionals who have worked so hard to give their employees good packages for their pay, travel, and even educational allowances for their children cannot fathom why, with all they have been given, these folks could possibly be depressed. When children express sadness at having to move once more, parents are often quick to jump in with some sort of, "But, Eduardo, just think about how much fun we're going to have when we get to Switzerland. We'll teach you how to ski and it will be great!" The problem for Eduardo is that he is actually looking forward to skiing and his parents are correct that it will be great, so he realizes he has "no reason" to feel sad that he is now leaving his home in Venezuela.

Another factor that takes away permission to look at the pain is based on the reason the parents went overseas in the first place. If they are in the military, how can TCKs mind when parents are literally protecting the very country to which they all belong? If parents are missionaries, how can the TCKs question their parents' desire to serve God? Surely whatever they have lost is worth it if God asked it of them. How can the child embrace both the pain and the joy of following God?

This goes back to where we began: the need to acknowledge and accept both the positives and the negatives of their experiences. But whenever others or the clients themselves have taken away permission for grief, again, there is no process for mourning the losses. And so, life goes on and the grief is buried.

### Lack of comfort  Yep.

Finally, there are some TCKs who do not deal with unresolved grief because there is no one to comfort them for their losses. In a way, this is an extension of lack *of permission.* A lack of emotional comfort is what happens when someone tries to encourage a person to go on before stopping to validate the feelings of the loss. Pollock and Van Reken state, "Offering comfort is a key factor in any grieving process—even when that process is delayed by decades. Remember, comfort is not encouragement. It is being there with understanding and love, not trying to change or fix things" (Pollock & Van Reken, 2009, p. 259).

Emotional comfort is different from encouragement. Encouragement attempts to fix the problem by wanting the other person to change their perspective and thus make it all okay. But what typically happens is when we begin with encouragement, the other person feels shame or frustration rather than comfort (Pollock & Van Reken, 2009, pp. 82–83).

It is through listening, understanding, comforting, and validating that we help our clients move towards healing. As we know, the loss the client experienced took place in the feeling part of the brain. Comfort gently touches the feelings. Once the feelings are affirmed and soothed, then the cognitive area of the brain can be engaged into action or an attempt to make sense of the loss. This is when encouragement comes into play. You need both, but before the client will listen to your words of encouragement and what you are encouraging him to *do*, he needs to know that you *feel with* him.

As a therapist, the best skill that you can employ is sitting and listening to your TCKs talk about their losses. If you attempt to reframe their losses as gains, the result is feelings of shame and withdrawal or anger. The result may be more hidden or delayed or unresolved grief and less willingness to proceed with therapy.

Henri Nouwen, a Catholic priest from the Netherlands and a well-respected author, talked about the role of comfort. *"When we honestly ask ourselves which person in our lives means the most to us, we often find that it is those who, instead of giving advice, solutions, or cures, have chosen rather to share our pain and touch our wounds with a warm and tender hand."* (Nouwen, n.d.)

But again, when there is no comforter, what do they do with the grief? Once more, life goes on and the grief is tucked away, only coming out in depression, anger, or anxiety.

## Additional Types of Depression

As you read these further possible reasons for depression among TCKs and TCAs, continue to keep in mind the underlying theme of loss. We have investigated the "normal" and inherent losses of any transition. But sometimes there are additional, and complicating, factors that add to the depth of the grief. It is important to understand these types of specific issues too. That's why taking a thorough history and paying attention to the Intake Form and follow-up questions I suggested in Chapter 3 are important.

Through them you can begin to uncover some of the more complicated issues for grief, loss, and thus depression in your clients. Here are a few more thoughts to consider when listening for the deeper story of the TCK in front of you.

How the parent left a system or a sector is important. If a parent got fired from his or her job and had to return to the home country, the ripple effect on the children is much greater than when, say, a parent living in Sao Paulo, Brazil, loses a job and then finds a new one in Manaus, Brazil. Obviously the family in Brazil will feel the effects of the move, but they remain close enough to see old friends, and the culture and language are the same. But for the family of someone who loses an international job, loss impacts the children of that family on many levels such as education, friendships, home, caretaker and all that is familiar to them, and could result in feelings of significant grief. There are often feelings of confusion and anger at the organization that fired their parent(s). The resulting question becomes, "Who am I now that our family has been cast out of our sector or organization?" There can also be anger at the parent for apparently not being adequate to keep the job and thus disrupting the entire family.

If the parents returned to the home country because of problems with their children, particularly your client, he or she could be struggling with feelings of guilt and shame. Maybe the parents are overtly blaming your client with constant reminders of whose fault it is that they lost their dream job. Or the parents may not be blaming your client at all, but that doesn't stop the sense of self-blame. Alex :)

If the parents returned to their home country due to moral failure on the part of a parent or the parents' marriage is falling apart, then you have even more complicated grief issues with which to deal. If a parent was involved in an affair and that parent stayed behind in the host culture in order to maintain that relationship while the other parent and children returned alone to the passport country, then that complicates the grief process as well.

The layers of grief can be many. You will need to focus on all types of adjustment and loss feelings—divorced parents, step-parents, new schools, visitation of the non-custodial parent, new rules within the family, the new culture, new friends, and the list goes on and on. It can be a nightmare. Then, add the piece where neither parent is paying attention to what is going on

73

with the children because they are completely distracted with their own chaos. Sometimes TCKs wind up with parents on two continents. What does a person do with all of that grief?

## How to Help

### Helping to identify the hidden losses

When working with an expat client (and that can be a citizen of another country living as an expat in your town) or a TCK who is struggling with depression, I always want to first explore this place of potential hidden loss. I give them the following homework assignment in order to help them process the depth of their losses. They are to put at the top of a sheet of paper the name of the country where they lived. For some clients it can be up to five sheets of paper. Then they are to divide the sheet in two columns. On each sheet of paper, they list all they lost in one column and what they gained in another column by leaving their previous place and moving to that place. They do this with each country where they lived. They list all their losses and gains. Most of the time, they return with about ten things listed for each place.

We then spend a session working together to explore what other losses they may have experienced. If their list includes only obvious, tangible losses, I ask, "So what else did you lose when you could no longer wake up in your home in Thailand (or wherever)? Maybe they will say, "The sound of the rooster crowing at daybreak." During this process, I will explore all of the senses. "What smells, sounds, feelings, have you lost by leaving that country?" "I miss the smell of the dust as we traveled through the mountains during the dry season." "I miss the sound of the bullet train as it came to a stop at my station." "I miss the feel of the masses as we rode the public bus through the city." The client is often amazed at the length of the list.

### Dealing with children

When working with TCKs who are children, I have used the same resources that I use with children whose parents go through a divorce as they deal with loss and how their home life has changed. We talk about their life *before* and their life *after* (the move). We talk about the confusion of emotions. We can talk about the happiness of visiting cousins and grandparents but the sadness as they left behind classmates and dear friends. We draw pictures of their home before and their home now. We look at photographs. We write letters to our peers who are left behind on how to make this transition or just tell them how much we miss them or think of them. The bookstores are filled with good books on how to help children deal with loss and grief.

There are also materials for children on moving which are good therapy tools to use with TCKs who are grieving. More and more resources are being developed to walk young TCKs through the many emotions of grief. Grief Therapy will be a reccurring theme of your work with TCKs of all ages. You can check my resource list in the Appendix for more ideas on how to use creative techniques with children as well as adults.

## Final Thoughts Regarding Grief

On the subject of grief, Doug Ota, an adult cross-cultural kid (CCK) and psychologist from the Netherlands states:

> *"I have learned that I can trust grief. That while it feels like it's burrowing around in the mud or in a dark cave, it is looking for something, and it knows what it seeks. I have learned that grief is looking for the same thing I am: a story that makes sense. Grief doesn't like stories that don't make sense any more than we do. Those stories hurt. The fact that entire systems of organizing life no longer seem to matter hurts. The fact that people and places we knew and loved go and leave us behind hurts. The fact that fundamental elements of identities can fade before our eyes hurts. But the hurt is temporary. The hurt is a gateway to something greater—just like the marathons I run nowadays to keep me from forgetting these lessons. I am no longer afraid of other people's dark places because I have explored so many of my own."* (Doug Ota, 2009)

*wow, good words.*

## Grief and Loss Issues and the DSM

If my TCK client is a child or a youth and is dealing with grief regarding his or her last move or the family's frequent moves, I will probably label it as an Adjustment Disorder with Mixed Anxiety and Depressed Mood as the symptoms mostly occur within three months of the onset of the stressor and do not persist longer than six months. I will double-check the DSM IV to be sure this meets the criteria for an Adjustment Disorder and it does not fit the criteria for another specific Axis I disorder. I will go with the lesser diagnosis rather than the one that is more severe.

But in most cases, if my client is an adult TCK or a third culture adult (TCA), and if he or she is dealing with grief resulting from his or her frequent moves, a difficult move, or a major conflict in a relationship or marriage, that person often fits the criteria for a mood disorder such as a Depressive Disorder or an Anxiety Disorder.

Again, go to your DSM manual and see if your client meets the criteria for either Clinical Depression or some form of Generalized Anxiety. In my treatment of the ATCK and TCA, I will do a lot of Cognitive Behavioral Therapy, working with them on their self-statements and their thoughts around their losses or relationships, as well as intertwining their beliefs around their life outside their passport country and today. With these clients I will utilize several of the creative techniques described in Chapter 8 to help them work through or resolve the conflict or bring the grief down to a level where it is no longer paralyzing their current behavior.

With the TCK or TCA, evaluate if you need to refer them to a psychiatrist for medication. It is my preference to try and help my client walk through their grief first. But if they are too far into the depths of grief or anxiety and there is a family history of either of these disorders, I may recommend that they set up an appointment with a good psychiatrist. Medication can help the client gain the emotional energy to walk through what is troubling them, regain their stability, learn good coping skills, and ultimately get off of all medication.

# Things You Should Know

1.  A major reality for the globally mobile is that their lives are filled with chronic cycles of separation and loss. For the globally mobile, the cycles are chronic and often relatively severe.

2.  The Stages of Transition developed by David Pollock are: Involvement, Leaving, Transition, Entry and Re-involvement.

3.  Clients present for counseling due to a varity of needs, but many times there are deep, unresolved grief issues buried underneath the presenting problem.

4.  The key reasons for unresolved grief are: lack of awareness of what they lost, lack of time to process grief due to a fast-paced life, lack of permission to grieve since they do not seem to have a "reason" for their sorrow, and lack of emotional comfort since the losses are hidden.

5.  TCKs may not recognize all they have lost in their many transitions—language, friends, routine, pets, caregivers, special foods, views, hobbies, homes, etc.

# Discussion Questions & Activity

1.  How do you help a client walk through deep grief? What grief model(s) do you use most frequently? Does it (or do they) fit in this case?

2.  Discuss how you would work differently with a client with visible losses versus a client with invisible losses.

3.  When does grief and loss move from an Adjustment Disorder to Clinical Depression? Talk about how this is more difficult to figure out with the TCK.

4.  Activity on doing delayed grief work: Think of a time when you had to delay dealig with grief, such as the need to get through an unrelated situation (like final exams) or a related situation (like planning the funeral). Some people delay grief so they can get their own children through the situation. Other people delay it by AVOIDING grief because they are fearful of it. Talk about how you felt during the delay. Explain how you later worked through the grief or why you still have not dealt with the grief.

# Chapter 5

# Working Through Adjustment Disorders:

# "Who Am I, Really?"

*"I arrived from Rome the 20th of June. Everything here is still utterly unknown, so totally different for me: our house and our car and our neighborhood, the streetlights and the food and the stores.*

*I'm carrying eight years of friendships and experiences and sights, of small, unnoticed knowledge and love for small, 'unthought-of' things that have no link to or acknowledgement in this new place.*

*Physically, I am here. But everything that belongs to me, everything that defines me, is on the other side of the Atlantic Ocean, in the old, sunny streets where my Italian friends laugh and yell, in impossibly far away Rome . . ."*

Ursula Lindsey, age 15 (Lindsey, 1994, p. 55)

*i get this*

Elizabeth, a bright young woman with parents of Jamaican descent, had grown up in England where she was born. As her dad climbed the corporate ladder, the family moved to South America for several years, where Elizabeth learned to speak Spanish simply by living in a Spanish-speaking world. There she went to a British school, but the students represented many different nationalities. One day her father came home with the news that they would be moving again—this time to the United States. He had just taken a high level-job with an international corporation based in Indianapolis.

At first, Elizabeth thought it would be another grand adventure. She even knew the language! But the move had not gone as smoothly as she expected.

The first problem was passing the entrance exams a local school gave her in their efforts to place her in the right grade. What did she know about inches and feet when she had been taught in millimeters and centimeters? The curriculum for math in a British school taught math concepts in a different order than in the U.S., so she had learned things that kids her age in the U.S. had not studied yet, and vice versa. The standardized admission tests for children her age relied heavily on a working knowledge of American currency, especially identifying currency by the president on the front and using colloquial names for each coin. Because she had just arrived in the U.S., Elizabeth had no idea how to answer those questions. Those who assessed her also said she didn't know how to spell because too often Elizabeth used an extra 'u' for words like colour and behaviour. She did so poorly on the test that the educators insisted on placing her one grade below other students her age.

Two months later, after she had joined grade-level social groups such as the Girls Scouts and gotten a bit more used to the way of doing school in the United States, the administrators realized they had misplaced her, and put her back into the upper grade. So for the rest of her time in that school, Elizabeth had totally separate groups—her classmates during the school day and those she socialized with outside of school.

When she came to see me, she felt despair. She told me how, at one point, she had been on a panel where she was asked the question, "What is the hardest thing about being a TCK for you?" She replied, "When people see me, they think I am an African American, but I'm not." A Black man in the audience had taken exception to her statement.

"Why do you want to be White?" he asked.

"I don't want to be White, but I'm not African and I'm not American. My roots are from Jamaica and I am British," she had tried to explain, realizing that if *he* did not understand, she could hardly expect others to understand.

Elizabeth expressed one of the most common issues TCKs face as they move on into life: "Who am I, really? The way other folks see me or the way I see myself?" The two biggest challenges I see among adult TCKs are the unresolved grief discussed in the last chapter and questions of identity to be explored in this chapter.

## Struggles with Identity Issues

One of my favorite movies is a perfect example of how many TCKs may be feeling when they come to your office.

The Disney cartoon *Tarzan II* begins where Tarzan is the young adolescent struggling to fit in with his peers. Remember, he is a human who is raised by apes. Throughout the movie, Tarzan attempts to answer the question about his identity. He tries to act like each of his friends and fit into their worlds. He attempts to be an ape, a giraffe, a bird, a fish, and various other animals— only to realize he cannot fit in. And if he were to find another human in the jungle, he would not be like them either since he was raised by the apes. Throughout Tarzan's search for identity, the words of this song declare his struggle.

"Who Am I?"
sung by Tiffany Evans
in *Tarzan II* by Disney

*Sometimes everything seems outta my reach,*
*No matter how hard I try.*
*Sometimes I feel like nothing at all inside.*
*Everything that I try to hold on to*
*Just seems to slip away*
*And though I fall, it keeps calling me back again,*
*But I keep looking.*
*I'll find myself; I keep searchin' for the real me.*

*Who am I? Tell me.*
*Where do I come from?*
*Who am I? Tell me.*
*'Cause it's like I don't fit in at all.*

*Sometimes I feel like runnin' away*
*And leaving it all behind.*
*And try to find a place where I belong.*
*If I keep lookin',*

*I'll find myself. I keep searchin' to find the real me.*
*Who am I? Tell me.*
*Where do I come from?*
*Who am I? Tell me.*
*'Cause it's like I don't fit in at all.*

(Evans, 2005)

At the end of the Disney movie, his friend Zugor answers his plea with the simple statement, "You are a Tarzan." Tarzan realizes that, instead of being a "nothing," he is a "something" in the jungles.

An earlier movie about Tarzan (made in black and white years before the Disney version) depicts the grown-up Tarzan's venture into the civilized world (New York City)—and he does not fit in at all there either. Why? Because he is a Tarzan of two very different worlds: He is a combination of the animals in the jungle and the humans in the city. In the old black-and-white movie, Tarzan returned to the jungle to live out his years with his human wife Jane, and eventually their own little boy who learned to swing on the vines through the trees like his father. Tarzan was a part of the jungle and was fluent in the language and ways of the animals, and yet he was also a man with all his own human characteristics.

## Who Am I?

So many TCKs are "a Tarzan" searching for their identity among their friends who cannot answer the question, let alone understand just why they are even asking the question. Some phrases that I have heard TCKs use to describe themselves are:

- cultural misfits,
- confusion of cultures,
- uniquely me,
- mixture of cultures,
- neither here nor there, and
- one foot in the door and one foot out the door.

Just like Tarzan, no matter how much they try to be like those around them, it never quite works. It's as if they are lost between worlds. Why do so many TCKs feel this way? Is it truly some sort of new disorder? Can we help them move from seeing themselves as misfits to understanding how they, like Tarzan, can use who they are in productive ways in whatever world they move into as adults?

To help sort out what is normal in this realm for TCKs versus what is pathological, let's look first at the basic idea of the interplay between culture and identity and then see how this applies to the TCK experience.

## How Culture Relates to Identity Formation

Identity is formed at least in part as a result of the messages about ourselves that we absorb from the society or culture around us—our family, our peers, our faith, and others in our community. Another way to say that is that when we look at others, we see the mirror of what we are supposed to look like, be, and do in our cultural world. In the days when these worlds around children stayed stable, learning a sense of "Who am I?" was usually not too difficult. Each component of the surrounding world reinforced the same message: "You are one of us." Or "You are not one of us."

If, however, the cultural environment is constantly changing as it frequently does for TCKs, then it becomes much harder to sort out the question of "Who am I?" Like Tarzan, for years many TCKs have asked, "How do I choose which is *my* culture or world from all of those I have been part of?" No matter where they look, there is no clear mirror that reflects who they are both outside and inside.

Traditionally, in a more stable community, people learned the cultural rules as children, then tested them as teenagers, and eventually assimilated them and moved out into the world as adults, confident that they knew how to get along in this group and society. In such a world, all the mirrors around the child reflected back the same clear, consistent message. "You are part of us." Or, in rarer cases, "You are *not* part of us. You are a 'them.'" How these children related to that community was not in doubt. As children learned the ways of their world, they were in "cultural balance"—knowing how this world operated without any longer having to stop and think out each action or custom before proceeding with daily life. For most, this led to a sense of belonging and confidence.

This stable, essentially mono-cultural community is not the world in which TCKs grow up. Just when they should be testing the cultural rules, they are often moving to another country where all the rules and customs of the world around them instantly change. What is approved of in one culture may be a complete blunder in another. By the time TCKs might be feeling they are in some sort of cultural balance, their parents come home and tell them it's time to take off again to still another world. While all this cultural mixing and matching may be interesting and part of how TCKs ultimately develop intercultural skill sets that serve them well in later careers, for children who are trying to sort out a primary task of childhood—understanding who they are and where they belong—such changes can be disconcerting.

## Growing Cultural Complexities in Today's World

The growing cultural complexity many children face as they try to grow up with parents from different races, different cultures, and different languages and who may now be living on different continents adds even more factors for therapists to consider as it adds to the struggles some have to develop a clear sense of "Who am I?"

Here is a great example of this type of cultural complexity so many people are now experiencing.

Pico Iyer is currently a journalist for *Time Magazine* and travels the world, just as he did in his childhood. He grew up in three cultures, never lived on a continent where he had relatives, could not speak the mother tongue of either of his parents (they were from different parts of India), and never stayed long enough anywhere to be able to vote. He describes himself as "The son of Hindu-born Theosophists, I was educated entirely in Christian schools and spend most of my time now in Buddhist lands; ...and, though, I spend most of my year in rural Japan or in a Catholic monastery, I've nonetheless accumulated 1.5 million miles on one American airline alone" (Iyer, 2000, p. 23).

He goes on further to describe his life, "The country where people look like me is the one where I can't speak the language, the country where people sound like me is a place where I look highly alien, and the country where people live like me is the most foreign space of all. And though, when I was growing up, I was nearly always the only mongrel in my classroom or neighborhood, now, when I look around, there are more and more people in a similar state, the children of blurred boundaries and global mobility....the very notion of home is foreign to me as the state of foreignness is the closest thing I know to home" (Iyer, 2000, p. 24).

In order to give more language to discuss this global change, Van Reken introduced the idea of the broader category of Cross-Cultural Kids (CCKs) mentioned in the first chapter of this book. She described this phenomenon more completely in chapter 3 of the revised edition of *Third Culture Kids* and continued to raise these important questions in an article she and Paulette Bethel wrote for *Intercultural Management Quarterly* (Van Reken & Bethel, 2012, pp. 10−11):

> How, then, do we handle the growing 'cultural complexity' or 'hidden diversity' of today's younger generations? Which culture shall we presume is before us when interacting with a Korean, born and raised in Korea for seven years, who then spent five years as an immigrant's child in the U.S. before his family moved to Kenya, where he finished his pre-university education at an international school? Do we refer to him as a Korean? An American? A Kenyan? A third culture kid? As none of the above, or all of the above? Growing up in many cultures is not the problem—it is trying to fit into pre-assigned slots in adolescence and adulthood that causes difficulties.

In order to understand why this matter of sorting out their identity while growing up cross-culturally is such a major issue for many TCKs—regardless of how relatively simple or complex their cultural history may be—take a moment to look at one model of culture and then how that applies to the TCK experience.

## The Iceberg Model of Culture

One of the most fascinating models of culture is Dr. Gary Weaver's Cultural Iceberg. He is the founder and director of the Intercultural Management Institute at the American University in Washington DC. I heard him explain how his concepts on culture in general relate to TCKs specifically.

Dr. Weaver used the metaphor of the cultural iceberg, which was introduced by the writings of E. T. Hall in the mid-1970s, to explain how cultural clashes or misunderstandings often take place. He noted that culture is divided into two basic parts: the *visible or surface layer of culture* and the *invisible or deeper layers of culture*. The *visible layer* includes the parts of culture we can observe such as food, traditions, dress, and the language used. The *deeper layers* of culture include unseen, but powerful, driving forces. It is here we store our values, our beliefs, and our assumptions of how the world works, also known as "world view."

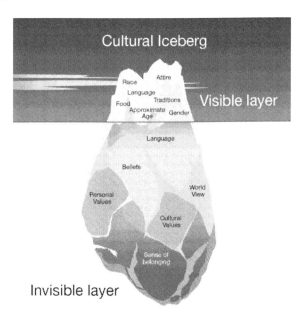

### Adaptation of Dr. Gary Weaver's Cultural Iceberg

According to Dr. Weaver (2011), the interplay of the visible and invisible layers serves two basic functions: First, the surface layer of culture is how and where we *express* the unseen values, beliefs, worldview, and even nuances of language that are stored in the deeper layers of culture. For example, in an Asian culture we will see a person bowing to someone who is older. This reflects an unseen cultural value of respect dependent on age rather than different factors such as social class that another culture might use. Religious beliefs may be fleshed out in a particular style of dress or artifact. A woman wears a burka because she believes true modesty means certain parts of her body must be covered when in public. Another person wears a gold cross around her neck as a sign of her Christian faith.

The second function of the two layers of culture is to help give us clues about who the other person is when we first meet. If we go over to meet our new neighbor and extend our hand for a welcoming handshake and this person bows to us in return, we assume they must be from a culture other than our own. When we see the burka, we will indeed assume this woman is of Muslim faith. Spotting the gold cross leads us to believe the other woman is of the Christian faith. These can be helpful clues to knowing if we are relating to this other person as an "us" or a "them"—a very important matter, by the way, if we consider why sports teams wear different colors or a team logo on their jerseys! We cheer for one team or another based entirely on what we see, not necessarily what we know about each particular person.

But what happens if someone bows to you because he or she lives in a place where this is the cultural norm, but it is not a reflection of a deeper cultural value this person has? Or if that woman wears a burka simply to be socially correct in certain countries or situations? Or if the second woman had the cross passed down by her grandmother as an heirloom and wears it as a reminder of her grandmother but is not a Christian at all? Our assumption about their beliefs or values in the deeper layers of culture could be quite wrong based on appearance. That means our expectations for how we will or won't relate as "us" or "them" are also false.

This is the area where, according to Dr. Weaver, cultures clash—beneath the surface. The Titanic didn't sink because it smashed into the visible layer of the iceberg but rather when it hit the unseen part. So it is with culture. When we see "difference" as we meet another person, it is relatively easy to expect that we may not view the world in a similar to how they do or share the same beliefs or values. We are prepared for that and relate from that context. When we see "likeness" and are correct, our expectations that we are operating from a similar set of values, beliefs and worldview will be right. Our new relationship will hopefully go well because both of us know, and abide by, the same rules for this relational game.

Dr. Weaver also pointed out that in today's world, cultural clashes are likely to increase because the visible layers of culture are rapidly changing and becoming much more uniform. For example, people from many different countries and cultures shed their national dress for attire such as the T-shirts and jeans that seem to have become the universal dress code for certain ages. Weaver warns that when the visible layers of culture begin to "look alike," we will presume that the invisible parts of who we are culturally will also be "alike."

The truth is, however, that it takes much longer to change values and beliefs in the places we cannot see than to change a sari for jeans in the places we can see. Weaver says because of this reality, the traditional role of the visible layer as a means to give us clues about whether a person we meet is an "us" or a "them" is no longer accurate. In other words, when we meet someone who basically looks like us, we still expect that we and the person we are meeting will think alike. But in today's world that isn't necessarily so and the cultural clashing can be more severe because we are unprepared for the unseen differences that serve as the drivers for our various responses and behaviors. We begin to wonder what is "wrong" with a person rather than understanding there is a cultural conflict at play.

## The TCK Identity Iceberg

So how does all of this relate to a therapist working with TCKs? Understanding the cultural iceberg is critical to understanding the common questions TCKs bring to the therapist regarding their confusion of identity and repeated attempts to figure out where they belong. This concept of the seen and unseen worlds of culture makes all the difference in whether or not the therapist is able to look at the TCK's story for what it is or interpret visible behavior and symptoms through traditional lenses only. Who people expect TCKs to be by appearance may have little to do with the reality of who they are by experience and cultural shaping. And this is what leads to unseen cultural clashing between TCKs and those around them. Their deeper places of culture—worldview, values, and beliefs—have been shaped in an entirely "other" place and way than those meeting these TCKs would ever guess by the visible aspects alone that they can see.

So these become critical questions for doing therapy with TCKs: How do I, as the therapist, view the identity of my TCK clients? How do they view themselves?

Because I am such a visual learner, it helps me to have a picture in mind as I develop my treatment plan. This is how I could picture the TCK experience on a personal level as it relates to the idea of Weaver's cultural iceberg.

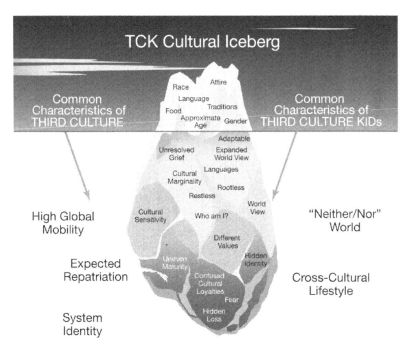

### The TCK Identity Iceberg Model

This model has three components—the two layers Weaver mentions and an additional component that helps us understand the TCK story more clearly.

- The visible layer – the external factors others see quickly when meeting TCKs

- The invisible layer – the internal realities common for many TCKs that are driving forces behind behavior and thoughts expressed

- The cultural "ocean" – characteristics of the third culture itself that shape and develop much of this deeper layer of TCKs

## *The visible layer*

When therapists meet any client, all we see initially is the visible layer. This TCK iceberg shows some of the ways we make assessments of them (and, in reality, all clients) from that first look alone. What is their race? What is their gender? Can we guess their nationality? Based on what language and accent they use, can we figure it out? Do they sound as if they are from mid-America, or Australia? Maybe English is an additional language for them? Are there clues from their attire? If they bow rather than shake our hands, what does that tell us?

Depending on our initial assessment of what we are seeing or hearing, we make assumptions about which social or ethnic group in our community they likely belong. Usually this first look gives us little reason to differentiate between our clients who are TCKs and those who are not. Even if we figure out that clients might be from another country, we most often think of them as "internationals" and easily forget that they may be TCKs as well. Remember, TCKs can be from any nation or culture in the world at this point, not just your own country. In fact, "international families" are raising TCKs right on your soil! Note: It is particularly important for university counselors working with international students to realize that some of these students are also TCKs and have had a very different life experience than other students from that same country.

## The invisible layer

As good therapists, we begin asking questions to explore the parts of our clients that we can't see—the invisible or deeper layer. We ask what brings them to our office.

Sometimes their answers surprise us based on our original assumptions about this client. This woman has a good job and life here in the local community. Why does she want to move every two years? From what we see, it appears she would fit into this place perfectly. Another client, like Don in our first chapter, seems obsessed with "how materialistic everyone is." Why is this such a focus? Don presents himself as an educated, well-groomed professional and it appears he would have no trouble getting a high-paying job himself if he wanted. What's behind this anger he displays? Other clients, like so many stories we have already read, talk of depression but seem to have none of the contributing factors that usually go along with this symptom.

If you look at the deeper layer of the TCK iceberg above, you will see some of the common "drivers" of their presenting symptoms, even if they themselves are unaware of these underlying factors. The rootlessness and restlessness some TCKs feel inside is exhibited in frequent career or academic moves. The expanded worldview gives Don a different outlook on the importance of wealth and material objects than others might have, and the unresolved grief plays out in depression or anger.

Even though the TCK characteristics listed in this deeper layer are not universally true for every TCK, if you become aware of them just as you would common characteristics of those from any national or ethnic culture, you will expand your capacity to listen with understanding and deeper insight to the presenting story that your TCK clients offer to you.

## The "ocean"

At this point, we realize we must know more about their context—the cultural "ocean" in which this person has lived and their identity has been formed. What are some factors that might be contributing to these characteristics that are resulting in negative or confusing patterns of thoughts or behaviors that have now become so severe that these TCKs have come to you, hoping that somehow you can help?

As a therapist, particularly a marriage and family therapist, I look carefully at the family or environment in which my client was raised. That's why the Intake Form in Chapter 3 is so critical. With it we can quickly see not only the usual factors we look for such as family history, employment, and so forth, but it is where we can also see if one of the shaping pieces of this client's story is this third culture ocean. If so, it is necessary to look at the environment of the third culture for that client just as you would consider the ethnic or national culture for any other client. This helps give understanding and meaning to what lies below the surface for your client.

Look at the "ocean" in which the TCK iceberg is placed and you will see it is a pictorial form of what Chapter 2 said about the common characteristics of the third culture. These factors of growing up in a cross-cultural world with high mobility, expected repatriation and a neither/nor world are realities for virtually every TCK you will see. They are part of the things that have shaped the development of their values, worldview, and other typical characteristics. In other words, because the high mobility has made moving so common, some TCKs can't imagine ever settling into one place, so the sense of restlessness and feeling of rootlessness are born and grow. Living cross-culturally means Don has likely seen poverty at a level that most people in his passport country have never seen and it has changed how he places value on things. The cycles of transition and resulting losses, if never dealt with, lead to the unresolved grief fueling the depression like Sandra has. These are just a few examples of how the cultural ocean of TCKs relates to the factors that will bring them to your office.

Of course, as with anyone who lives in only one national culture, there are specific differences in each TCK's personal experience that also impact him or her. Such things as family of origin, the values of the passport culture instilled by the parent from that country, and the organizational system under which each went overseas are also factors in developing a sense of identity. All of these areas—in addition to the third culture experience—will need to be explored to have an accurate diagnosis and treatment plan.

For now, however, I want to take all the pieces we have discussed regarding the TCK iceberg and pull them together to continue to show in more detail how and why the cross-cultural component of the globally mobile childhood impacts identity.

## How the TCK Iceberg Tells the Story

The more we understand about a globally nomadic childhood, the more we realize how few accurate clues the visible layer of TCK's iceberg gives to reveal what is underneath or to glimpse the worlds in which they have grown up. Ruth Van Reken and Paulette Bethel (2005, pp. 8-9) call this reality for TCKs a "hidden diversity— *a diversity of experience that shapes a person's life and world view but is not readily apparent on the outside, unlike the usual diversity markers such as race, ethnicity, nationality, etc.*"

Because the term "diversity" has come to have many implicit meanings related to race and equity, I prefer to call this difference between how others perceive the TCKs to be and how they see themselves a *hidden identity*. What you see is often not what you get. As with Elizabeth's story above, those around her assumed she was an African American because she appeared black and was living in the U.S., but, as she said, she was neither African nor American culturally or by citizenship. Her true identity was hidden from those around her.

"So what?" you might ask. "Lots of people are different from who they appear to be. One person's comments shouldn't ruin Elizabeth's life forever."

This is a very logical response. But for a child already struggling with the basic life task of establishing some sense of identity, to feel chronically at odds with how others perceive him or her to be is both painful and confusing. It can also engender a major backlash against individuals or a group they feel is trying to put them into a box. Take a look at a few ways the "what you see is not necessarily what you get" motif can play out for TCKs.

As we said earlier, based on appearance alone—particularly how they look compared to the dominant culture around them—TCKs, like all others, will be quickly judged as being an "us" or a "them." The conclusion others reach in that first moment sets up expectations for how each particular TCK will behave. In their passport country, people most often presume the TCKs are an "us" and expect them to think and act like others who have grown up in this culture. If they don't behave "properly," no one considers it a potential clash of cultures because "obviously" they are from this place and they "should" know how life works here. Those around the TCK assume this TCK is simply being a bit "weird" and the TCK certainly gets the message:

"Somehow I don't fit in here." Some call this a "hidden immigrant" experience. The TCKs can be as culturally clueless about their supposed "home culture" as any true immigrant, but no one will give them allowance for their ignorance, or clue them in like they would an obvious immigrant, or see their aberrant behavior as a cultural faux pas rather than a personal failure.

When in their host countries, TCKs are often presumed to be a "them." Because they do not look like others in this land, the presumption is that they are clearly foreigners. No one expects them to act or think like the locals do, nor do they expect it of themselves. This gives the TCKs more freedom to pick and choose which parts of the local culture they do or do not want to participate in without personal condemnation because no one expected them to be "the same" in the first place. This acceptance of living amicably with differences between them and others is one of the great gifts of being a TCK—learning how to bridge and negotiate among different cultural worlds. But it also means TCKs can have a hard time understanding why this ease of moving in and between different cultures seems to change when they repatriate to their passport culture where it then seems others expect them to be the same as everyone else. They don't realize the mirror has changed and they are now seen as "us" instead of as "them."

There is a caveat here, however. If it happens that the TCKs physically resemble others in that host country—for example, a Chinese American growing up in Hong Kong, a white Canadian TCK living in Germany, or a Nigerian child raised in Botswana—people meeting them on the street in their host country presume they are an "us" as well. This can cause disgust or disdain from the locals in a way that doesn't happen when the TCK is a clear foreigner. Again, all these different reactions are dependent on whether expectations based on the visible layers of culture are or are not being met.

Another challenge is when the TCKs may not look like the surrounding culture but internally are more like that culture than others presume. Perhaps they've simply lived in this other world so long, it has become their own, or they have gone to school locally and become integrated into the culture in a way that surprises others who wonder how they fit in so well when they look nothing like their peers from the local culture. The TCKs may have a great time with those peers, and feel quite insulted when others assume they are not part of this group because they look different from their peers or, even worse, when in later years they cannot get a visa to return to this place they once called home. Again, who they appear to be to others isn't how they see themselves. This can create another dimension of identity confusion

Of course, some TCKs look around and see what they feel is an accurate reflection of themselves—that those in the community mirror back that they are an "us" and they feel and think like "us." This may apply to TCKs who spent relatively little time as TCKs living in another country, or they did it at such a young age their experience didn't fundamentally change how they thought or acted before they returned to live permanently in their home country. Some TCKs feel like mirrors if they happen to grow up in a culture where they do, in fact, physically resemble the dominant culture around them. One white U.S. American adult TCK who grew up in France told me, "In France I feel like a mirror. In the U.S., I feel like a hidden immigrant."

For example, because I have brown hair and brown eyes and speak fluent Spanish without an accent, it gets very confusing when I go to a Mexican restaurant here in Indiana. If I speak Spanish to the waiter, they usually will stop and look at me and say, "What are you, a North American or a Latin American?" I am a hidden immigrant in my own country. And when I go to Honduras, my friends frequently say, "You are not a North American, you are a Honduran." I am a mirror in Latin America.

In other words, when people see TCKs as clear foreigners or clear mirrors and they are right, life isn't so confusing for the TCKs. Who they are inside and out matches the message of the community's mirror, and that is helpful. But when the internal place doesn't match the assessment of others—when they are hidden immigrants or have adopted the host culture as their own in a way others can't see—then the confusion can continue to grow unless they understand what is going on. Due to mobility, of course, the message of the mirrors is also changing and this also adds to normal confusion in trying to answer the question, "Who am I, really?"

### Why Appearance as Related to Surrounding Culture Matters in Therapy

This idea of how the TCKs relate to the surrounding culture by appearance may seem like a relatively minor point to belabor, but it can offer some major clues to what is behind certain behaviors or feelings. I find when a younger TCK comes in and either hates being back in the passport country or seems adamantly against going back to the land where the parents are working, many times it relates to this matter of how they are being perceived by the surrounding community. They may feel they are losing the sense of identity or the freedom to be themselves that they had before in the land their hearts call "home" as others seemingly try to squeeze them into a particular cultural mode in this place that is now suddenly supposed to be "home."

If they look like others in their host culture, they may not want to return because they have had a similar feeling there. Or, increasingly in today's world, some children who are clear foreigners in a host culture don't want to be so visible even for safety's sake if this is a country that is at political odds with their own. The point is: Do not to ignore this generally overlooked factor of how a child relates to the surrounding dominant culture in terms of physical appearance when you are working with a child whose parents don't understand a sudden obstinacy about either staying or going.

One other reason parents will bring younger TCKs to see you can relate to this matter of the visible layer of the TCK iceberg. Sometimes when children are adjusting to life in their "home" country during leave or permanent repatriation, the child is facing some degree of bullying at school because other children perceive them to be "different." They don't know all the nuances of such things as dressing according to that year's fashion edicts or they are ignorant of some unwritten code such as where kids sit on the school bus depending on their grade in school. When they talk about the countries where they've lived, other kids can think they are bragging or lying and mock them for that. Sometimes TCKs who don't want to return overseas feel teased or bullied in their host culture.

Bottom line, when a TCK comes in and talks of "Who am I? Where do I fit?" I find it helpful to validate that they have, in fact, lived in a world where the cultural mirrors around them reflecting back their identity have often given different messages depending on where they have lived. This is an important beginning step in normalizing these feelings for them (and you) and can open the way to discussing other areas that need to be explored to make an accurate assessment of what is going on for them.

## How Re-entry Creates Extra Stress on Identity

Traditionally, in a more stable community, people learned their culture's rules as children, tested them as teenagers, assimilated them as teens and early adults, and moved out into the world as adults, confident that they knew how to get along in this group and society. This is not the world in which TCKs grow up.

There is one time where a TCK's hidden identity can create enormous, and often unexpected, stress. That is when TCKs make the permanent transition to their passport culture. Because growing up internationally and in the ocean of the third culture is as normal for them as any other way of growing up is for other children, most TCKs haven't stopped to think of how they have been shaped by this experience just as others have by whatever culture they grew up in. In most cases they assume they will fit right in with their supposed home culture because they have visited this place each suregularly when the family went on leave and it has always been fun to be with their grandma and cousins, doing special things together.

But after a time, the cultural clashes begin. Friends talk too much about the "weather." Don't they care that a nation this TCK lived in has just begun a civil war? They call the Super Bowl winners "world champions" and seemingly don't realize American football is just that . . . pretty well relegated to the United States as compared to the global impact of soccer.

Reentry can happen and be stressful anytime and at any age for TCKs (and their parents!) but Tina Quick points out in *A Global Nomad's Guide for University Transition* that this can be a major unseen factor for whether or not TCKs adjust well to beginning their time at a college or university. If they are simultaneously reentering (or entering) their passport culture after much of their childhood lived outside this land, these unseen realities can be disorienting and take them to a counselor's office for help. Younger TCKs usually reenter with their parents so that they at least have the grounding of the family during this transition, but many university students are navigating these cultural waters of reentry without close parental support because the parents are still overseas. This, of course, simply adds to the normal challenges of reentry.

For one student, the process of reentry became more mystifying when, ironically, he was in a Cultural Psychology class at university. Independent educational consultant Rebecca Grappo told me this story.

The Cultural Psychology professor asked each student to: "Describe how your family celebrates Thanksgiving." The TCK in the class was confused about answering that seemingly simple question: "It depends on where we are at that time as to how we celebrate Thanksgiving." The professor tried again, "Well, describe how your family celebrates Thanksgiving culturally." Again, the TCK did not know how to respond to the question and expressed his inability to answer this question since his family had made so many transitions between cultures. The professor kept interrupting his questions and restating the assignment, "How does your family celebrate Thanksgiving?" At this point, both the TCK and the professor were frustrated—their cultural worlds had unknowingly collided. The professor of Cultural Psychology was completely unaware of the multi-cultural world of the TCK and it hadn't occurred to the TCK before that it was so unusual to have celebrated Thanksgiving in so many ways. (As told in Cross-Cultural Symposium, Butler University, Indianapolis, IN, Oct. 13, 2011)

Why didn't this professor of Cultural Psychology understand how his simple question could be so complex to this student? The answer is that this TCK looked and spoke like the other white, U.S. American students in the class who had all presumably grown up in neighboring cities or states. Throughout the U.S. everyone knows that Thanksgiving is on the fourth Thursday of November every year and is celebrated with turkey, dressing, sweet potatoes, green bean mushroom soup casserole, and cranberry sauce. Apparently the professor figured that deviations from this norm would indicate some cultural diversity among his students, but it didn't seem to have occurred to him that a *single person* might have many answers. Such is the world of TCKs and gives further meaning to why it is so important for therapists to take the time to discover more about the context of each TCK's story.

## Understanding Individual Context for Each TCK's Story

In addition to the general characteristics of the third culture "ocean" and finding out if my clients belong to a well-defined and structured system (see Chapter 6), I want to understand a bit more about their unseen world. Did they live in a rural setting or city? Were they in a developing country where they likely saw a lot of poverty and injustice or a highly developed metropolitan area with access to all the latest gadgetry technology has to offer? The point is that under the shared experience of growing up or living internationally, each client still has a unique story just as all clients do. As always, it is important to understand the context from which that client is coming in as much detail as possible.

Once I understand the world where my client lived and grew up as a child or young person, then I am better prepared to look at who my client is as *this* person. Never forget TCKs are first and foremost persons along with the rest of the human race and other, human issues that affect all people can also be present here.

## How the TCK Iceberg Applies to TCAs and Other CCKs

While once more the previous discussion has focused on TCKs, the concepts are critical when working with adults who have been living cross-culturally for a while as well as others who grew up cross-culturally for other reasons. While these third culture adults (TCAs) may have a strong sense that they are whatever nationality the passport says is theirs, they too have lived in the third culture ocean and their lives have been changed by that experience. One of their most difficult times is also re-entry because they once knew how to live here well and in sync with others. They, too, are surprised when the deeper levels of how they view life and their own culture now make them feel like outsiders in a land that they once knew as "mine." And for other types of CCKs, for many different reasons, who they are internally is often not how others see them. The principles of the TCK iceberg apply directly to them as well in terms of the dissonance between the expectations and the reality of who they are—even outside of the reality that they also have grown up cross-culturally, the other characteristics of their cultural ocean may have different components than in the TCK model.

## How to Help Them Sort Out Who They Are

While there may be many TCKs who struggle for a while with wondering who they are or where they belong, once they understand the reason for their confusion and that these feelings are within a normal range for others of like experiences, most go on and embrace the various pieces of their life rather than feeling as if they only have an either/or choice to decide who they are. But for those who come to your office, there are two simple exercises I do to try to help them begin to sort out a clearer sense of who they are. I also try to help them see how lessons from the cultural iceberg apply to their situation as well.

1.  Paper Bag Representation: One activity that is frequently done with clients is to ask them to make a picture of the person the rest of the world sees when they look at the TCK. Have them cut out pictures from old magazines and glue them to the outside of a large paper bag. Then cut out other pictures of who they feel they truly are and drop them into the paper bag. As the therapist and the client talk, the client shares just what part of them they reveal to those around them, how they arrive at the decision whether or not to share what is IN the bag to those select few, and what their true identity is.

2.  TCK Identity Iceberg: Another exercise is to give them a picture of the cultural iceberg and ask them to put words on the top for how they believe others perceive them to be and then in the lower section, to put the driving forces or values or cultural reasons for those things they have named above and particularly if there are any seen things with very different reasons for them in the deeper levels than others may presume.

3.  Acknowledging Identity: Identity questions are terrifying to the TCK since they brush up against the huge, core question of "Who am I?" This is such a complex question. When you attempt to work on this directly, it seems to trigger their defenses and they respond with, "Of course, I know who I am!" Josh Sandoz, the founder of the International Therapist Directory, suggests, "One way that works is in an indirect manner. How? As you notice particular cultures in their actions or mannerisms, you might state, 'You are so Brazilian.' Or you can say, 'You remind me so much of my friends from Brazil when you do that.' Apply this to whatever culture they are displaying, but please make sure you know it IS Brazilian, and do not say that if you really do not know." (Sandoz, Personal Email Exchange, February, 2012) Sandoz commented he helps them to enjoy the

different parts of themselves, noticing the various emotions and loyalties and conflicts that are stirred up within them. That can lead to the TCK's ability to better tolerate his inner tensions and start addressing those "Who am I?" questions for himself.

As the TCK slowly learns he is both the insider and the outsider at the same time, he comes to grips with his own identity. To have those parts recognized and valued while being welcomed and respected into the group or culture where he resides, he learns to accept himself. Although he cannot control how others respond, he can respect that restlessness due to his heritage of many cultures. This is why I love Pico Iyer's term "Global Soul" when he describes the TCK.

## Identity and the DSM

Life would be so much simpler if we lived in a world where we did not have to come up with a diagnosis for billing purposes immediately after that first session. In most cases the diagnosis would be an adjustment disorder or a mood disorder. If Elizabeth, whose story I shared at the beginning of this chapter, were a child, some might wonder if she meets the criteria for Oppositional Defiant Disorder since she seems to meet some of the criteria with her response to the black man. She seemed to "argue with adults," "actively defy or refuse to comply with adults' requests or rules," and was "often touchy or easily annoyed by others" (APA [DSM IV], 1994, p. 68).

But if you were to listen carefully to her story, you would realize that she was not trying to deliberately argue with the man. She was trying to *clarify her identity* to him. She was struggling to understand her own story, let alone trying to explain it to a non-TCK adult. How *does* a therapist tell the difference both for treatment's sake as well as for insurance and billing purposes?

In most cases, if the ATCK is trying to figure out where they fit in this big world and just who are they and where are they going, I see most of them fitting into an Adjustment Disorder with feelings of anxiety or depression. Of all the diagnoses in the DSM, I believe the Adjustment diagnoses carry the least stigma in the field of mental health. I want the ATCK to understand that they are very normal. The world in which they grew up was not normal.

# Things You Should Know

1. Traditionally, in a more stable community, people learned their culture's rules as children, tested them as teenagers, assimilated them as teens and early adults, and moved out into the world as adults, confident that they knew how to get along in this group and society. This is not the world in which TCKs grow up.

2. Dr. Gary Weaver's Cultural Iceberg Model shows the interplay of the visible and invisible layers. The invisible layer is the area where Dr. Weaver stated that TCKs clash—beneath the surface. This concept of the seen and unseen worlds of culture makes all the difference in whether or not the therapist is able to look at the TCKs' story for what it is or interpret visible behavior and symptoms through traditional lenses only.

3. In the case of the TCK and the TCK Iceberg Model, we need to look at the third culture in which the TCK has been raised. This helps give understanding and meaning to what lies below what we initially see in our client.

# Discussion Questions & Activities

1. Draw your own iceberg and identify what you observe about yourself above and below the water. What have you learned about yourself. How will this make you a more effective therapist for TCKs?

2. Ask yourself the question, "Who am I?" and create a list of characteristics. Which of these characteristics could make you a good TCK therapist? Which characteristics are more of a challenge to you?

3. Activity: Do the Paper Bag Representation in this chapter.

4. Activity: Create a TCK Identity Iceberg for yourself. Share your icebergs in a small group.

# Chapter 6

# Discovering Answers to Adjustment Disorders such as "Where Do I Belong?"

*"The place to which you feel the strongest attachment isn't necessarily the country you're tied to by blood or birth: it's the place that allows you to become yourself. This place may not lie on any map."*

Jhumpa Lahiri in *New York Times* article "American Children"
(Schillinger, 2008)

### Home – Where Is It?

The two most difficult questions for a TCK to answer are: "Where is home?" and "Where are you from?"

A variety of TCKs served on a panel at a conference I attended. These panel members were asked, "Is 'where is home?' a more difficult question than 'where are you from?'"

The answers they gave were typical:

- The first question is easier as you respond with where the emotional place is that you call home while the second question is more cognitive.
- You might answer "where is home" with the location where you currently reside. It can also depend on your audience.
- The second is a harder question. "Where are you from" is harder. I have to decide or ask, "do you mean lately, or where I grew up, or where my parents live?" I might answer with a place where I had some favorite memories. Or I may define home by my age at that time. It depends on the context of the question.
- Home is a fairy tale. It doesn't exist anywhere.
- The world is my home.
- Do you want the long answer or the short answer?
- Where my suitcase is.

In our last chapter, we talked about how TCKs struggle to find identity. But this search is for more than simply making a mental assessment of "Who am I?" We know by intuition and Maslow's hierarchy of needs that each person in this world is a relational being. Because of that, we all need to have a sense of belonging to some place and to some people.

Given the transient nature of the TCK experience, this is a great challenge for many TCKs. The longer they go without finding a way to satisfy this need, the more alone and depressed they can feel. Simple solutions like joining the YMCA or attending a small group at church aren't so simple to them because they continue to have the cultural challenge of living between and among various worlds but not quite as a part of any—so joining another group further complicates their identity questions and gives them yet another group to which they have to try to explain their identity. This is the very thing they don't need or want.

For now, we'll look a bit more closely at why TCKs often struggle with these feelings of not belonging and how the various systems they belong to can be part of the solution or can add to the challenge. Again, as therapists we are trying to normalize the essence of this experience to help us recognize the places where therapy is needed so we can help them move through those places and on from the challenges that have gotten them stuck along the way.

## The Issue of Rootlessness and Restlessness

We saw in the deeper places of the TCK Iceberg that "rootless" and "restless" are common characteristics that lurk below the surface for many TCKs. Why is that?

One of several reasons for feeling restless is being drawn to a sense of adventure which is brought about by a life lived exploring new places. TCKs know there is a big world out there to explore. That can be a positive reason for many—being willing to do things a bit outside of the box, which becomes a gift, a characteristic that is sought by companies in the 21st century.

Another reason relates to the two hardest questions many TCKs dread: "Where do you come from?" and "Where is home?" When asked where they are from, TCKs have to first figure out exactly what the person is asking—if he or she really cares or if it is just a social question like "how are you?"—and how much does the TCK want to self-disclose at this point in the relationship? Eventually most TCKs

> A sense of rootlessness is at the heart of the restlessness. Help them begin to consider options for creating a sense of roots and belonging in a more intentional way.

figure out a way to answer this without having to tell their entire life story. "I live in Quebec now." Or, another option is, "My parents are from London." Or, some simply say, "I grew up in different places but now I live here."

This gives the listener a chance to ask more if they really care and it gives the TCKs a way to find out if this was a true question or just part of a polite greeting. But I have a lot of fun when I ask new people this question because I do listen carefully to their reply. If they give me any of the above answers (or something else like "It's a long story"), I will always ask more because I often find a TCK behind such an answer!

But the real issue behind those perfunctory answers remains. TCKs struggle through the thought process: "Where *am* I from? And what does it mean to be 'from' some place? Does that mean the country my passport says I come from? Is it where I live now? Where I lived before? I don't even know what the question means!"

And then, of course, the question right behind that is: "Where is home?" In the answers the panel gave, some said this was easier to answer than "Where are you from?" because it was an emotional place. Even those who don't know what geography they connect to will often say, "Wherever my family is." Or they remember the night skies of Africa and say, "When I see clear stars, I feel at home." In fact, some can list several senses of home while the "Where are you from?" question seems to ask for them to pick just one answer.

For some TCKs you will see, however, a migratory instinct seems to control their lives —manifesting in frequent job changes, moves to new locations, and constantly changing relationships. I believe that for them, a sense of rootlessness is at the heart of the restlessness. They can't settle down, even when they want to. After several cycles of destroying potential relationships and careers through this compulsion to move, they may come to see you. This is one time it is essential to remember where these feelings stem from so that you can first normalize at least the roots of what by now they feel is a compulsion. It is essential for you to help them begin to consider options they have for creating a sense of roots and belonging in a more intentional way.

## Finding Identity and Belonging in a System Identity

One of these options is to look at the various systems in which these TCKs have grown up. Often TCKs do find their sense of identity and belonging in terms of relationships rather than geography. For many it is the family system. All the regular issues that families face—for good or for bad—relates to TCKs, of course, since this is their first place of identity and belonging, Research done by the MK Consultation and Research Team/Committee on Research and Endowment (MK/CART/CORE) on ATCKs clearly indicated that the number one predictor of whether a TCK was going to use the gifts of his or her background well was how he or she related to his or her family of origin (Andrews, 2004, p. 369). Those who talked about close family ties despite geographical moves or distance ranked the highest on the well-being scores. Those who struggled in the family system had similar outcomes to non-TCKs who came from dysfunctional families. Surely an international experience doesn't magically change any of that. So use your good skills as a therapist to explore that reality.

> The number one predictor of a TCK who is going to use the gifts of his or her background well was how he or she related to his or her family of origin.

But for some TCKs there is another huge piece that is often overlooked. That has to do with the organizational system in which they grew up.

## The Potential Power of an Organizational System for TCKs

You will also see that one of the factors of the third culture ocean includes the possibility of the TCK having a strong identity to a system. Usually as therapists we look at family systems in detail. This is no different for TCK clients. But many TCKs also have a strong sense of identity with the organizational system, or sector, which is the reason their parents went to another country or culture in the first place and began this globally mobile lifestyle they have known.

Some have asked me, "Why do we need to look at the possibility of an organizational system identity for TCKs any more than other children whose parents work for organizations or corporations in their local community?"

To answer that, we must first consider how much an organization or corporation that sends families overseas functions in a parental/family role. In many cases, the sending agency or corporation makes decisions about the most fundamental issues that affect a child's life. Which country will the family live in? Where will the child go to school? (While the corporation or organization may say they give the parents a choice, often they will only pay for a particular type of schooling.) When will they move again? It often depends much more on the corporation or organization's needs rather than a simple choice by the parents. Where people shop is essentially preordained by the system in some sectors (such as the military).

Compare that dynamic to former eras when parents traditionally climbed their career ladder while staying in the same geographical area. If a parent worked for a local bank, it had no branches in foreign lands. At that time, a person might begin as a teller and rise to president but could live in the same house or community for his or her entire career. What went on at work didn't directly affect the family, outside of perhaps a parent coming home a bit grouchy after a bad day! Children in that banker's family went to school in the local community with other children who, for the most part, also lived in a non-mobile environment. The banker's children never had to move because of a change in the parent's role at the bank, and ultimately parents made the decisions that directly affected their family's life and choices. Most likely, the company or organization for which the parents worked in those eras had no idea or concern about anything related to the child's housing, schooling, or shopping preferences.

Because of how strongly the organizational system of many TCKs resembles a family, it is logical to understand that just as the dynamics of a family structure affect the children who are part of that family, so the dynamics and unspoken messages of the organizational system in which TCKs grow up also affect them. Whether that system is healthy or not can shape a child's life in vastly different ways.

## How TCKs Often Find Identity within the Organizational System

Because many TCKs struggle to find a clear sense of personal identity when the usual markers of place, community, culture, and even family are constantly changing, the very system in which they are growing up (or grew up) becomes the one constant mirror for defining themselves. It is not uncommon to hear someone say rather proudly, "I'm a military brat" or "I'm an Aaramco kid" or "I'm a missionary kid." This identity with a particular group is, in fact, another example of how many TCKs find their sense of belonging in terms of relationship rather than physical place—their life in relationship to an organizational system. It is here, with others of shared experience, that they often find the deep sense of belonging so absent when, for example, they try to repatriate to their passport country.

To understand this type of connection, take a look at the types of communities that often form for those living as expatriates because of an international career. Whether it is military, Foreign Service, missionary, or corporate, families who belong to these communities frequently live in a strong local community such as a military base or Foreign Service enclave. Since most expatriates in these situations are away from their blood relatives, they form a dynamic that is similar to the role of the extended family "back home." In the missions community the children refer to the expat adults as "aunts" and "uncles," which makes that bond feel even tighter.

> It is with others of shared experience that they often find the deep sense of belonging.

In addition, as they move from place to place at the company or organization's request, they often reconnect with those from their group whom they have known before. In many ways, it's like a family reunion. The "brand name," such as "I'm a corporate kid" or "I'm a missionary kid" or

"I'm a military brat" serves to identify where and to whom they belong in much the same as a last name identifies a child with his or her family of origin in the Western world. It can be such a strong tie that if a therapist dares to question any of the common practices of that system—perhaps for missionary kids the idea that they were sent to boarding school at age six or for a military kid that by policy the family moved at least every two years—they will not only become defensive, but stop the therapy.

On the other hand, if they have been in a system that has been very controlling, or even totally sheltering, sometimes the transition away from that can lead to full-blown rebellion or an inability to know how to function in today's world as they have become accustomed to others caring for all of their needs.

> If a therapist dares to question any of the common practices of the system, they will not only become defensive, but stop the therapy.

In this arena your skills in systems therapy can work effectively once you understand the depth of impact some of these systems have had on your clients. Appendix A will help you explain to your clients what a system is and how it can control them through its spoken and unspoken edicts for years to come. Appendix A is also available as a printable handout for your clients at: www.quietstreamscounseling.com

**What to do:**

1.  When your TCK client is beginning to get restless, try to brainstorm with them what they might do that will not involve moving, such as moving the furniture around in their home, going to a movie in a foreign language with subtitles in their language, hanging out for a couple days in the international section of a nearby large city, or playing their favorite music from home. The idea is for them to feel it is okay to go and "touch their international roots" for a while.

2.  Sometimes, it is helpful to have the client write a letter (not to be actually mailed) to the president of the organization who sent their parents overseas and share their concerns, suggestions, joy, anger or whatever they want to share with the president. Just thinking out

their feelings and how they might suggest to leadership that they could change things for the next generation is therapeutic.

3. In order to help the client deal with the pain resulting from a decision made by a system, I have them write this sentence at the top of a piece of paper: "How dare you...." And then they address it to a particular person or position in the system and complete the sentence. They may use the entire sheet of paper(s) to complete their thoughts or write out their emotions.

## What's the Diagnosis?

As far as the diagnoses for clients struggling with these issues, I believe they would be the same as in Chapter 5. They probably would fall into some type of an Adjustment Disorder.

# Things You Should Know

1. For some TCKs you will see a migratory instinct that seems to control their lives. I believe that for them, a sense of rootlessness is at the heart of the restlessness. This is one time it is essential to remember where these feelings stem from so that you can first normalize at least the roots of what they feel is a compulsion and then begin to consider options they have for creating a sense of roots and belonging in a more intentional way.

2. One of the characteristics of the third culture includes the possibility of the TCK having a strong identity with a system. The fundamental issues of life of the TCK are affected by decisions made by the sending agency or corporation.

3. The system in which TCKs grow up becomes the one constant mirror for defining their identity. Often TCKs do find their sense of identity and belonging in terms of relationships rather than geography.

# Discussion Questions & Activities

1. Have you experienced rootlessness and restlessness? If so, unpack your experience (with the group if you are going through this in a group setting) with the purpose of developing empathy for TCKs.

2. How did your parents' vocation impact your world as you grew up? Talk about the advantages and disadvantages of the impact or lack of impact. How did that affect you emotionally?

3. Think of your first year-round job. How did you feel near the end of May when you realized you would not have a summer vacation? How did you deal with your feelings? Share your thoughts in groups of two or three.

4. Think of a time when you broke up with someone (or lost a best friend) you had been close to for at least 6−8 months. How did that impact your regular routine, identity, shopping habits, entertainment choices, and sense of belonging? Describe any feelings of being lost or feeling like a misfit you may have experienced. Relate this discussion to the TCKs and how they might feel as they struggle with identity and belonging as they move among countries.

# Chapter 7

# Understanding Adjustment or Mood Disorders: "Why Do I Get Along with Everyone Else, Except You?"

*"'Tis better to have loved and lost,*
*than never to have loved at all."*

Alfred Lord Tennyson

## The Paradox of Relationships

The area of relationships is an amazingly paradoxical reality for those who have grown up globally. The gift of making friends leads to the challenge of relationship building.

> Portia knew she loved him. Her husband of two years, Edward, was loving, kind, and affirming, and he adored her. They had such fun being newlyweds—going to the movies on weekends, learning to cook together in the kitchen, or repainting the little house they had bought. Life should have been idyllic, but something marred that calm and beautiful surface.
>
> "I just don't understand it," Portia told me on her first visit. "I love Edward so much, but every time we begin to get really, really close, I find something to fuss about. He forgot to bring in the newspaper. Or he didn't take the garbage out. It's all stuff I could even do myself, so why do I keep doing that? It's almost like I deliberately push him away each time we are close like that. I think closeness is what I want; yet I spoil it every time. Why?"

On one side, TCKs have met so many people of so many backgrounds, their lives are filled with absolute richness. They may not keep up daily with their friends (although Skype and Facebook are surely helping today's generation to be able to do that now), but when they meet, even after long absences, they can often pick up right where they left off. It seems they haven't missed a beat. Through these interactions with friends, they learn of other people, cultures, and places in a way that others could spend a lifetime reading about, yet never know anyone personally from such a place. Surely, for many, the richness of relationships is one of the great gifts of a global childhood and life.

## The Impact of Cycles of Mobility

But there are also very real challenges. These cycles of separation due to airplane rides across oceans impact friendships as well as the individual in several ways. First, some TCKs never learn to deal with conflict because they know if they simply outwait the situation, or ignore it, they or the other person or persons will be gone. Then no one has to "worry about it" anymore. This does not serve well in adulthood where conflict management in careers as well as home is a needed skill.

Kay Eakin in her writings for the United States Family Liaison Office in Washington DC made this statement, *"There is some indication that TCKs often do not learn problem-solving skills in handling interpersonal relationships. With a built-in rotational cycle, there is a temptation to simply leave a problem without resolving it. Because of the importance of people rather then [sic] place, this baggage gets carried on to the next location and may re-emerge and impact the development of new relationships."* (Eakin, 1999, p. 20)

Second, the fact that virtually every friend they have made on this global journey has been lost by at least one of the two of them moving away is significant. After awhile, not only for the kids but for some adults as well, the potential pain of saying Goodbye outweighs the fun it might be to have a friend—if even for a short time. Why seek to go through that painful event again if it can be avoided?

For many, the only lasting relationships are within the family. This can lead many globally mobile families to a special closeness. Research shows that those TCKs who are deeply connected to their families do well in the long-term outcomes, but even family stability is becoming harder to maintain (Andrews, 2004). Sadly, divorce hits these families as well; afterwards, parents are often living continents away, not just a city or a few states away.

Third, sometimes TCKs form friendships with those who have never moved. This can be a very healthy thing because TCKs can learn new patterns of in-depth and long-term friendships. But expected patterns of how friends interact or even what it means to be a friend can be wildly different. Some ATCKs find they disappoint or offend friends who may be used to an ongoing daily text or frequent visits from those they consider friends. This is different from their long-distance friendships. Soon they can begin to feel "boxed in" to the high demands these newfound friends require and withdraw from the relationship altogether.

## The Impact of a Cross-Cultural Upbringing

If we go back to the metaphor of the cultural iceberg and think of how people appear to be visibly with who they are in the invisible places of their lives, it's not hard to see the many ways that growing up among different cultural worlds can shape people in ways that are invisible to those around them. Again, in a world that even operates "diversity" programs in large measure based on race or gender, this becomes a particular challenge.

Where are some of the areas where the invisible world of the TCKs can produce unrecognized clashing? Four common areas are:

- School or university
- Friendships
- Parents
- Marriage/Partners

## Relational Challenges within the TCK's Community

### Schooling

Schooling is a key place where assumptions based on appearance are critical.

Franz, a 10-year-old from Belgium, began schooling in a suburb near Colorado Springs, Colorado, when his mother took a job with an international corporation headquartered there. His white skin matched the color of many of his U.S. American classmates and he quickly learned to speak "American" so he could blend in.

One day his math teacher announced a contest. Each student was given a math problem and was to estimate the answer first. Then, at their turn, each would go to the board to solve it and the team whose members could do the entire group of math problems fastest at the board would win.

Franz's team started to pull ahead of the others. Everyone was cheering. It was Franz's turn to go to the board. He went, put the problem on the board quickly. His team was cheering more loudly than ever as he sat down.

Then the teacher spoke up. "Franz, I saw that you copied the problem on the board from what you had worked on your paper. You were not supposed to work it out first, just estimate it. That's cheating. Your team loses because of that."

You can imagine how devastating this was for Franz. He knew English to a degree, but not well enough to understand what was meant by the term "estimate." He looked and spoke like many other Americans. While the teacher might have taken this into account for an obvious immigrant, she never considered this might be a cultural matter rather than a "cheating problem." After several similar incidents of miscommunications, his parents took him out of the school and, ultimately, cut short their assignment with the corporation and returned to Belgium.

## Friendships

Years ago I ran across a model for the five levels of communication as developed by the Jesuit priest, John J. Powell, a professor at Loyola University in Chicago, Illinois, and a popular author. Powell (1969, pp. 47-53) categorized communication into the following five levels:

> **Level Five:** _Cliché Conversation_ – There is no conversation at this level, only the exchange of statements such as "How are you?" or "How is your family?" or "It is really good to see you."

**Level Four:** _Reporting the Facts_ – We expose very little about ourselves at this level; we simply report facts. We talk about what others have said or done. It is nothing about our life.

**Level Three:** _My Ideas and Judgments_ – On this level there is some talk about our own selves. At this level we share ideas and reveal some judgments and decisions, yet we remain very guarded in what we select to disclose at this level.

**Level Two:** _My Feelings (Emotions)_ – On all of the previous levels we do not share what truly makes us unique. It is at this level we share who we truly are when we share what we are like at our "gut level" or talk about our emotional reactions. Often we do not share at this level because we fear possible rejection by the other person.

**Level One:** _Peak Communication_ – In order to attain this level of communication, one must first have attained Level Two; that is, the sharing of your feelings. In Peak Communication there is complete openness and honesty.

For whatever reason, one characteristic of TCKs is that many of them jump directly into level three. Pollock and Van Reken (2009, p. 133) hypothesized that because TCKs move so often, they realize there isn't necessarily a lot of time to develop a relationship and so they need to get started quickly. Others believe they are more likely to self-disclose because they or the other person will be moving, so it seems safer to share more deeply since they won't bear any long-term consequences. And, of course, how we develop relationships is also very cultural. One German ATCK looked at this list and said, "Where I come from, we always start with politics. We love to argue about them and we are still great friends at the end."

But this is something important to look at if your clients come in saying that they can't make friends in the local communities. If people in the local community are used to a different rhythm for establishing friendships, what does this new pattern do to them? For many, it scares them off! It seems too intense. Perhaps others deem the TCK as too nosy. On the positive side, when they run into another TCK they skip levels and immediately go deeply into the friendship, causing the onlooker to think they most certainly have been childhood friends. Why? Because this is how their "third culture" works.

Tina, another TCK, and I did not allow any grass to grow under our feet as we quickly formed a close friendship a few years ago. We are two ATCKs from two very different worlds. Tina is a military brat who lived in various countries in Europe and Africa. I am a missionary kid who lived in various countries in Latin America.

When we first met, we quickly learned we had both played basketball in high school, loved sports, and Tina had ridden horses in the rodeo while I had ridden horses in the mountains of Central America. We quickly fell into telling stories of life in other parts of the world.

Recently, we made the strange discovery that our parents live within fifteen minutes of one another in different retirement communities in Florida. Other than that one strange coincidence, our worlds were very different, yet the common bond and characteristics of the TCK helped us form a quick and tight friendship, and completely skip the beginning steps of forming a friendship. We skipped some of those basic questions such as: What are the names of your daughters? What does your husband do for a living? Where did you go to college?

A couple of weeks after I met Tina, we were chatting away about our ideas for future presentations, our past experiences, and our shared views on the world. Jim, a friend of mine, was listening in on our non-stop chatter. Finally he was able to squeeze in a question, "How long have you all known each other?"

I responded with, "Oh, I don't know. Maybe two weeks."

Another big reason to pay attention to this difference in the ways that TCKs commonly try to establish relationships is that it can be easily misinterpreted by others as some sort of "come on." I have heard many stories of ATCKs who thought they were merely being friendly to someone else in what would have been the usual way in their expat groups, only to find out the other person presumed they were interested in a far more intimate relationship than they intended. So don't overlook the differences in ways various cultures, including the third culture, form friendships and what can happen when neither side understands they are playing by different sets of rules.

## Relational Challenges within the TCK's Family

### *Between parents and children*

This is where the idea of the third culture and how it shapes developmental patterns begins to be particularly important. Parents frequently presume that their children see the world as they and the generations before them have seen it because they share a common national passport, so they are rudely awakened when a child does not behave according to expected practices.

Musa had been born in Nigeria but moved to the United States in his pre-teen years when his father took a job with an international bank. In the early years, he had to learn to speak up when adults were around instead of respectfully (according to his past teachings) keeping his eyes focused downward when older folks were talking to him. In time, he became used to the U.S. culture and others who saw him would have assumed he was a happy, well adjusted African American teen.

One day, a newly-arrived Nigerian family went to Musa' family's home. When the family entered, Musa was sitting on a chair and didn't get up to give his chair to the senior man in the family. His father was horrified. "Musa, give your chair to the Old Pa."

"Why?" he asked. "Then I won't have a chair to sit in."

There was loud arguing that night between father and son. How could his son have so disgraced them all? How could he not "know" how he was supposed to act around older people? Didn't they share the same genes? As far as the father was concerned, Musa had totally and completely shamed the family that night. How could it be so?

It is because these types of situations that parents may bring their child or teen to you to find out what is "wrong" with them. Sure, there are the normal teenage issues of seeking independence from parents, but the wounding is deep for the parents when their TCKs turn out to think and behave in way so completely unlike them or the child has given up the old cultural values in their home.

### *Between partners*

Of course, there is another huge area where family relationships are significantly impacted. In today's world, I can't imagine any family therapist who has not had to deal with the issues related to cross-cultural marriages. Marriage is challenging for all couples but when the two partners come from two different cultures that have different value systems, traditions, worldviews, languages, and so forth, the stresses are magnified.

Elsie Purnell spent many years talking with and helping adult missionary kids. She put her findings regarding missionary kids (MKs) and marriage in the book *The Family in Mission*. She listed several reasons MKs might make poor decisions regarding marriage (2004, pp. 145–153):

- Need security after so many separations,
- Want independence due to a desire to escape an enmeshed, controlling family,
- Desire to rescue another person,
- Drawn into intercultural marriages or attracted to another TCK because they feel understood,
- Do not recognize that when they marry a monocultural person, it is a cross-cultural marriage,
- Attempt to adapt to their passport country by seeking stability and roots in marriage, or
- Decide not to marry due to repeated losses and fear of intimacy.

There are, however, a couple of special nuances for ATCKs and marriage. The first occurs when two people of the same nationality, race, and even faith marry, one a TCK, the other someone who has grown up locally. They do not think they are entering a cross-cultural marriage since all the traditional markers are "the same." Again, back to the iceberg: Their world views and values may be almost polar opposites. However, since they are unseen, and each one thinks his or her own way of looking at things is "right," the source of conflict can be less obvious than if it was a traditionally defined cross-cultural marriage.

The second nuance is when one person is a clear "other" or even "foreigner" by typical standards but is also a TCK. At times the therapist may address their conflicts by looking primarily at the two "national cultures." While each can have a part in the conflict, often the TCK's part is less from his or her national culture, and more from the issues relating to the TCK part and the "third culture," which are playing out big-time.

Nabil carried an Indian passport, but he and his family had moved to several countries before he was 16 because his father worked with refugees. When he was 16 years old, his father took a job in the United States, and eventually in Indiana. At age 18, his girlfriend, Marilyn, became pregnant and, wanting to do the "right thing," he married her.

Marilyn had never lived outside of Indiana and her only travels were to neighboring states. Now 17 years and three children later, they were in my office, deep in marital conflict. Nabil had recently moved out of the home.

In reviewing the Client Intake form and noting his many international moves and seeing his skin coloring, I began to explore his multi-cultural world. When I asked him if he were Indian or a citizen of the U.S., he gave me a lengthy explanation to a supposedly simple question. Then when I asked him where was home for him, I knew for certain he was a TCK as he struggled to answer another "simple" question. I quickly noticed that with each of my questions about Nabil's history, Marilyn began to get angry.

Hoping to win her over, I began to check on her history and pointed out that one difference for her and Nabil was that her family had lived in the same community for several generations. Next I tried to explain some of the characteristics of the TCK to her. She exploded in anger at me, "He is an American and not an Indian. He needs to stop speaking his Indian dialect with his parents and use only English in our home at all times. He needs to forget that world and meet my needs."

After trying to re-stabilize the discussion, I suggested a book for them to read regarding TCKs. Nabil wrote down the name of the book, but Marilyn just glared at both of us. The more I talked about what it meant to be a TCK, the more his face lit up; he felt understood. However, it was just the opposite for her. She got angrier and angrier because she felt misunderstood and shut out.

> I finally stated, "In order for this marriage to make it, you will need to attempt to understand each other's world better."
>
> She responded, "I do not see the need for me to understand his world. He is not in India anymore. He needs to just get over it."
>
> The following day she called and cancelled their next appointment. I've not seen either of them since.

That isn't how it usually goes when I work with a couple composed of a TCK and a non-TCK. Most of the time, they grow together in their understanding of one another and the non-TCK slowly learns to recognize the impact on the spouse and their marriage of the other one's having grown up in the third culture. There needs to be an understanding that this is, in fact, a marriage between two (or more) cultures.

Another issue for many marriages, like Portia's at the beginning of this chapter, is that ATCKs often replay their protective mechanisms of the past. They will let the partner get "just so close" and then begin to push them away. The risk of a Goodbye is too much if they put all their eggs in that one basket, and years of protecting their deepest places can be a self-fulfilling prophecy.

While on one level it seems TCKs often rush into friendships, they also can do the opposite by withdrawing from any intimacy out of fear that someone may move. If they do this, they are left in the uncomfortable position of risking sharing their heart with another who could hurt it, or going through life alone and never enjoying the pleasure of a close friend.

An ATCK with whom I worked regarding friendships would always talk about her new apartment she was sharing with a relatively new friend. In asking her what she had contributed to the furnishings of the apartment, her response was, "I am only getting things that I can fit into my car. I never stay any place too long." Before she was even settled in with her new friend and roommate, she was already planning her next move. TCKs find it difficult to stay in the same location as a friend for an extended period of time.

**What To Do**

Helping your TCK client work through some of the basic steps in forming friendships may be valuable. How do they make the decision regarding whom to befriend? What is the right pace and what are the right things to discuss with a new friend? What are the assumptions and/or expectations that are made in friendships? What do you do if there is a misunderstanding? What are the proper cultural boundaries? Helping them learn to walk through the various levels of friendship and learn how to determine if someone is trustworthy are necessary skills which they often skip or have never learned due to their fear that they or the other person will move.

Working on good social skills can help TCKs who are struggling with friendships. From learning how to move through the introductory phases of forming a friendship to establishing a healthy marital relationship with their spouse and not run away to work or some other socially accepted activity which keeps the other person at a distance is a challenge for many. Friendships can be an unexpected learning experience.

How do they learn to deal with friendships? The best and healthiest way is by experiencing friendships through learning good communication skills and conflict resolution, and by risk-taking, and talking about what happened as a result of that risk with you, the therapist, so that they can figure out (with your guidance) how to maintain the friendship.

For a homework assignment, I have had TCKs walk through the steps of forming a friendship with a newfound friend. I call it "lab work." Each week we talk about what took place in the new friendship, what seemed to go right, what went wrong, how to tweak the plan, and how to make the decision of whether to continue to develop the friendship. It is hard work for many; they say they feel like they are learning social skills that most of their peers learned in high school, or even middle school or before.

When working with a couple where one is a TCK and the other is not, I often will recommend the non-TCK partner read books that describe TCKs. I want them to learn from the experts regarding the psychological and cultural makeup of their spouse. (See Appendix for several recommendations.) Besides unresolved grief, there can be struggles because of the hidden identity of the TCK. Others may see their spouse as not being any different and not recognize they belong to the third culture. I want the spouse to learn about it from other sources besides their spouse and the therapist.

Another activity that you can do with your couple clients is to have them both complete their Identity Iceberg and talk about what is the same and what things are different from one another. Then have them evaluate how this might play itself out in their relationship as a couple and in their relationships as a family.

## The DSM and Relationships

What might be the proper diagnosis for an ATCK who is struggling with relationship challenges? This is a tough question. It would depend on the severity of the problems, the length of time they have been encountering these challenges, and if they meet certain criteria in the DSM. In most cases, they meet the criteria for either an Adjustment Disorder or a Mood Disorder of some type.

## Things You Should Know

1.  Kay Eakin in her writings for the United States Family Liaison Office in Washington, DC, made this statement, *"There is some indication that TCKs often do not learn problem-solving skills in handling interpersonal relationships. With a built-in rotational cycle, there is a temptation to simply leave a problem without resolving it. Because of the importance of people rather then [sic] place, this baggage gets carried on to the next location and may re-emerge and impact the development of new relationships"* (Eakin, 1999, p. 20).

2.  TCKs tend to develop close friendships quickly due to a fear of moving because it is easier to share deeper things with someone you will not be with long-term, or it is the cultural style in the country where they were raised. This pattern can be easily misinterpreted.

3.  Parents who presume that their children see the world as they and the generations before them have seen it because they share a common national passport can be rudely awakened when a child does not behave according to expected practices.

4.  A marriage to a TCK has its own unique challenges. Marriage can be stressful for all couples, but when the two come from two different cultures that have different value systems, traditions, worldviews, languages, and so forth, the stresses are magnified.

## Discussion Questions & Activities

1.  What book comes to mind that may be a "good read" for a TCK in knowing how best to relate to people in their present context/culture?

2.  If you are not a marriage and family therapist, what professional development activities can you participate in that will help you respond to TCKs who need assistance with family of origin, dating, or marriage and family issues?

3. How can you guide a TCK in the healthy and practical use of social media as a way to establish and maintain relationships?

4. Activity: Start a new friendship with someone you have never known. After each meeting or interaction, write notes about what happened and what each of you talked about and asked. Try to determine what level the friendship is on and how it is progressing.

# Chapter 8

# Questioning Post-Traumatic Stress Disorder: "Where is the Abuse, Kidnapping, War Crime, or Life-Threatening Event?"

*"Life is raw material. We are artisans. We can sculpt our existence into something beautiful, or debase it into ugliness. It is in our hands."*

(Better, 2010)

### Post-Traumatic Stress Disorder or Not?

I can't stress enough the importance of looking at the *whole* story for every client, and in particular at the invisible pieces and world they have known when you recognize they are TCKs. Why? Because many of them may come with what you feel are signs of Post Traumatic Stress Disorder (PTSD), but when you listen to their initial story, nothing seems to warrant the label of a major trauma that would result in this diagnosis.

However, there are some particular places to examine closely in the lives of many TCKs that can lead you to the events in their lives that caused the same symptoms as those who have experienced a major trauma such as a rape or kidnapping. Once you identify those life-altering events, you will be amazed at how your skills in working with this diagnosis for other clients will apply here as well.

> Suzy's parents worked in a village deep in the jungles of Ecuador. When she was ready for the first grade, she was taken to boarding school—a trip of a couple of days away from her parents. When her parents left her, they did not cry or prolong the Goodbye like many of the other parents. They had been advised not to do so because this would make the Goodbye more difficult for Suzy. However, Suzy internalized the feeling that her parents really did not want her with them—perhaps because she was a bother to them. Suzy then began a pattern of not bothering anyone about anything for fear of rejection. Her conclusion was that, "No one wants me. I am not loveable."

In her years in boarding school, Suzy was not a good student and feared asking for help from her teachers or her classmates. She did not want to bother anyone else since they too could reject her. She barely passed each grade until it was time to return to her passport country, England, where her parents presumed she would enter university. Suzy didn't want to do that because she feared disappointing them if she didn't pass her classes. Rather than talk to her parents about her fears, she kept all of her anxieties and questions close to her heart, along with the nagging thought, "No one wants me. I am only a bother to people. I am not loveable."

When Suzy arrived in England, the fear of failure didn't go away. But for the first time, she found young men who were there to "help" her out and show her the ropes. She began to depend on them to rescue her in times of emotional or physical need. As a result, Suzy ended up in one abusive relationship after another. In the end, she came to anticipate hurt and rejection in all of her relationships and began to strike out in a rage to anyone who attempted to get close to her. Sadly, she soon created her own worst nightmare and slid into one addiction after another until she was living on the street. It was at this point Suzy reached out to a local counselor.

Obviously, when clients walk through our doors, TCKs or not, the first thing we want to know is why they have come. Behind the presenting symptom, however, we also seek to understand what may be driving a particular behavior or emotional state. Suzy came in saying, "I want to get off of drugs," but other clients come in saying the same thing. Why does *she* use drugs? What might be some hard realities inside that drugs keep her from facing?

## Possible Reasons for Post-Traumatic Stress Disorder Among the Globally Mobile

### *Living in places of high risk*

Trauma has become a frequent experience of many expats. When I was a child, I would be aware of expats who could not live the expat life due to all of the physical hardships of strange diseases such as typhoid fever, hepatitis, snake bites, dengue fever, and other mysterious illnesses. It was only on very rare occasions that we heard of expats who had to return to their home countries due to emotional issues or a traumatic event. Not that traumatic events did not take place, but rather expats just did not return to their passport country because of them.

But the times have changed. We learn of horrible atrocities around the world on a daily basis. Kidnappings, civil warfare, bombings, or mass murders are rapidly increasing in all parts of the world. For most of us, these events happen daily on our TV screens or in streaming video on our computer screens or smart phones. "This is so sad" we say, and we wonder what is happening to our world. But they don't particularly impact our personal lives.

That is not so, however, for the expatriates who are in those situations and the countries where these events happen. Particularly for those who have lived in that place for several years, and for their children who have come to see this as "home," these events happened in 3-D. They were there, even if no one would connect them to that place by their passports. When the embassy was bombed in Kenya, a U.S. American teenager was in the basement getting some papers he needed to go with his college application. In another African country, three eight-year-old TCKs were in a car pool on their way to school when the car was hijacked and all of them were forced at gunpoint to get out and watch the gunman threaten to take the life of their driver, one of the children's mother. In South America, a young expat teen was shot in the leg by bandits who jumped from a speeding taxi and stole her cell phone as she sat on the curb chatting with her friends.

Don't forget to think and ask about the political climate of the country or countries in which your globally nomadic client has lived, as an adult or child. The point is that when an event such as the terrorist attacks on the United States that took place on September 11, 2001, there were many grief counselors sent to the scene to work with those impacted by this event. Those who witnessed the event, either in person or via the media, forever carry it in their collective memory. But when similar traumas happen in remote places, and your clients were there, one of the additional traumas is that *no one was there* at the time to help in processing the trauma and many do not even know about the horrific trauma that took place. So they come to you now, hoping you can help them stop the nightmares and flashbacks.

If my client is a child or a youth, and the parent tells me of a life-threatening event that took place in their family and they are now seeing a developmental regression or unreasonable fears in their child or the child is suddenly acting in a fashion that is not typical of that child, I will begin to explore PTSD in that child and adjust my treatment accordingly as I do with the adults.

## Living in places of increased human suffering

In addition to the human-induced traumas, many who have lived overseas have witnessed terrible famine and extreme poverty firsthand. They have seen human suffering up close and very personally. This can take an enormous toll on people, particularly those whose job it is to try to relieve such suffering. They see it every day and it can become overwhelming for the aid worker or for their children who also see these realities. When they recall the cries of those who were suffering whom they or their parents could not help, it impacts their enjoyment of life today.

In places where child mortality rates are high due to malnutrition or other reasons, expatriate children learn about the realities of death at an early age. Perhaps it is through the death of a child of the person who works in their home, perhaps it is their good friend, perhaps someone they knew in the community, but in any case, some young TCKs have seen several people die and this can create high anxiety and a certain symptoms of trauma.

Other types of suffering that can impact all members of globally nomadic families include the times they may be in a country where a major earthquake, tsunami, or other natural disaster took place. They have heard the loud, nonstop blare of the radio passing along messages to family members who live in remote areas or the long list of names of those who have died as a result of the natural disaster. Again, they have been eye-witnesses to what most from their passport country only casually read about in the paper or on the Internet with their morning cup of coffee or their evening glass of wine.

## Coping with universal traumas

And then, of course, there are the types of traumatic events that can happen in anyone's life—some type of airplane or other vehicular accident, drowning, or the suicide of someone they love. Again, one of the main problems on top of the actual loss is that if it happened in the expat's homeland and they received word about it while overseas, folks around them have no mental picture of the person they have lost. They will be sorry, of course, but it's not the same as being where others are grieving with you because they also know the person or situation. And, of course, the opposite can happen. People can be back in their passport countries and hear news of a friend they loved overseas who was killed in a bad accident and no one in that environment can truly grieve with them either.

The point is that living globally doesn't make anyone immune from these types of things, but because they often happened half a world away, your clients may think you do not care about political events "over there." Most ATCKs or TCAs will not add most of these events to their initial Intake Form as their reason for seeking therapy. But they may list anxiety or depression.

## Living with the realities of boarding schools

Another invisible place for many therapists is the issue of boarding schools, particularly for ATCKS who are middle-aged or older. For many of them, boarding schools were the norm because the plethora of international schools now available were non-existent during their childhood years. For some children, just going away to boarding school created a wound so deep and traumatic that it resulted in PTSD from the sheer pain of the separation from their parents. Like Suzy in our story, many in this older group left their parents for school at the age of six and basically lived hundreds of miles from home in all types of schools for nine months a year. While this is no longer the norm, it was for them and for many ATCKs. This is a more important part of their story than even *they* realize. Many struggles of attachment can be related to some of these early separations. So if your TCK client spent time in a boarding school, spend a significant amount of time evaluating that experience. Here are some things to think about.

First, one size does not fit all. It's easy to make a blanket judgment, depending on your own history or awareness of these past days of expat living, regarding whether or not boarding schools are a good or bad idea. It may or may not be how your client sees it. And if they went to several boarding schools, some may hold good memories and some may hold painful memories.

Second, remember that each family member will have his or her own story of a particular boarding school. Why is this true? There are many factors that impact the long-term view of the ATCKs regarding their boarding school days. The age of the children when they go away to boarding school can make a difference in their experience and the emotional impact. The frequency of the parents' visits or contact with their child and that child's interpretation of that contact can make a difference.

Third, different personalities respond in different ways. Some kids shut down emotionally for one reason or another before they ever got to boarding school. One child in a family may have had plenty of friends and did not have the same struggles as a sister or brother who could not deal with the school cliques or the extreme loneliness once the lights were turned out and they were alone in the dark with their thoughts of home.

And finally, the school itself can make a difference. What were the rules and/or types of punishment at the time your client attended the school? Were the expectations different or the same for day students? What was the atmosphere among not only the students, but also the house parents and the teachers? Did they love kids or were they there because they had no other options. Some TCKs struggle in boarding school and spend many years in the offices of therapists trying to get emotionally on top of that experience, while others may be filled with primarily good memories of boarding school.

Apple Gidley, a TCK who attended a boarding school in England for several years and thrived in that environment, was facing the difficult decision of whether or not to send her own TCKs to boarding school due to the nomadic life her own family was experiencing. She makes this observation about life in boarding schools:

> It is an emotive issue with no hard and fast answer. Add to the mix
> the cultural divergences between countries, and within countries,

particularly with regard to boarding schools and you have a crucible of opinions. Britain, Australia, Canada, and some Asian and African countries and increasingly Russia, consider the boarding school option as potential, not punishment . . . But for many on the nomadic trail, boarding school can offer teens a chance to thrive in a stable environment through some of their most important educational years, without going through the dislocation of multiple moves in an already turbulent time of their lives. It gives a child the opportunity to experience continuity with peers, consistency in curriculum, and a sense of community, exempt from the upheavals of a mobile life, while still benefitting from the global experience with family during vacation time. (Gridley, 2012, p. 144)

Along with the positive press for boarding schools, there were far too many TCKs (one is too many) who were physically, sexually, or emotionally abused in boarding schools. Without a doubt, a boarding school is a perfect place for an abuser, or even for peer abuse to occur because contacts are limited with their parents and letters written home can be screened. Often the abuser is someone who all others would consider an upstanding member of the community.

The DVD *All God's Children: The Ultimate Sacrifice* is a gut-wrenching story of the years of abuse that took place in a missionary boarding school in Mamou, Guinea, and the struggles these now-adult TCKs and their parents encountered in trying to get the sponsoring organization of their boarding school to legally deal with the abuse. The book *Too Small to Ignore: Why the Least of These Matters Most,* written by Dr. Wess Stafford, the President of Compassion International, is the heartbreaking story of Wess' own experience as a child in that same boarding school.

This is the story of just one boarding school, but unfortunately, I hear many very similar stories shared by TCKs from all parts of the world. I have a growing file on reports that have been filed on boarding schools from past generations. Abuse many times goes undetected as TCKs live or go to school in some of the most remote parts of the world where it goes unnoticed by parents or authorities. Or it can take place in the middle of a large city.

I worked with several ATCKs who were all sexually abused by the same man. His parting words to each of them was, "If you tell anyone, I will come back and hurt one of your family members on your birthday." Even though these TCKs were now adults and were living in their home country, they dreaded each and every birthday.

Abuse of TCKs does not take place only in school, but it can take place wherever the TCK lives just like with any of your clients. Often it is buried because they do not want to negatively impact their parents' job. Many believe the lies of the perpetrator and feel that it was the fault of the child. And there are some TCKs, particularly missionary kids, who are hesitant to bring a bad name to the organization for whom their parents work. As is typical in some cases of severe trauma, TCKs have learned to "split" or "dissociate" in order to deal with stress.

Be careful as you are checking for abuse and what you label as abuse. It may not be abuse in the culture where the TCK was raised. The definitions of abuse vary from country to country and generation to generation. What may be abuse in one era may not be seen as abuse at all in a former generation. A good example of this is how the view of spanking of children has changed in various cultures and countries.

Today, there are several organizations and individuals who are hard at work to do better screening and training for agencies. One group is the Child Safety Protection Network (http://childsafetyprotectionnetwork.org), which is a collaborative network of mission agencies, faith-based NGOs and international Christian schools intentionally and strategically addressing the issues of child protection. There are new programs springing up in all sectors and many countries as progress is being made to protect children.

## Revisiting Suzy

Let's go back to Suzy's story. We left her in the story as she finally sought a therapist. Suzy's life was going from bad to worse until she ended up in a halfway home. The social workers recommended a therapist who worked at the halfway house, Peter, to work with her. Peter happened to be a TCK from Africa and had a big heart for those less fortunate in life. He discovered in an early session that Suzy was a TCK and had traveled the world with her parents just as he had as a youngster.

Peter and Suzy began to swap stories. As long as Peter kept things on a surface level, Suzy enjoyed talking to him. But when he attempted to get to the core of her feelings regarding life in Ecuador and in boarding school, she would angrily shut down. This went on for months, until finally one day when he once again attempted to ask her about going to school at the age of six, she exploded on him.

Peter remained calm and did not defend himself or shame her for her angry charges against him. Suzy was desperately trying to push the therapist away and make him reject her like she felt everyone else had done all of her life. When she finally calmed down, he quietly told her that he was not leaving, but would continue to work with her.

Suzy got up and slammed the door as she bolted out of his office. For weeks, she would not schedule an appointment with Peter, although she would carefully observe him go in and out of his office at the halfway house.

After several weeks, she went into his office. Suzy asked him, "Do you still want to work with me?" When he responded "yes," she broke into tears, "For the first time in my life, someone is sticking with me even though I have really messed up."

Through his patient interaction with Suzy, Peter had already begun to slowly change her self-statement of "No one wants me. I am not loveable." As Suzy experienced Peter sticking with her, she began to slowly entertain the idea that maybe others would too.

Peter could have originally just labeled Suzy with a Personality Disorder and believed she was unable to conquer her past demons. However, once he heard about her being left alone in boarding school at a very young age to fend for herself against a few older students whose mission seemed to be to torture and tease the younger kids, he understood Suzy. When he learned how the adults in the school would chasten her for her tears and not hear her pleas for help, her behavior and coping skills made complete sense. My young therapist friend realized he was dealing with underlying issues of loss and grief, PTSD, and many years of being alone.

When Suzy had returned to her home country of England, she felt like an outcast with her peers and was raped by her boyfriend. All of this was confirmation in her mind that there was something terribly wrong with her. She believed she was worthless as a human being and could not do anything meaningful with her life. But upon encountering this new therapist, Suzy felt understood, cared for, supported, and respected. She felt it was a safe place to explore the repeated trauma in her life. After many months of hard work, she was able to change her self-statements, make peace with her inner world, and establish herself in a career with the police department helping other rape victims.

## Beware of the Triggers

I have worked with clients who have been through several traumatic events and did well in their childhood—only to have all of this past trauma triggered by a classroom assignment in graduate school. A movie can trigger past trauma in a TCK. A good example of this is the movie *Hotel Rwanda,* which can be too overpowering for the TCK or TCA who was evacuated from a war-torn country while their friends were left behind. Or the movie *The Patriot* may seem just fine until the TCK who grew up in boarding schools sees the scene where the young child must tell her father Goodbye as he goes off to war. Like most who go through some major trauma, they seem to be okay until a later time and something triggers the release of that memory.

Then there are some ATCKs who end up with symptoms that look like they must have endured some form of terrible abuse and yet the therapist cannot figure it out as there is no history of abuse. Could the repeated Goodbyes to a caregiver, beloved nanny, best friend, and family members result in trauma symptoms? I believe so.

## Compassion Fatigue and Vicarious Trauma

Trauma work is emotionally draining even for seasoned therapists. It takes a toll on all of us as we listen to stories of pain, suffering, and trauma. As therapists, we need to be emotionally healthy, have our own support systems in place, and have some form of supervision. This is necessary in order to help us not only give our clients the best care, but also to monitor our own self-care. We need to have a supervisor or coworker who can debrief us as we hear and feel our client's trauma. If we do not take good care of ourselves we will burn out as we vicariously experience the trauma of our clients.

One of the best resources currently on the market is the classic book written by Dr. Charles R. Figley titled *Compassion Fatigue: Coping With Secondary Traumatic Stress Disorder In Those Who Treat The Traumatized.* Figley talks about "the need for balance; the use of external resources; self-atonement; connection; and the need to foster one's sense of meaning, interdependence, and hope" (Figley, 1995, p. xx).

It is my belief that we need to disengage from our client's trauma after the session by doing something completely different from our work in order to give our minds and emotions a rest. Our work as therapists can take a toll on us. We need to practice what we preach to our clients.

**What to do:**

1. If you do have a client struggling with Post-Traumatic Stress Disorder, Eye Movement Desensitization and Reprocessing (EMDR) therapy is an excellent new type of therapy that has a good track record of success with clients who have been through abuse or trauma. If you, as the therapist, are not trained in EMDR, then have them see someone certified by the EMDR International Association (EMDRIA) for a few sessions. Once the client has completed the EMDR, you can continue to work with your TCK on other issues. See www.emdria.org for a therapist trained in EMDR in your area.

2. If they do fit the criteria for PTSD, then as a therapist, I know that I need to not only address topics around their identity as a TCK, but also put into place some good trauma work with the client around the particular trauma that took place before they can focus on any other aspect surrounding their growing up as a TCK. I have to make sure they are stabilized before I rip open any new wounds.

## PTSD and the DSM information

When does a client receive the diagnosis for Post-Traumatic Stress Disorder (PTSD) on an Axis I?

In describing PTSD the DSM-IV (1994, p. 209) states:

> The person has been exposed to a traumatic event in which both of the following were present:
>
> 1. The person experienced, witnessed, or was confronted with an event or events that involved actual or threatened death or serious injury, or a threat to the physical integrity of self or others.
>
> 2. The person's response involved intense fear, helplessness, or horror. Note: In children, this may be expressed instead by disorganized or agitated behavior.

Some of the traumas that we have looked at in this chapter would most certainly fit in one of the categories above. Traumas such as witnessing kidnapping, violent crime, or warfare, or experiencing sexual or physical abuse, or suddenly being evacuated from an area or a country are obvious. And for some, trauma would include going away to boarding school, especially if they felt intense fear and hopelessness as they watched their parents drive away or suffered in relationships with other students or boarding school staff.

As I look at the list of behaviors, I am drawn to several that I have frequently seen with ATCKs:

- efforts to avoid thoughts, feelings, or conversations associated with the trauma,
- inability to recall an important aspect of the trauma,
- restricted range of affect, or
- sense of a foreshortened future

Whenever I have any client whose behavior fits any of the above description or who begins to describe a life-threatening event, I will question my client carefully about the trauma he or she experienced. I might even pull my DSM manual off of my shelf and begin to walk through the criteria for that diagnosis with my client to see if they fit the criteria for PTSD.

# Things You Should Know

1. Some of the possible reasons for symptoms of PTSD are due to the TCK living in places of high risk, seeing increased human suffering, witnessing universal traumas, being sent to boarding schools, or being subject to actual events of abuse or trauma.

2. Repeated Goodbyes can result in symptoms that look like PTSD.

3. The definitions of abuse vary from country to country. Also, what may be abuse in one era may not have been seen as abuse at all in a former generation.

# Discussion Questions & Activity

1. How do you listen to and experience traumatic stories? Have you found that your own beliefs about the world are altered and possibly damaged?

2. How do you care for yourself as a therapist who is privy to such stories?

3. How much do you know about Compassion Fatigue and Vicarious Trauma in the helping professions? Have you learned how to prevent and/or transform it?

4. How has your definition of trauma changed as you have read about the affect of transitions on the individual?

5. Activity: Watch the local, national, or international news on television for 3–5 days. Tally how many "bad news" items are reported each day. Note how many murders, rapes, kidnappings, and robberies are reported each day. If you are watching international news, note how many instances of bombings and other civil disturbances are reported. Then note how you feel after watching the news. Note any lingering thoughts later that day (or evening) or the next day. Report back to class and compare notes with a partner or the whole group.

# Chapter 9

# Using Creative Techniques in Therapy

### *Is This Home?*

> *Mountains, valleys, tall stately pines*
> *Jungles, parrots, cool rushing streams*
> *Orchids, coffee beans, white deserted beaches*
> *Is this home?*
>
> *Horns, dust, uneven broken sidewalks*
> *Buses, bicycles, slow moving oxcarts*
> *Buildings, beggars, narrow winding streets*
> *Is this home?*
>
> *Bunk beds, story time, climbing mango trees*
> *Swimming, hiking, letter writing Mondays*
> *Boarding school, duffle bags, green painted desks*
> *Is this home?*
>
> *Reading, short-wave radios, board games*
> *Adventures, brush forts, slow plodding donkeys*
> *Firecrackers, tree houses, homemade paper dolls*
> *Is this home?*
>
> *Airports, suitcases, numerous delays*
> *Lonely, exciting, fearful, new adventures*
> *Passports, visas, long stamped documents*
> *Is this home?*
>
> *High school, confusion, United States*
> *Cliques, hatred, lonely, grieving silence*
> *Outcasts, anger, useless world knowledge*
> *Is this home?*
>
> *Television, drinking water, white snow*
> *New friends, strangers, big extended families*
> *Lawn mowers, fast cars, money, money, money*
> *Is this home?*

*El Hatillo, Raymond, Tegucigalpa, Marion*
*Ohio, Indiana, Texas, red Georgia clay*
*Honduras, Mexico, Costa Rica, United States*
*Is this home?*

*Accepting, listening, wandering nomads*
*The world, family, friends scattered far and wide*
*Belonging, understanding, rich multicultural souls*
*This is home.*

(Bushong, 2004)

His mother had brought Jeremy, a 15-year-old TCK, for therapy with me. The family had been working in Europe for an NGO over the last ten years. However, her husband had decided he no longer loved with her but, was in love with a coworker with whom he was spending many hours while doing a special project for the organization. Jeremy's mother had brought their three teens back to her hometown, while her soon-to-be ex-husband stayed in Europe. They were going through a messy divorce and Jeremy's father only called the children about once a month. He claimed he was too busy. Jeremy was the child who seemed to be struggling the most with this sudden transition.

One afternoon in our session, he was trying to tell me just how much his life had changed with the move. Remembering that he had shown me some of his pencil sketching in his diary, I pulled out a white sheet of paper and a pencil and handed it to him.

"Jeremy," I said, "draw me a picture of how your life has changed." His face brightened when he saw the pencil and paper. And he quietly began to think and sketch.

When he was done, I saw exactly what he was talking about as we talked about the picture he had just drawn. On the left side of the paper, he had drawn a rough sketch of a young boy walking barefoot, with a blindfold over his eyes across a turbulent ocean, trying to hang on to about seven balloons. Each balloon was labeled with something meaningful to him such as "friends," "soccer," "Father," or something else he was trying to hang on to in the transition. On the right side of the picture was a picture of a cement jungle with a huge banner that said, "Welcome to High School," and next to it was a long list of rules all written in quite lengthy detail. There were knives pointing his direction, sticking out of the buildings.

Jeremy thrust the paper my direction and muttered, "This is what it feels like."

One of the ways TCKs or ATCKs can convey their story to you, or even to themselves, is through the use of the arts, like my poem at the beginning of the chapter or my having Jeremy sketch his feelings. It is an effective method to make their story or thinking come alive. Although they may not be skilled in the artistry of words, their natural skill may be music or pencil sketches; TCKs are typically very good in at least one of the arts. Some of them had to develop their own entertainment as children, while others were exposed to the great works of art throughout the world.

As a therapist, I am sure you already know how important it is to let the client use the form of creative therapy they are most comfortable using to express their deep feelings of love, joy, conflict or pain. Trauma therapists believe that emotional wounding takes place in the "right brain" which is the feelings and creative part of the brain. Therefore, in order to help healing take place the use of the arts shows amazing results in these clients.

> One of the ways TCKs or ATCKs can convey their story to you, or even to themselves, is through the use of the arts.

When TCKs use the art form they love to communicate their deep feelings, they seem to come alive in therapy. If it is not something they do naturally, they get stuck in the cognitive mode as they try to figure out how to use that particular artistic technique and don't move into their feelings. For example, dance would not be my voice. If you were to ask me to choreograph a dance to express my feelings, I would freeze, ask you ten thousand questions, not be able to figure out which foot is my left foot, fall into a fit of laughter, or just skip out of therapy. But if you were to ask me to draw a rough pencil sketch of a scene from my childhood, I would focus on what I wanted to draw and the details around that scene to communicate my feelings. Use what is comfortable for the client rather than *your* preferred method.

Let's look at some of the more common creative techniques that I have used with my TCK, ATCK, and TCA clients. This is not an exhaustive list, but should help you start thinking about how you might use the creative arts with your clients.

## Art

When a therapist is trained in art therapy, it is wonderful. But unfortunately many of us are not trained in this form of therapy. I stumble around in this area, but I love it. I have taken several workshops on the use of art therapy and I have used it many times with my TCKs and ATCKs who love art. I have seen wonderful works of art done by ATCKs displayed in galleries and I have seen simple drawings that told of wonderful adventures in childhood.

What can you do with art therapy? I frequently ask my client to draw different concepts for me. I might suggest:

- "Draw a picture of you, in each of your host countries. Draw a picture of you today. How is today's picture influenced by yesterday's picture?"

- "Draw a picture of how you see your future."

- "Draw me a picture that depicts your life as a TCK."

- "Draw a picture of home."

- "Draw a picture of your grief."

- "Draw a picture of your family and how they deal with transition."

- "Draw a picture of the community or compound where you spent most of your childhood."

- "Draw a bridge with your childhood life on one side of the bridge and your future on the other side of the bridge."

- "Draw the scene you are describing for me right now."

They then draw in any format they desire (pencil, crayons, fine art, graphic art on the computer, decoupage). I might ask them to do this activity as homework or I might have them draw it right there in my office. We follow this activity by spending a large chunk of time talking about the picture, noting things like, "I see that the sun is out and the sky is blue in these pictures but not in these. Tell me why you did it this way." "Why is your brother missing from this family scene?" "Talk to me about this part of your drawing where your mother is swimming in the ocean and the rest of your family is in the boat." or the simple, "Tell me about your picture."

Are individuals' eyes shut? Some art therapists state this could mean the individuals were not aware or did not want to be aware of what was going on around them. Do they have faces on their people? Note what is included or not included in the scene. At times they leave out a family member or draw them on the far edge of the paper with a lot of space between them and other family members. What period of time in their family history did they decide to draw for you? Why that time period?

If you can pick up a basic book on art therapy such as the *Handbook of Art Therapy* edited by Cathy A. Malchiodi (2012—see full information in *Resources* at the back of this book), it will give you some wonderful guidelines on what to look for in pictures or photography.

> If art is the voice of your client, it is rich with meaning as you explore the colors, objects, details, and themes of the artwork.

I was in a workshop where the ATCK participants were asked to draw a timeline across the top of a sheet of paper and mark those points on the timeline when they made a move. Each attendee was given a list of different types of roots, such as strangler roots, surface roots, drought-resistant roots, parasitic roots, taproots, fibrous roots, etc. The next directive was to either draw in or print what type of root he or she put down in that new location. It caused each participant to think about how deeply they were planted, or not planted in the culture where they lived at various stages in their lives. If art is the voice of your client, it is rich with meaning as you explore the colors, objects, details, and themes of the artwork.

## Photography

"A pictures is worth a thousand words" is commonly said. If the client can bring in pictures of themselves, homes, friends, schools, family or whatever they select to share with you, it can give you valuable insight into the emotional impact of each transition or just the global lifestyle on the family. As you look at the pictures, note who is next to whom in the pictures as well as the expressions on the faces. There are some TCKs who do not have any pictures—as they were lost in transition. That is a significant loss to discuss.

> Photographs of the client and their family, homes, friends, schools, or whatever can give the therapist valuable insight into the emotional impact of each transition.

I recall working with a TCK who was a doctor. His family had gone through many traumas during his youth, including kidnappings and civil unrest. Added to those traumas were the effects of his father's several major bouts of depression. Ultimately they left their international post. As I looked at all of the family pictures, my eyes were drawn to his mother's face in each of them. In the "early days" his mother's eyes were bright and clear with a big smile on her face. His father's face was stoic without any expression. In the "later days" the brightness was gone from her eyes, the smile had left her face, and she looked almost angry. His father was still stoic, but he also had developed a hard look on his face. The children were not in the later pictures.

But now the son was in my office dealing with depression, confusion, and tremendous grief over all the losses in their numerous planned and unplanned transitions. Although he was in the middle of his own career, he was questioning his career choice, thinking about another move, and contemplating working internationally. He was wondering what kind of an impact his choice would have on his children, even though he was an adult TCK.

He talked about not noticing the tired expression in his mother's eyes and began to tell stories about the struggles they had experienced over the years. Before that day, he had seen it all through the eyes of a child and teen and thought of it as a big adventure. That day he looked at the pictures. As he studied the eyes of his parents, he began to list the various things he would do differently as a father and a spouse. Photography can capture the feelings of the individuals which otherwise might have gone unobserved.

There are some TCKs who are wonderful photographers and love to use this medium for self-expression. Several years ago, I saw the photography of Steve Robbins, an adult TCK from Latin America. Steve is a very gifted photographer whom I first met when he was a young teen riding across an open field on his horse and I was a college student visiting the community where his family lived in Bolivia. I was thrilled to meet him at a local Mexican restaurant to renew this friendship, and even more so when he brought his portfolio to share with me. There were two pictures that struck me in Steve's portfolio.

Used by permission of Steve Robbins

Used by permission of Steve Robbins

Steve shared with me that he had titled his photography *Feet in Two Worlds*. His description of it was the following: "I was struggling to understand who I was as an adult TCK. I placed the area of sharpest focus on the baby—since my childhood was clear to me. I composed the photo so that it does not show us where the path came from, or where it goes. . . . I wanted to convey my feelings of not really knowing who I was" (Personal email exchange in 2010). The second photo was after he was able to better grasp his identity as a TCK and felt more solid on the path of life.

If Steve were my client, we would have discussed the symbolism of the strong tree and its maturity in the center of the photograph. We would discuss the composition of the photos. We would look at the broken branches strewn throughout the yard. We would explore the symbolism of the baby—that is, its nakedness, hard cold texture, sharp focus, and distance from the tree. And we'd talk about where the path may have originated and where it is going. When did he lose his feeling of not being grounded on the path? What helped him to once again feel grounded in the second picture? We would explore if there were any events that led to feeling invisible. What events helped him feel visible?

So much can be explored in looking at all of the different aspects of a photograph as the client looks inward and studies how it relates to his or her own life story.

> Much can be explored in looking at all of the different aspects of a photograph as the client looks inward and studies how it relates to his or her own life story.

Recently, research psychologist Dr. Anne Copeland developed a set of pictures that can be used in a therapy session to help the client talk about their transition experience. The information about this resource, *Reflection Photos*, is listed in the *Resources* section in the back of this book.

## Music, Film, and Dance

If the client is musically inclined, have him or her find music that describes his or her world. There is more and more music out there produced by

> YouTube is a wonderful place to find music or video about or by TCKs.

ATCKs. Recently a friend of mine posted on Facebook a short video of her son, a young TCK, performing a rap he composed. YouTube is a wonderful place to find music about or by TCKs. If you just type in the words "third culture kid" in YouTube, you will find many excellent pieces of music and film around the theme of the TCK.

At times a song comes along which tells their story. The pop singer Michael Bublé recently has a song titled "Home," which talks about his longing to go home again. It quickly became a favorite among ATCKs as it talks about that longing for home. What I find interesting about the ATCKs' fascination with that song is most ATCKs cannot tell you where IS home, but this song resonates with them as they long for home, wherever it might be located. It makes for an interesting discussion in a session regarding where is home and why this song speaks so strongly to them.

An artist of my generation is John Denver who was not a traditional TCK, but a domestic TCK. He grew up in the military and knew what it was to be rootless and lose so much due to repeated Goodbyes. If you listen to several of his songs such as, "Goodbye Again," "Fly Away," or "Leaving on a Jet Plane" you will hear some of those TCK themes and their struggles with saying Goodbye over and over again . . . yet, they choose to keep moving even though they do not have to do so.

Another example of a popular song of a few years ago that tells the story of the TCK is found in the movie *Namesake* and is sung by Nitin Sawhney. It is titled "The Same Song." The entire movie tells the struggles of a young Indian TCK trying to figure out his cultural identity at that vulnerable stage of the young adult.

> *How many roads have I wandered?*
> *None, and each my own*
> *Behind me the bridges have crumbled*
> *No question of return*
> *Autumn leaves like discarded dreams*
> *trampled underneath a tide of careless feet*
> *it's the same song playing*
> *everywhere I go*
> *it's like an army marching right through me.*
> *Nowhere to go but the horizon*
> *where, then, will I call my home?*
> *Summer spent, in the high grass*
> *or just fragments, ransacked memories*
> *dark river snakes, across this murky hall*
> *boatman sings his downstream melodies.*
> *How many roads have I wandered?*
> *None, and each my own*
> *Behind me the bridges have crumbled*
> *where, then, will I call my home?*

(Sawhney, 2006)

If your client is so inclined, have him write his own lyrics or musical arrangement. Or if she plays an instrument, have her play a selection that reflects her feelings. If he plays with a band, have him bring in a recording of his group. It may not be your choice of music, but it sings the story of your client. I have certainly listened to more than my share of rap music and heavy metal.

Music is the language of the heart. Some clients love to go home after a difficult session and bang on their drums or piano or a favorite instrument from another culture such as a bamboo flute. Or when they are feeling homesick for "home" they will play the music of another language that is a part of their identity. I have my folder of Spanish music on iTunes that I play from time to time, depending on my mood.

The same is true of the film industry. There are numerous examples of TCKs describing their world on YouTube on the Internet. And documentaries regarding TCKs are popping up at a rapid pace. A listing of some of the movies produced to date that depict the life of the TCK are listed in the appendix in the section labeled *Resources*. As the number of TCKs increase, the number of films depicting that life is on the increase.

In Chapter 11 is a wonderful example of a TCK using dance to convey her feelings. Dance may or may not be a realistic medium to use during a one-hour therapy session, but with a little creativity on your part, your client will be able to use it to help you understand him or her a bit better.

## Writing

Journaling is an often used form of expressing what the client is currently feeling as he or she is processing events from his or her past or current world. The poem at the beginning of this chapter was one I wrote as I thought about my adjustments to many countries and cities and what I longed for from each of those places. If I were in therapy, my therapist would have me walk through each of the lines and talk about those places, sights, smells, and sounds.

Whenever I assign a client the homework of journaling, I ask him to just write and not edit his writing or try to write in a politically correct manner. I want him to just write using as many feeling words as possible. Some do well writing in a little notebook that they carefully hide from prying eyes. Some love to journal in another language. Some write in their private journal on a password-protected computer. I have noticed that today's

> Whenever I assign a client the homework of journaling, I ask them to write without editing or worrying about being politically correct.

youth are journaling online and calling it blogging. Some have a formal blog under their own profile. I know others who have a fictitious profile where they blog those thoughts and feelings they are fearful to share with others because of their fear of rejection, yet they do it on the Internet.

I have the client bring to a therapy session whatever they want to share of their writings. I have them read it to me as it helps me understand and get a feel for the emotions they felt as they wrote, rather than my reading it silently or to them. We then go through it piece by piece.

In whatever creative form the client uses, I do not believe there are mistakes. Sometimes it is in the mistake—wrong word, slip of the crayon, crack in the voice—that a window is opened to the subconscious and what lies in the soul of your ATCK or TCK client. Any of the above forms of therapy can be used with an adult or a child.

Be creative as the therapist in helping your TCK tell you about their world and their feelings associated with that world. Some of the best work that my clients have done has been the result of an impulsive idea where they communicated to you in a casual way a hobby or skill they might have had where they could lose themselves, but which they left behind in one of their moves.

I had a young man from Asia share with me how he was struggling with his therapist whose only form of therapy was Cognitive Behavioral Therapy. As we chatted, he casually mentioned that he loved to relax by playing a traditional instrument from one of the countries where he lived as a child. I asked him what would happen when he played? He replied, "I am flooded with emotions which I cannot verbalize." I asked him if he ever took his instrument to a therapy session and played it for his therapist. "No," he responded, "my therapist knows I play, but he said he doesn't do music therapy. He only does CBT." My suggestion to the young man was to play and play his instrument as he continues to work on healing. I felt his music was the language expressing the emotions of his heart.

Be creative in your use of the arts in therapy. Use what is available and let your client lead the way. It is a powerful and fun medium.

# Things You Should Know

1. Let the client lead the way in choosing a form of creative therapy (art, music, journaling, photography, dance, etc.) he or she is most comfortable using to express deep feelings of love, joy, conflict, frustration, or pain.

2. Trauma therapists believe that emotional wounding takes place in the right brain, which is the feelings and creative part of the brain. Therefore, in order to help healing take place, the use of the arts shows amazing results in the client.

3. Have clients read to you what they wrote as it helps the therapist understand and get a feel for the emotions they felt as they wrote.

4. Be creative as the therapist in helping your TCK tell you about their world and their feelings associated with that world. Some of the best work that clients have done has been the result of an impulsive idea.

# Discussion Questions & Activity

1. If you are not creative, which technique from this chapter seems the most do-able for you? Explain why.

2. If you are creative, what other techniques come to mind?

3. What technique(s) are you most experienced and effective in using? Can they be used with TCKs?

4. Do one of the activities suggested in this chapter for yourself. Choose one that appeals to you. Share with a partner or small group about what you did and why. Will it be easier to use creative outlets with your clients after doing it yourself?

# Chapter 10

# Evaluating Theories, Therapy Models,

# and TCKs

*"The problem with Facebook is there is only room for one home town."*

A complaint by a TCK

I met an adult third culture kid one day who was sharing with me his experiences with therapists over the years. I found his philosophy very interesting.

He stated, "I've had therapists of different persuasions: a Caucasian woman, a Japanese-American woman, a Chinese-American man, and a gay man. I have tried traditional psychoanalytic therapy as well as Gestalt and an unconventional method that used Mindfulness meditation and CBT. I have also participated in group therapy for artists. It's amazing that my desire for novelty will even play out while seeking therapists (some would say it would be better if I just stick to one), but I find the different perspectives much more valuable at getting to the 'truth.' And I do give adequate time with each—at least 6 months, reaching to over a year with one."

When this young man told me of his experiences with therapy, I had to smile. Why? Because so many of us get stuck trying to decide just which therapy model or theory is the best. Or, if we have made the decision to work with the globally mobile, we ask what is the best theory to utilize with this particular population? The young man in our story used a good variety of models and therapists. I am not promoting this method for our clients, but he sure was creative! Yet, I am left with the question, what IS the best theory or model?

While there are many useful approaches and models and my message has been that you can use the therapeutic skills you already have, here are the models I use most frequently and how I apply them to TCKs.

## Attachment Theory

The Attachment Theory model developed by Dr. John Bowlby (1907–1990), a British psychoanalyst and psychiatrist, has as its primary focus the impact of the distress on infants (all young children were referred to as infants) when they are separated from their parents for a long time period at an early age. The main belief is that individuals need to experience an attachment (bonding) with a primary attachment figure for the child to grow up emotionally and socially healthy. If the infant, who is dependent on the parent for care and protection, does not experience this attachment, it results in "attachment behaviors" such as crying and searching. Bowlby believed that it is around this attachment that all of life develops.

Dr. R. Chris Faley, an Associate Professor of Psychology at the University of Illinois, wrote an article titled "A Brief Overview of Adult Attachment Theory and Research," where he made the following statement regarding Bowlby's attachment theory:

> The attachment system essentially "asks" the following fundamental question: Is the attachment figure nearby, accessible, and attentive? If the child perceives the answer to this question to be "yes," he or she feels loved, secure, and confident, and, behaviorally, is likely to explore his or her environment, play with others, and be sociable. If, however, the child perceives the answer to this question to be "no," the child experiences anxiety and, behaviorally, is likely to exhibit attachment behaviors ranging from simple visual searching on the low extreme to active following and vocal signaling on the other. (Faley, 2010)

Bowlby stated in his book *A Secure Base: Clinical Applications of Attachment Theory* (1988, pp. 26–27):

> Nevertheless for a person to know that an attachment figure is available and responsive gives him a strong and pervasive feeling of security, and so encourages him to value and continue the relationship. . . . The biological function attributed to it is that of protection. To remain within easy access of a familiar individual known to be ready and willing to come to our aid in an emergency is clearly a good insurance policy—whatever our age.

156

Bowlby believed it is a strong tie of affection that binds a person to an intimate companion. Our primary motivation in life is to seek and maintain that attachment no matter our age. He went on to state if grief, loss, and separation are not resolved through a primary attachment, then pathological symptoms such as anxiety and depression will develop.

David J. Wallin's book *Attachment in Psychotherapy* (2007, p. 12) spelled out the three principles around which attachment theory is formed.

1. Seeking, monitoring, and attempting to maintain proximity to a protective attachment figure.

2. Using the attachment figure as a "secure base" from which to explore unfamiliar settings and experiences.

3. Fleeing to an attachment figure as a "safe haven" in situations of danger and moments of alarm.

Wallin described the goal of Bowlby's attachment theory as "not only protection from present danger but also reassurance of caregiver's on-going availability" (Wallin, 2007, p. 13). The attachment figure was not just physically present, but also emotionally responsive. What was important was the child's appraisal of the parents' availability.

We need to be emotionally attached to another person and have that person be available to us in order to experience security. Some refer to it as "being known" or "to exist" in someone's mind. A. A. Milne (1994, p. 284), creator of Winnie the Pooh, expressed it best in the old children's classic, in a conversation between Pooh and Piglet.

> Piglet sidled up to Pooh from behind. "Pooh," he whispered.
>
> "Yes, Piglet."
>
> "Nothing," said Piglet taking Pooh's paw. "I just wanted to be sure of you."

Think of the TCKs who left home at a young age and went away to boarding schools. How did that impact their ability to reattach to their parents? Or ponder the impact of the repeated losses of significant attachments, such as primary caretakers like nannies, in the lives of TCKs. What about the TCK who was attached to a caretaker in Germany and was then moved to Hungary where she reattached to a new caretaker, and soon after that to France to do it all over again? Ultimately, it impacted his or her ability to reattach to anyone.

Could this be why it is often healing for TCKs to hear the words, "I am still here"? When they mess up, remind them, "I am still here." When they are afraid, remind them, "I am still here." When they are having a tough time, remind them they can check in with you via a voice message or a text just to know you are STILL there. In order to calm down their anxiety after an emotional session some need to just drop in on a close friend, because they need to know or feel "their good friend is still there."

The subtle, often repeated message that you, or that person with whom they may have a tentative attachment, are still there helps them as they set out from their "safe haven" or "secure base" to venture out into their world. Like Piglet said to Pooh, "I just wanted to be sure of you." After the client learns they can attach properly to their therapist, they can then replicate that with significant others in their lives.

As I work with the TCK, I will continually work with them on forming secure attachments to individuals who will be able to be that secure attachment for them. We may look at their nuclear and extended family, their friends, and safe individuals who might provide that "safe harbor" for them in times when they perceive danger or alarm

## Cognitive Behavioral Therapy

Cognitive Behavior Therapy (CBT) seeks to replace irrational thinking, behavior, and emotion so that the individual can better handle challenging circumstances. It is often used in the treatment of anxiety and depression. The belief is that changing the irrational thinking or maladaptive behavior can change the feelings of an individual.

Usually people are not aware of the constant chatter going on in their heads. Try this little experiment. Right now, stop and ask yourself, "What am I saying right now as I am reading this paragraph?" Hopefully it isn't "I don't understand this section at all." That thought would certainly lead to feelings of boredom and confusion. The resulting behavior would be your quickly skimming through the chapter or skipping it altogether. But if you are saying to yourself "this is really interesting" and you really do feel interested in it, the resulting behavior will be to carefully read the chapter. Why is this? Action eventually joins feelings and self-statements. The third will eventually join the other two, whatever the combination.

With that in mind, we know we cannot control what we feel, but we can control what we say to ourselves and how we act. Since we cannot control how we feel, it is crucial that we watch our self-statements and our actions. CBT uses the belief that clients can change their feelings about a situation as they replace irrational self-statements with rational statements and appropriate behavior.

How is CBT played out in a therapist's office? When I am working with clients and attempting to help them comprehend the impact of their self-statements on their feelings and actions, I will do so by utilizing a diagram. On the left side of the paper I will write the word "Event" and draw an arrow to the middle of the paper where I write the words "Self-Statements/Thoughts" and draw an arrow to the right of the paper where I write the word "Feelings."

Let's say Rhonda, as a college-age TCK client, is dealing with spending her first Christmas away from her parents since she is in Turkey in college and her parents are in Russia. I write under the word "Event" the words "Christmas without family." Then I ask her what she is saying to herself about this upcoming event. Rhonda responds with, "I hate being a TCK. Why can't my family be normal and live close by so I can go home for Christmas like a normal family?" I write her words under the "Self-Statement." Then I ask her to tell me the feelings that she experiences when that statement rattles around in her head. Rhonda responds with "anger, sad, lonely."

At this time, I ask her to think of a new self-statement that is realistic and truthful but not as negative and more hopeful. After several attempts, let's say she ends up with the new self-statement, "It will be different to spend Christmas away from my family and I will miss them. This is my chance to start a new tradition and experience a new adventure with my friends here."

Once we evaluate if the statement is indeed realistic, I ask her what she feels within herself when she gives herself that statement.

Rhonda replies, "When I say that to myself, I feel some excitement, still some sadness because I will miss my family, but it is more manageable. I feel a sense of freedom to design a new adventure. I believe my anxiety will drop once I have a new plan in place."

Note that she has replaced most of her intense, unpleasant feelings with feelings that are more manageable. Rhonda feels more in control. The belief is once the client has the new self-statement and the actions working together, the feelings will change.

I have drawn out what this CBT model would look like on paper.

---

### Example of Cognitive Behavior Therapy

| EVENT | SELF-STATEMENT | FEELINGS |
|---|---|---|
| First Christmas without family | "I hate being a TCK. Why can't my family be normal and live closeby so I can go home for Christmas like other families?" | Sad ↑ Angry ↑ Anxiety ↑ Control ↓ Lonely ↑ |
| First Christmas without family | "It will be difficult to spend Christmas away from my family and I will miss them. This is my opportunity to start a new tradition of doing something unique with my friends or family." | Sad ↓ Anger ↓ Anxiety ↓ Control ↑ Excitement ↑ |

---

Another way I may use CBT with TCKs or TCAs is to listen to their statements regarding their past or their future. I listen for unrealistic statements that are negatively impacting their feelings or actions. Some examples of these statements are:

- These people will not understand my world. They don't really care.

- Why should I make friends? I will move soon, so why try?

- I will not like this place.

- Nowhere feels like home.

- People will think I am weird if I tell them where I grew up.

The client might rephrase these statements to one of these:

- I may have to teach my friends about my world to help them understand me be a little better.

- Yes, I may have another friend move or I may move, but to not take a risk by making new friends guarantees that my life will be lonely. I have to take the risk.

- This place may not be (fill in the blank), but I will make it as homey as I can.

- I can share a little bit about my past and see how others respond to my world. There just might be someone who really is interested in my world.

As ATCKs and TCAs learn to recognize irrational thinking surrounding their past experiences, they will be more accepting and appreciative of their current environment.

## Family Systems Theory

Murray Bowen is seen as the father of Family Systems Theory. Bowen was a psychiatrist whose main work was at the Menninger Clinic and at the National Institute of Mental Health in Maryland. Before Bowen, therapists looked at their clients as individuals rather then looking at the entire family system. The focus of this theory "conceptualizes the family as an emotional unit, a network of interlocking relationships, best understood when analyzed within a multigenerational or historical framework" (Goldenberg & Goldenberg, 1991, p. 147).

Bowen believed family members were strongly influenced in their thinking, feeling, and behavior by the family system. He saw the client as part of a larger family system. Therefore, in order to do good therapy with the client, the therapist needed to go back and look at the entire family system. The therapist needed to look at the environment in which the client had grown up.

The Family Systems therapist attempts to understand and ultimately help the client to understand the impact of past family messages on his or her current behavior. Together they look at the influence of the system on the individual within that system.

When working with TCKs, the therapist cannot look at only the immediate family of origin for the patterns of behavior in the Family Systems, but must also look at the many other systems in which that expat lived and worked (or grew up in). Often these play a much more influential role in the TCK's life than they do in the life of an individual in a family that does not (or did not) move around the world into and out of various cultures. One must look at the cultural system(s), vocational system of their parents, expat community in which they lived and/or worked, and extended family system.

How did each of those systems deal with communication of emotional data? Was there a choosing of sides regarding major decisions? Were there emotional and communication cutoffs of individuals? If so, why, and for how long had this pattern been in place? Where was their family in the ranking of the system of the organization for which the parent worked—Supervisor, Vice President, laborer, etc.? Society also places tremendous influence on the family and the individual within the family to act based upon their feelings rather than their intellect. And if that society changes frequently due to the family moving here and there, then those messages can change quickly. Could this be why so many TCKs are quick to become the chameleon?

Bowen would have had a heyday working with ATCKs/TCAs. He would have realized that counseling TCKs is not looking at just one system or a couple systems, but many layers of systems and their influence on this world traveler. What were the messages and patterns passed on to them, influencing their current thinking and feeling patterns as an adult?

> TCKs are rooted in systems (family, sector, educational, local) because their highly mobile lifestyle prevents them from being rooted in a place like most children. That is why it is so painful for the TCK if he or she feels rejected by one of those systems that was influential on him or her during his or her developmental years.

This view of the client helps the therapist understand why some of their clients struggle with sorting out their feelings from their actions or the family actions from their feelings. TCKs are rooted in systems (family, sector, educational, local) because their highly mobile lifestyle prevents them from being rooted in a place like most children. That is why it is so painful for the TCK if he or she feels rejected by one of those systems that was influential on him or her during his or her developmental years.

A poorly undifferentiated TCK might tend to blame himself, having feelings of guilt and shame, if his father had lost his international job. Another way to determine the level of self-differentiation in your client is to look at how he deals with stress or anxiety. Does he let feelings guide his behavior?

Some months ago, I met a young man from Asia who shared his story of rejection by his family. His story broke my heart. Why? Often the only constant system in the lives of TCKs is their family. If the TCK is struggling with numerous losses and then in the midst of it all, they lose their family, just think of the tremendous loss on so many levels. Let me have my young friend share his story with you in his own words.

I first came out as gay to my family when I was 15 years old. This was shortly after my repatriation to the U.S. I was born in Washington, DC, but my family left shortly thereafter, and thus began my life growing up in three countries in Asia and the South Pacific.

The transitions between my dad's postings overseas were quite stable. I accepted the internationally mobile lifestyle as the reality of my life, and I did experience it as an adventure—my most cherished childhood memories, which have shaped my life forever, are from when my family traveled. We were in a fortunate position to travel plenty, and we traveled well—whether it was to the U.S. or to Indonesia, where my mother is from, and everywhere in-between. I truly came to love the world.

Leaving certain friends behind was certainly sad, but what grounded me was a sense of closeness to my family that didn't wane in spite of the relocations. My father was an extremely organized, pragmatic, and thorough individual. I remember him always making sure to call to the airline to "reconfirm" flights (do we still do that these days?). My mother was always extremely supportive and gave my sister and me a sense of security with her generous, graceful care.

This is why it was an immense shock when their reaction to my coming out was not one of acceptance. I had not wanted to "return" to the U.S. —I knew the losses would be more than in my prior moves. I would lose my identity as an expat in the international school system and I would lose the community of friends in the same situation as my family and me. I resented that I was expected to somehow behave as an American and fit right in with kids.

My family was my only real sense of belonging during this time, and when I came out, I felt like the scaffolding supporting me had fallen apart. My classmates at the time had grown up in the place where they currently lived with one another.

Looking back more than a decade later, what makes this easier to understand is that I know my parents did not hurt me intentionally. After many, many conversations, which grew calmer over the years, I have gained my mother's acceptance, for which I am very grateful. She has said that unfortunately they were not ready for such news and had no preparation for dealing with such a shock. I have also begun to see that while they did not accept something about me that I felt was important, that it doesn't mean they didn't love me.

It took many years of therapy for this young man to recover from the rejection of his family system that up to this point had been his only constant system. The messages of the system were devastating. If he had been my client, as a Family Systems therapist, I would have spent much time looking at all of the various messages which had been passed along to him, not just by his nuclear family but also his extended family and the other systems in his life. We would have sought understanding about his parents' reaction to his lifestyle, mixed with a lot of grief work. We would also have worked on communication skills so that he did not create any emotional cutoffs with his family and we would have explored how he might individuate and form his own identity. It would not be an easy or quick journey.

In Appendix A you will find a more in-depth look at the impact of a dysfunctional system on the TCK. There are also suggestions for working with the TCK.


## Structural Family Theory

Salvador Minuchin was born and educated in Argentina and served in the military with the Arab nations. He received his training in child psychiatry in the United States, where he eventually settled, and developed the Structural Family Theory along with his colleagues who included Jay Haley, Harry Aponte, and Braulio Montalvo. Structural Family Theory looks at the invisible way in which a family organizes itself and relates presently with each other.

Goldenberg and Goldenberg (1991, p. 168) describe it as: "In essence, the structure represents the sum of the rules the family has evolved for carrying out transactional patterns between its members, governing how, when, with whom, and in what manner family members interact." These structures are not seen as permanent, but serve for a brief purpose.

The family is made up of various subsystems that serve to carry out the wishes of the family at large. Each of these subsystems has their its rules, boundaries and alliances (Goldenberg & Goldenberg, 1991, p. 169).

The therapist looks at the various family subsystems, boundaries, alignments, power structure, and coalitions in order to better understand the family structure. As Goldenberg and Goldenberg state, "The ultimate goal is to restructure the family's transactional rules by developing more appropriate boundaries between subsystems and strengthening the family's hierarchical order" (Goldenberg & Goldenberg, 1991, p. 182).

When a family system is "enmeshed" (overly involved) or "disengaged" (not involved), then dysfunction can take place. Parents can become too strict or too lax in allowing their children to develop their own autonomy. This is evident primarily when the family is under stress as they revert back to whatever their family of origin did to handle the stress.

Systems Family Theory deals primarily with insight and understanding about why the family is behaving in certain ways (based on the history of the family) while Structural Family Theory is dealing more with present-day behavior.

Therapists can use the theory from the Family Systems models even though they are working with just one individual in the family. The therapist will work with that individual in the context of their relationships in the family.


## Erickson's Developmental Model

Erik Erickson described eight stages of individual development that are crucial for the healthy development of an individual. (See Okun and Rappaport, 1980, p. 15)

> Stage 1: Infancy: Birth − 1 year
>
> Stage 2: Early childhood: 1−3 years
>
> Stage 3: Childhood: 3−6 years
>
> Stage 4: School age: 6−12 years
>
> Stage 5: Adolescence and youth: 13−22 years
>
> Stage 6: Young Adult: 22−30 years
>
> Stage 7: Adulthood: 30−50 years
>
> Stage 8: Mature age: 50 years − death

Each of these stages has its own developmental challenge that is either met or not met. In their book *Working with Families: An Introduction to Family Therapy*, Okun and Rappaport (1980, p.14) describe these developmental challenges outlined by Erickson's model as "the alternative outcomes to how the individual meets the challenge . . . described by a pair of concepts. One concept [listed first] indicates the positive growth that is inherent in successfully meeting the developmental challenge; the other indicates the consequence of an unsuccessful resolution of the challenge." The developmental challenges are:

Stage 1:  Basic trust vs. Basic mistrust

Stage 2: Autonomy vs. Shame and doubt

Stage 3: Initiative vs. Guilt

Stage 4: Industry vs. Inferiority

Stage 5: Intimacy vs. Isolation

Stage 6: Generativity vs. Stagnation

Stage 7: Integrity vs. Despair

Erickson believed that an individual must successfully complete one developmental stage before they could move on to the next stage. Why is this important when treating a TCK?

I would want to know at what age the TCK made each of his or her major transitions. If there was any type of trauma, how old were they? Do they show any signs of being stuck at one stage? And if so, what took place at that age? Does their behavior or their speech appear to be that of someone much younger than their actual age? And if so, what took place? If they lost a nanny as an infant, they would be stuck at stage one, per Erickson. This is where the therapist would begin their work, to help the client attain healing and thus move on to the next developmental stage.

It is interesting to look at Stage 5, where a person would typically land if he or she had successfully negotiated all of the previous stages. It is during adolescence people seek to develop their identity. This is the stage where TCKs experience a tremendous amount of influence on their lives by their peers, leaders, and heroes. Yet, this is also precisely the time when many of them make a major transition back to their passport country where they suddenly have a substitution of peers, leaders, and heroes—people with whom they have little connection or history. It is those TCKs who continue a positive relationship with their peers and role models who are able to be resilient in the midst of all of this transition.

The adolescent that is unsuccessful in forming his identity during his youth and early adulthood becomes mired in "identity confusion." Or, to state it in everyday language, this is the individual who cannot decide on a career, does not commit to long-term relationships (for example, marriage or where he will live), and waffles on so many other crucial decisions. These are necessary decisions to make if one is to navigate into the next developmental stage of adulthood.

Malia Morteimer (2010, p. 16) made the statement in her dissertation presentation for a Ph.D. in psychology: "In Ruth Useem's study, prolonged adolescence and difficulty with intimate relationships were cited as some of the most prominent problems for TCKs. According to Erikson's theory, this makes sense because it is during these two developmental stages (adolescence and early adulthood) that TCKs usually return to their passport country or go off on their own."

It would be interesting to do further research into Erickson's Development Model with the TCK in mind. Some have attempted to do so, but much more needs to be done and published as I feel it has much to tell us about the TCK and could help parents and teachers with their TCKs.

As I conclude this chapter on therapies and theories and working the ATCKs and TCAs, I want to end where I began. The theory or therapeutic model you use is not the determining point as to whether or not your client will reach their goal. Models come and go. The ones I have discussed are the ones that I use most frequently with the types of presenting issues that ATCKs and TCAs bring to therapy. Use the language, theory, methods, or styles that are most comfortable for you and your client. Most therapists are not purists; most of us are eclectic.

> Use the language, theory, methods, or styles that are most comfortable for you and your client.

# Things You Should Know

1.  Some of my favorite theories or types of therapy to use with TCKs are: Attachment Theory, Cognitive Behavioral Therapy, Family Systems Theory, Structural Family Theory, and Erickson's Developmental Model.

2.  Use the language, theory, methods, or styles that are most comfortable for you and your client.

3.  <u>Attachment Theory</u>: The repeated moves that have taken place in the lives of TCKs have affected their ability to attach.

4.  <u>Cognitive Behavioral Therapy</u>: As TCKs learn to recognize irrational thinking surrounding their past experiences, they will be more accepting and appreciative of their current environment.

5.  <u>Family Systems Theory</u>: The study of the TCK family involves more than the nuclear family; it also includes the cultural system(s), vocational system of their parents, expat community in which they lived and/or worked, and, to a much lesser extent, their extended family system.

6.  <u>Structural Family Theory</u>: The TCK family operates not only under the invisible structure of the family unit but also the invisible structure of the culture where they live(d) and the systemic rules of the employer.

7.  <u>Erickson's Developmental Model</u>: A TCK can become stuck in an earlier, developmental stage which corresponds with a major transitional change in his or her family.

# Discussion Questions & Activity

1.  Which theories or therapy models in this chapter are new for you?

2.  Which theories or therapy models in this chapter are familiar to you?

3. What professional development activities interest you as a result of reading this chapter? You may want to explore the websites of the organizations listed under *Resources* and attend one of their conferences or webinars.

4. Activity: Break into groups of four and convince the others in your group that your favorite theory is the best theory to use in counseling TCKs.

# Chapter 11

# Leveraging and Launching TCKs

*"You can't tell a story without a listener."*

(Doug Ota, 2009)

Beate Sirota Gordon's story appeared in *The New York Times*. Although she was not a lawyer or a constitutional scholar, in 1946, post-World War II, Beate, at the young age of 22, had written the women's rights into the Constitution of Japan. *The NY Times* stated, *"Her work—drafting language that gave women a set of legal rights pertaining to marriage, divorce, property and inheritance that they had long been without in Japan's feudal society—had an effect on their status that endures to this day."* The article asks the question, *"What kind of a 22-year-old gets to write a constitution?"*

She was born in Vienna to Russian Jewish parents. Her father was a concert pianist and a teacher. When she was five, they relocated to Tokyo, Japan, where she attended a German school and the American School of Japan. In 1939, when she turned 16, she left Japan and went to college in Oakland, California, while her parents remained in Japan.

After the attack on Pearl Harbor in 1941 Beate lost contact with her parents and could not afford to fly to Japan to search for them. Due to her fluency in English, Japanese, German, French, Spanish, and Russian she was able to land a job at a United States government listening post in California and it was her task to monitor radio broadcasts from Tokyo. Later she transferred to the United States Office of War Information.

She graduated from college with a bachelor's degree in modern languages and she became a United States citizen the same year. Even with her Office of War job, she was unable to find out if her parents were alive. She could not travel to Japan as a U.S. citizen, so in 1945, she got a job as an interpreter on General MacArthur's staff. Later that year she was finally able to travel to Tokyo where she eventually was reunited with her parents.

> One of General MacArthur's first tasks was to draft a constitution for postwar Japan. Beate was the only woman on the constitutional committee, resulting in her being deputized to write the section on woman's rights.
>
> In the 1950s she joined the staff of the Japan Society in New York. By the 1970s she was the director of the performing arts at the Asia Society in New York. When she retired in 1991, she was the director of performances, films, and lectures.
>
> A documentary film *The Gift From Beate* was made about her life and in 1998 the Japanese government honored her with an *Order of the Sacred Treasure* award. She died in 2012 at the age of 89.
>
> (Fox, NY *Times* newspaper online, January 1, 2013)

Beate Sirota Gordon was an adult cross-cultural kid who leveraged her growing up years and made a difference in her world. Her story shows us how one young college student, who lost contact with her parents due to a war, took all of the pieces of the different cultures, languages, observation skills, resiliency, and creativity and turned them into an incredible contribution to Japan and the United States. She left no scrap tossed aside as she took all of the ups and downs of her story and wove them together into the fabric of her future.

In Chapter 5 we looked in detail at the struggle some TCKs have in sorting out a clear sense of identity when they grow up among many cultural worlds. Now we look at the flip side. Dr. Barbara Schaetti is herself a bi-national ATCK who did her Ph.D. research on identity formation in TCKs. In her book *Strangers at Home* (1996), Barbara wrote a chapter titled "Phoenix Rising: A Question of Cultural Identity." She describes the concept of marginality with the global nomad:

> Cultural marginality is in and of itself neither bad nor good, although the experience has the potential to be both. It is characterized by . . . feeling at home nowhere and, on the other hand, feeling at home everywhere. (Schaetti, 1996, p. 178)

She goes on to state that we can let ourselves become "encapsulated" by cultural marginality or learn to use it "constructively." When someone is encapsulated, that person sees himself or herself as being isolated, "perceiving their circumstances as so unique that they do not, cannot, envision a peer group with whom they can relate" (Schaetti, 1996, p. 179).

Dr. Janet Bennett, co-director of the Intercultural Communications Institute, calls this "terminal uniqueness." She and Dr. Schaetti believe:

> The constructive marginal is able to move easily and powerfully between different cultural traditions, acting appropriately and feeling at home in each, and in doing so, simultaneously maintaining an integrated, multicultural sense of self. Rather than the "either/or" identity of the encapsulated marginal, constructive marginals experience their movement between cultures as "both/and." (Schaetti, 1996, pp. 180)

They realize that they will not feel at home in any one spot in the world but "rather [will find a sense of belonging with] a group of fellow marginals with whom [they have] more in common than with anyone else" (Schaetti, 1996, p. 181).

As therapists this is what we want to do—to help our clients foster their multicultural identity, rather than ignore it or state that it does not matter as that was then and this is now. We need to encourage them to embrace their multicultural self, and leverage it in our multicultural world. This allows our global nomad clients to be who they are rather than deny the wealth of culture that is the very fabric of their being. It is essential to move them out of feeling "terminally unique" into the company of peers with a similar identity.

Dr. Schaetti concludes with the powerful statement:

> As global nomads, we owe it to ourselves and to one another to encourage the experience of constructive rather than encapsulated cultural marginality. There is so much power, so much to celebrate, in the constructive expression of the global nomad experience! (Schaetti, 1996, p. 188)

## Leveraging the Past into Today's World

Throughout the final stages of therapy, I take advantage of any opportunity to help TCKs explore how they can use their skills in today's world. Their story may not be as dramatic as Beate Sirota Gordon. Yet the ability of the TCK to adapt to various cultures, their fluency in languages, the ability to blend in with those around them, the skills to listen and observe, and even their sense of loyalty for systems, can serve them well.

Some travel the world, while others stay in one place all of their adult life and use those things they learned growing up among worlds. I have seen TCKs leverage their history through involvement in the military as translators or spies as they blend in so seamlessly into the culture. Some have joined musical groups who perform in various languages. TCKs work for international companies in the foreign language division, do translation work, produce international movies and documentaries on their lifestyle, become international correspondents in either television or the written news, or teach or serve as counselors in international schools or large universities around the world. I have seen TCKs become involved in humanitarian organizations either in their own neighborhood or in some scientific project on an island that is not even on the map. Some return to serve alongside their parents in some form of missionary involvement. My own brothers work in the area of photography and media production for international agencies.

The number of mental health counselors and psychologists who are TCKs is growing as we seek to tap into our heritage. Many of us counsel in various languages and work with organizations that are helping refugees or immigrants who have moved into our neighborhoods. Some serve as consultants to international agencies or as coaches to employees relocating on the other side of their world.

A couple of years ago I met Beth Eisinger, a TCK, who was raised in Turkey and is a good example of a TCK leveraging her past. Beth works for a state museum, but her hobby is art. I have several pieces of her artwork proudly displayed on the walls of my office. Beth does a lovely job of depicting her life as a TCK. Much of her art has as its theme roots, plants, chameleons, or other symbols of the life of the TCK. (See or purchase Beth's work at www.thefinetoothedcomb.etsy.com) Whenever I have seen her art on display, there are usually a number of TCKs crowding around her display and the I often hear them exclaim, "This is me!"

I recently asked Beth how her artwork helped her tap into her heritage of growing up globally mobile. Her response was,

> I think my artwork has been most helpful to me in getting to the core of what I am feeling because it takes me outside myself. Looking inside, my thoughts feel murky and abstract. By going through the process of transferring these feelings into a picture it is like my feelings have put clothes on and they suddenly have a form that I can grab hold of and deal with. (Eisinger, personal email, 2012)

She described her use of roots in several of her works of art:

> This is how it was for me when I made these paintings about my cross-cultural upbringing using the imagery of roots. Before I painted them I often struggled to articulate what my upbringing was like. Afterwards, I felt like I had established for myself a reservoir of pictures and metaphors to draw from to explain to others the particular struggles that come with living cross-culturally. (Eisinger, personal email, 2012)

Used by permission of Beth Eisinger

This particular piece of art is one of my favorite pieces. *Three Places at One Time* is the name of the drawing. She described it to me.

> I painted this to help express how it feels to have lived for significant amounts of my childhood in three different countries. In each of the countries I lived I had to put down roots in order to survive. Even when I was uprooted and planted in a different country, some of my roots remained in the previous country. Today, I may look like I am a normal plant on the surface but underground I have an extremely expansive root system that struggles to straddle all the different places I have lived. (Eisinger, personal email, 2012)

Another TCK I have watched leverage her past is Alaine Handa of A.H. Dance Company (www.alainehanda.com). Alaine is a TCK from Indonesia, Singapore, and the United States. She choreographed a piece she titled *Chameleon, the Experience of Global Citizens* which she and her dance team have performed in the United States, Canada, and Asia. She describes the Chameleon piece as drawing on "the insight and experience of Third Culture Kids: those who have spent a significant period of time in a culture other than their own." (taken from www.alainehanda.com)

Some TCKs teach their children the values they learned as a TCK. They go to great lengths so their children can have the opportunity to travel the world, even if it is only during their holidays from school. They encourage them to study a foreign language in school, or take a year off to study abroad. They teach their children to cheer for soccer teams from their past host countries. And many welcome exchange students into their homes.

My own non-TCK niece, Elizabeth Ewer, was often encouraged to broaden her view of the world by her TCK father. One day, after cheering for the Honduran soccer team to triumph over the United States, Elizabeth commented to me, "My problem is that I really wanted the U.S. to move forward. I guess I get to cheer for Honduras. I always have mixed emotions during the World Cup qualifying. I wish it were more black and white." I, as the true TCK responded, "It is black and white to me. I am cheering for Honduras to tromp the United States."

## How Do I Do This?

In order to help the TCK take advantage of their rich heritage, I might have them read or watch documentaries about TCKs in order to broaden their minds on what they might do with their future. (A list of resources is found in the Appendix.) They are encouraged to seek out other TCKs who are using similar skills and befriend them. I encourage them to embrace their complete identity as a TCK rather then compartmentalize it. It may not end up as a vocation as with some, but a hobby as with Beth.

If the TCK is looking to make a career change, they can take a vocational test and see what is the best career for their skill set. Then as I look at the results of the tests with my client, we talk about what other skills they might possess which the vocational test was not designed to measure—for example, those things found on the Identity Iceberg—and explore how they might integrate the two.

Why is it best to wait until the final stage of therapy to begin to do this activity? They have now resolved whatever issue brought them into therapy; they are now ready to think what parts of their history they want to weave into their current world. They now understand who they are and how they fit into their world. They are now free and able to embrace their identity as a TCK and thrive as they reach their full potential.

## Saying Goodbye, or the Termination Process

Ultimately, there comes that time when both you and your client realize that they have met all of their goals in therapy and are ready to fly off on their own. They no longer need your help. It is time to say Goodbye. This can be an emotional time for you and your TCK client.

Why? After walking through the depths of the soul of your client and feeling the deep emotions they have shared in their sessions with you, it is hard to say Goodbye. As the therapist, I am thrilled my client has met his goals and now feels emotionally strong and healthy enough to launch out on his own. After all, this is the goal of therapy. But it is emotional to watch him walk out of my office for the last time.

Also, it is especially difficult for the TCK as you are now doing what brought them into therapy: one more Goodbye. We are preparing them to experience one more loss. Only now it is a Goodbye with the one who helped them work through the deep grief of repeated losses.

How can this Goodbye take place without re-traumatizing your TCK? How do you say Goodbye, grieve and remain whole? It will be an emotional time. And if you are a therapist who is also a TCK, how do you do this and not fall into a puddle of tears yourself? Goodbyes never get easy for TCKs, no matter their age, who they are, or what they do.

## When Do You Start the Process?

How do you know when to say Goodbye and discharge, or terminate, a TCK client? You begin the discharge process after the client has met his goals for therapy, developed healthy coping skills, and explored how he might leverage his past and what he has learned or experienced. You need to start the termination process when you find that most of your sessions involve only "checking in" with the client on how he did since you last saw him, you are not processing any new material, or you are lost in what to talk about with him. When you are experiencing a silence because there is nothing else left to discuss or work on in the therapy hour, this is when it is time to begin the process of discharging the client, or as we say in our profession "the termination session."

I do not like the term "termination" or even "discharge" session for this time of wrapping up the therapy process, especially when it comes to TCKs as it sounds so final. It can be emotional for a TCK whose antenna is attuned to the inkling of the "termination" of a relationship. Remember, he may have shared many parts of his life he has not shared with anyone else. You may be the first person that he feels truly "gets him" or understands him. In order to make this process more gentle for the TCK, I prefer to call it the "Graduation Process," which leaves the client with more of a feeling of completing something that was difficult and is now moving out into their future. I must admit that this is for my sake as well as the sake of the client.

Here are some guidelines on how to walk through a "Graduation Process" with your client in order to experience a healthy Goodbye. Read the list and then I'll talk you through it step-by-step.

# Termination Process

1. Set the "Graduation Date."

2. Review the "Presenting Problem" and Treatment Plan.

3. Talk about the grief that is normal with Goodbyes and how it applies to therapy.

4. Discuss how they said Goodbyes in their family of origin.

5. Talk about how they told their best friends Goodby in each country where they lived.

6. Ask: Do you have any "farewell gifts" that you were given? Did you give any "farewell gifts"? What was the culture around giving "farewell gifts" in the country or countries you call home?

7. Review the "mental picture album" of the therapy process.

8. Discuss what experience or homework was the most beneficial to the TCK in his or her journey of self-discovery? Why?

9. Talk about what was the least beneficial experience or homework and why.

10. Ask the client: What is one thought that you hope you never forget? (It encourages the client if you can return the favor and give him or her one thing you learned from him or her.)

11. Ask if he or she has any questions about you or the therapy process before you discharge him or her.

12. Review the client's self-care plan.

13. Talk about how the client can "check in with you" after being discharged.

14. Remind the TCK client he or she can return to therapy at any time if needed in the future.

15. Follow the rules of ethics in your profession regarding befriending a client after that last therapy session.

Let's expand on each of these points by looking at some general practices or guidelines for preparing to release your client:

1. Some therapists like to space out the sessions at the end of the therapy process in order to see if the client can function okay on their own. Others do not like to do it this way as they feel the client will just disappear on them without any proper closure to therapy. Many TCKs tend to fall into this category, as most will do anything to avoid a Goodbye. Others become quite upset if there was not a proper Goodbye. I believe the idea of setting an actual date when they will stop coming regularly to see you is dependent on how long the client has been in therapy with you or how well you have connected emotionally with your client. Like with all clients, particularly TCKs, if they will be moving again, you will need to conclude therapy. (Set the date with the client and begin to talk about it at least six months in advance, as you will want plenty of time to walk through the wide range of emotions that will spring up.)

2. I will pull out the Intake Form and review with the TCK their presenting problem(s). Has this or have these been resolved? If not, does the client need to be referred to another specialist or can he or she complete the process on their own?

3. Talk about the grief process of saying Goodbye one more time. I believe it is okay to self-disclose how you are also grieving this Goodbye, if it is the case. It can help your client to normalize their feelings when they realize they are not alone in their grief. It validates their grief and makes it okay, rather then having to deny it as so many did throughout their childhood. Also, if YOU are also a TCK, it normalizes that Goodbyes never get easy for any of us.

4. Ask your client how each member of their immediate family says Goodbye to those who mean a lot to them. Has this been a consistent pattern for them? If there ever was a time when they did it differently, why? What was the response of their family for how your client said Goodbye?

5. Pull out the client's time line and have your client tell you how he said Goodbye to those who were important to him in each of the countries where he lived. Ask him if he has had any further contact

with them since they said their Goodbyes. Does he need to go back and contact that friend once again and give a proper farewell?

6. Talk about farewell gifts. Ask your client if she still possesses any "farewell gifts" that she was given? Did she give anyone a farewell gift? What was the culture regarding giving farewell gifts in the country(s) she calls home? Some therapists are very strict in not accepting any gifts whatsoever from a client as they view it as an ethical violation. Review your code of ethics in your profession regarding this matter. In some cultures, the exchange of gifts is the proper way to say Goodbye. To reject the gift would be disrespectful. The gift can be a small meaningful token, a poem, a song, or a stone with a meaningful word on it. It is not the value of the gift, but the symbolism of the gift and the significance of the relationship.

7. As you recall your work together in the therapy process, have the client talk about the mental pictures that come to mind as he thinks of his journey through therapy. Why do those particular scenes come to his mind? Both of you can share the "pictures" that come to mind. I like to compare the emotional state of the client when I first began to work with him to today's snapshot and his current strength and emotional wholeness.

8. What experience or homework was the most beneficial to the client in the journey of self-discovery? Was it the TCK Identity Iceberg? Why was that particular homework assignment or session most beneficial? I find this question very helpful to me in knowing what worked and what did not work with my TCK client. So often the client does not tell me about a fantastic homework assignment I gave or my words of wisdom or wonderful skills as a therapist. But in so many cases they simply say, "You understood me and listened to me. That was the part that was most healing for me." Wow, and think of all the money I spent in learning all of those wonderful skills and it boiled down to listening to and caring for my client!

9. What was the least beneficial experience? Why? I do this for the same reason as the previous question. At times, the client will say something was not at all beneficial to them, and it may not have been, but it helped me to understand them. Other times, I may not

use a certain activity again based on their feedback. You can make the judgment about what you will do with their statement.

10. What is one thought that you hope you never forget? (It encourages the client if you can return the favor and give them one thing you learned from them as well.) This activity will help the client be able to define in a sentence what they learned in therapy and make it clear in their own mind. For the client to hear how you have perceived their growth is something they can take away with them and hang on to when they get discouraged. It is your gift to them.

11. Ask your client if she has any questions about you or the therapy process before you discharge her. This is a time where she may not have any questions at all, or she might ask you a nagging question such as, "Did you groan to yourself or roll your eyes every time you saw my name appear on your schedule?"

12. Review the client's self-care plan with him or her. Once again, you want to be sure that your client knows exactly how to take care of himself or herself once out of therapy. You want your client to be successful.

13. Talk about how the client can "check in with you" after he is discharged—send an email, leave you a voice message, send a Christmas card, or any other ways you have. Again, I have invested a lot of energy into helping my client achieve his or her goals. I want to know how he or she is doing after therapy. It does help the client to know he can reach out and "touch" you at least once a year. Again you are modeling to them how to say healthy Goodbyes. You do not want to re-wound your TCK as he has had too many people who were very meaningful in his life completely walk away.

14. Remind him he can return to therapy any time, if he would want or need it again in the future. It continues to amaze me how often clients think that once I have discharged them, they can never return to see me again.

15. Follow the rules of ethics in your profession regarding befriending a client after that last therapy session. Most rules in the United States

say that you must have closed the file for at least two years before you can establish a friendship with a client outside the office. One word of caution, if you move into a friendship with them if and when it is ethically appropriate, remember that if they ever need therapy again, you cannot be the therapist as you have now crossed that line into a friendship. TCKs can make friends that understand them, but therapists that understand them are difficult to find.

Finally, celebrate with your client a job well done. At times, clients will bring in cookies or some type of international snack for their last session. Celebrate their graduation from therapy and celebrate your own job well done. Celebrations in life mark milestones and provide a date and time for closure. Often we don't take time to truly celebrate, but actually celebrating will give both of you a feeling of satisfaction in a hard job well done, and will lift your spirits and those of your client in the future as you remember.

# Things You Should Know

1. Dr. Barbara Schaetti states, "cultural marginality is in and of itself neither bad nor good, although the experience has the potential to be both. It is characterized by . . . feeling at home nowhere and, on the other hand, feeling at home everywhere."

2. Take advantage of any opportunity to help the TCK explore how he or she can use his or her skills in today's world.

3. Goodby, or termination of therapy, can be emotional for a TCK whose antenna is attuned to any inkling of the "termination" of a relationship. Remember, your client may have shared many parts of his life with you that he has not shared with anyone else. You may be the first person that he feels truly "gets him" or understands him. Take your time in walking through the termination process.

# Discussion Questions & Activities

1. Think about Goodbyes in your life. How did or does each member of your family say Goodbye? Have you ever given or received "farewell gifts"? Explain. How did a "farewell gift" make the Goodbye easier or harder? Do you still have that "farewell gift"?

2. Activity: Play John Denver's song "Goodby Again" and note all of the similarities with the life of the TCK.

3. Activity: Watch the movie *The Interpreter* and observe TCK Silvia Broome (Nicole Kidman). How did she leverage and launch herself?

4. Activity: Watch the movie *The Best Exotic Marigold Hotel* and observe TCK Graham (Tom Wilkinson). How did he leverage his history of having grown up in India (for the first eighteen years of his life) to support his fellow retiree expat tourists?

# Chapter 12

# Wrapping Up:
# "We've Only Just Begun"

*"…Chile. That is the land of my nostalgia, the one I invoke in my solitude,*
*the one that appears as a backdrop in so many of my stories,*
*the one that comes to me in my dreams."*

Isabel Allende, a TCK
(Allende, 2003, p. 10)

Recently, I heard Kay tell this story about her daughter Katherine. It was an amazing story of pain, searching, not giving up, heartbreak, and ultimate joy. Kay persistently knocked on many doors in her attempt to find a therapist who understood her daughter. Katherine was a TCK struggling to deal with the grief of repeated transitions. Once again she was trying to fit into another new country and school in her passport country.

My initial reaction to the discovery of my sixteen-year-old daughter's eating disorder was that she had a problem that needed fixing quickly, though I had no idea who to call or where to start. Of our three children, Katherine was the one who found our relocations the most difficult.

Born in Singapore, she was a happy and confident little girl. But our moves to the U.K. when she was nine, then the U.S. when she was twelve, caused her great feelings of isolation, loneliness, and anxiety, culminating in her teenage years with depression and bulimia. Several years of inpatient and outpatient treatment and individual and family therapy, along with Katherine's persistent, intense determination led to her eventual recovery.

That Houston pediatric psychologist was the first of many psychologists to treat our daughter, but Katherine felt no special connection with her, and I felt totally excluded from my daughter's treatment. Yet I knew her problems started when she had her first international move and were exacerbated by each subsequent relocation where she found the challenge of new schools and forming new friendships so hard.

For many years Katherine felt her psychologists seemed more bent on digging into the past than arming her with coping skills. She felt there always seemed to be a search for one particular traumatic incident or relationship that may have triggered her mental health issues, whereas we know that many factors contributed, including our transient expatriate lifestyle, which though considered, was never dealt with at length. Striving to fit in is normal for a teenager, but this is enhanced in a TCK. With each move Katherine felt a fresh loss of identity and tried to change herself to fit in, but failed.

The turning point for Katherine was ten weeks of inpatient treatment where, in addition to her individual therapy, we engaged in family therapy. These family sessions were often grueling for us. We would have benefitted from family therapy years earlier as this could have lessened Katherine's feelings of isolation and helped lift the burden of shame and guilt she felt.

Katherine found an exceptional outpatient psychotherapist to work with who was experienced in treating eating disorders. She was sympathetic, understanding, and enabled Katherine to acknowledge her own uniqueness and value herself. Cognitive behavior therapy was employed, giving Katherine ways to cope with her anxiety and depression by recognizing thinking patterns and arming her with specific coping strategies as opposed to destructive eating disorder coping mechanisms. Now Katherine had her support team of family, psychotherapist, and psychiatrist, but paramount was her own intense desire to recover and her motivation to persevere with treatment so that she could come to terms with her illness.

As an adult now, Katherine has a proud and strong sense of identity, and she is grateful for the richness and diversity of lifestyle, cultures, and friendships she has experienced growing up on three continents.

Listening to this story, everyone in the room was glued to the edge of their seats, wondering what would be the outcome for this daughter who was in such emotional pain and the mother who was on a mission to find help for her daughter. Would Katherine end up on drugs or take her own life in despair? It wasn't until Kay finally got to the part where she shared they finally found a therapist who understood them that we began to breathe once again.

Tears of joy ran down our faces when Kay announced her daughter was now doing very well and was in our midst. We looked around the room to see who might be Katherine in our midst. Shyly, a young, attractive woman sitting at my table stood up. It was Katherine. The workshop broke out in applause as we shared the joy of victory for this mother-daughter team.

During the time of discussion that followed Katherine's presentation, the oft-repeated question was, "Where are the therapists that understand the TCKs?" Or a similar question of, "How can we help therapists understand our world?"

Now that you have walked through the process of understanding the third culture and its impact on the child who grows up in it, you have a much better understanding of each TCK that may enter your world. You now know how to recognize them and help them share their story with you if they are a little reticent in sharing their life with yet another person. I trust you have pulled out your DSM manual and tried to work with me to figure out the correct diagnosis that you need to use for insurance purposes. And you followed the discussion on the major presenting problems or "ticket in the door" of depression or anxiety and what common events in their life may have triggered these symptoms so that you now see the TCK standing before you in your office.

Hopefully, you have had a few "a-ha" moments as you looked at some of the identity questions TCKs have and their many "Who am I?" questions. We have looked at some of the reasons some TCKs flee from commitment in relationships, and yet crave that person that understands them and their world. Even as we walked through the chapter on "Therapy 101" stuff of various schools of psychology and different techniques that seem to work best with TCKs, I trust you were able to understand how they each help you in your practice with TCKs. Did you notice which therapy models helped Katherine in the end?

Then I explained to you how to wrap it all up with helping your TCK plan for his or her next step of leveraging that identity. And we concluded with how to plan and execute a good termination process with your TCK. It has been a fun journey of exploring and learning together how to work with TCKs. They always help me expand my world to new cultures and people. It is the Katherines and the Kays who call us to stretch and grow as mental health providers so we can be there to walk alongside them in their journey when it gets bumpy for them.

**My TOP TEN List**

In trying to condense all we have learned together as we have looked at the topic of counseling TCKs, I have done much scratching of my head and narrowed it all down to my "Top Ten Tips for Counseling TCKs." Let me share them with you.

### Top Ten Tips for Counseling TCKs

1. Always keep in mind they view their world through the lens of many cultures.

2. Do not assume anything about their world.

3. Listen and learn for they have much to teach you.

4. Read all you can about and by Third Culture Kids and make the application to others of similar experiences.

5. What may be pathology in one population may not be pathology in another.

6. Hidden losses and grief are frequently the root of their presenting problems.

7. Be creative in your therapy because the client may not fit into your typical counseling model.

8. You are closer to their world if you view them as internationals.

9. When dealing with identity issues, picture the TCK Identity Iceberg.

10. Model a healthy Goodbye.

Do these tips sound familiar? They are my themes on how to counsel TCKs. If you were to catch me between sessions at a TCK conference and hurriedly say to me, "I have a new intake this hour and he says he is a TCK. What do I need to do or know?" or, if you were to ask me, "What is your book about?" this would be the outline of my brief reply to you.

## "It is a beautiful world beneath the surface of the ocean!"

Several months ago off the coast of the island of St. Croix, I had my first experience of snorkeling in the crystal blue waters of the Caribbean. Early in the morning, one of my friends and I crowded into a small boat with about 40 snorkelers. All were chatting and excited to get this chance to catch the views of the mansions dotted along the shore as we sped out over the waves to our spot in the ocean. Some of us struck up conversations with those crowded close to us on our bench. We were from all nationalities, ages, and levels of experience.

When the boat stopped, our college-aged guide pulled out our equipment and began to give each of us our gear. She gave us instructions on how to strap on the life jacket, how to fix the mask tightly on our faces, how to breathe and when we should put on the large, oversized fins. Some of our group knew the routine and were quick to get ready. Others of us were novices and were nervous about the entire experience, so we had many questions. "Do I have my mask on right?" "I can't breathe." "Is this supposed to be this tight?" "You look funny." "I don't get to ease into the ocean?" "I am supposed to jump off the end of the boat into the ocean! You are kidding, right?"

This was not what we had expected. When we signed up for this experience, we thought we were going to ease into the ocean from off of some nice sloping beach. But that is not what it turned out to be like. We were to jump overboard right into the "deep end of the pool."

Some were fearless—and jumped quickly into the water, formed a small group, and swam away with a guide. Some of us rookies were a bit more nervous. First of all, it took me about three tries until I got a mask that did not fill up with water as soon as I lowered my head into the warm waters of the ocean. Second, it took another ten minutes to get the hang of breathing normally without hyperventilating. Third, it took another five minutes to actually let go of the edge of the boat and trust my life jacket. And I knew how to swim! When I was ready, a guide came over and tossed me a rope and told me to hang on and he would lead a couple of us away from the boat out to the coral reefs.

It was beautiful to just swim along behind the guide hanging on to the rope and enjoying the swim. I did this for some distance. Then, I worked up my nerve to try out my new skill and I stuck my face in the ocean to see what was below. Once I realized that indeed I could breathe through the snorkel and not drown, I was amazed at the world that was beneath the surface. I did not have a clue that there was all of this beauty beneath the surface waters. How long had I enjoyed the waves of the ocean and not seen this entire new world beneath the surface?

The brightly colored fish were brilliant yellows, blues, oranges, and stripes. The coral reef was amazing and had such intriguing shapes. Every once in a while a large school of fish would slowly swim right below our feet. I quickly forgot the mechanics of my snorkeling equipment and my feelings of panic as I got lost in the absolute beauty of this new world right below me. It had been there all along and I had missed it. It was an experience I will never forget. Sadly, it was a world missed by those who were too fearful to make that jump off of the boat into the water.

## Just Jump In . . . You Have a Safety Rope

I tell you this story because I see counseling TCKs just like this experience. So often we get all of our training to be a good counselor, we listen to our guides, and we have all of the right equipment. When the time comes to jump into the deep waters of counseling, some of our group wants to ease into the field slowly from the security of a beach. Others come up with all types of excuses of why they should not even jump out of the boat into the waters, and never actually get involved in counseling. Others, in spite of their anxieties and a million and one questions, jump into the deep waters of counseling.

Then what happens? So many in our field are content to paddle on the surface with their clients and focus on what is around them and what can be easily seen or experienced. Their focus is to work with what is here and now. They stay close to the boat and all that is secure to them.

I am asking you to take this book and use it as your rope connected to a guide. Hang on, follow the guidelines, and look beneath the surface of the Third Culture into the deep waters wherein lies the beauty of the hidden identity of the TCK that the swimmer who stays on the surface never gets to see.

You will view an entirely different world that has been there all along. It is a world so many of us were not even aware was there—a world of many colors, many homes, and many schools that came in and out of their lives. Some sights are beautiful, some are troubling, some need to be further explored, and some will take your breath away. If you hang onto the rope, you will not get lost. You will slowly gain your confidence as you experience success in working with the TCK in their deep waters. And as you gain confidence and expertise, I challenge you to let go of the rope and launch out into new areas even beyond your guide. Hopefully, you will experience the same delight I do and you will look for every opportunity to go snorkeling. Counseling TCKs is most rewarding!

## Things You Should Know

1. Keep your eyes and ears open to hints that you may be working with a TCK.

2. Consider revamping your intake form.

3. Review the Top Ten Tips for Counseling TCKs.

4. Look for common life events as triggers for symptoms that bring TCKs into your office.

5. Delve into the "who am I?" and "where is home?" questions with a listening ear.

6. Be alert to trouble in lasting relationships. Inquire about losses and the grieving of those losses.

7. Review the different techniques for therapy and use what you are comfortable using with each client.

8. Be creative in therapy and employ the creative arts to help your TCK express himself and explore his own feelings.

9. Plan with your TCK for leveraging his or her identity.

10. Keep yourself healthy.

## Discussion Questions & Activity

1. Having read this book, ask yourself a *hard question*, "Am I the best person to help TCKs?"

2. Having read this book, ask yourself a *helpful question*, "What else do I need to learn?"

3.  Having read this book, ask yourself an *honest question*, "When will I know that I need to refer?"

4.  Share with someone else what you've learned about yourself as you've read this book.

5.  Share with someone else an "aha" moment you've had while reading this book.

6.  Activity: As a present or future mental health therapist, work with a friend or another therapist to list ways to stay balanced and healthy. What habits do you need to change? What are the signals your body gives you when you are failing at self-care? How will you be accountable?

# Bibliography & References

Allende, Isabel. (2003). *My invented country: A nostalgic journey through Chile.* New York: Harper Collins.

American Psychiatric Association. (1994). *Quick reference to the diagnostic criteria from DSM-IV.* Washington, DC: APA.

Andrews, Leslie A. (2004). Spiritual, family, and ministry satisfaction among missionaries. In L. A. Andrews (Ed.), *The family in mission: Understanding and caring for those who serve* (pp. 359–372). Palmer Lake, CO: Missionary Training International.

Association of Americans Resident Overseas. (n.d.). Paris, France: AARO. Retrieved from www.aaro.org

Better, Cathy. (2010, June). "The Inca weaving," by Johannah Helen Wetzel (Sidebar quote). *Among Worlds, 12*(2), 16.

Brembeck, Cole, & Hiler, Walker (Eds.). (1973). Third culture factors in educational change in *Cultural factors in social learning.* Lexington, MA: D.C. Heath.

Bowlby, John. (1988). *A secure base: Clinical applications of attachment theory.* New York: Routledge.

Bushong, Lois. (2004, December). Is this home? *Among Worlds, 6*(4), 23.

Cottrell, Ann Baker. (March 30, 2012) Private Conversation at FIGT Conference in Washington, DC.

DeParle, Jason. (2010, June 26). Global migration: A world ever more on the move. *The New York Times.* Retrieved from http://www.nytimes.com/2010/06/27/weekinreview/27deparle.html?pagewanted=all&_r=0

Dyer, Jill, & Dyer, Roger. (Eds.). (1991). *Scamps, scholars and saints: An anthology of anecdotes, reflections, poems, and drawings by third culture kids.* Australia: MK Merimna.

Eakin, Kay B. (1998). *According to my passport, I'm coming home.* U.S. State Department: Family Liaison Office.

Eisinger, Beth. (n.d.). *Three places at one time.* Retrieved from www.thefinetoothedcomb.etsy.com (used by permission)

Evans, Tiffany. (2005). Who am I. On *Tarzan II* (DVD). Burbank, CA: Walt Disney Home Entertainment.

Faley, R. Chris. (2010). *A brief overview of adult attachment theory and research.* Champaign: University of Illinois Psychology Department. Retrieved from http://internal.psychology.illinois.edu/~rcfraley/attachment.htm

Families in Global Transition. (n.d.). Warrenton, VA: FIGT. Retrieved from www.figt.org

Figley, Charles R. (1995). *Compassion fatigue: Coping with secondary traumatic stress disorder in those who treat the traumatized.* New York: Brunner-Routledge.

Fox, Margalit. (2013, January 1). Beate Gordon, long-unsung heroine of Japanese women's rights, dies at 89. *The New York Times.* Retrieved from www.nytimes.com/2013/01/02/world/asia/beate-gordon-feminist-heroine-in-japan-dies-at-89.html?pagewanted=all&_r=0

Gidley, Apple. (2012). *Expat life slice by slice.* Great Britain: Summertime.

Goldenberg, Irene, & Goldenberg, Herbert. (1991). *Family Therapy: An Overview* (Third Ed.). Pacific Grove, CA: Brooks/Cole Publishing Company.

Handa, Alaine. (n.d.). *Chameleon, the experience of global citizens.* Retrieved from www.alainehanda.com

Hugo, Graeme. (2006). An Australian diaspora? *International Migration, 44*(1), 105–133. doi: 10.1111/j.1468-2435.2006.00357.x

Humphrey, Keren. (2009). *Counseling strategies for loss and grief.* Alexandria, VA: American Counseling Association.

Interaction International. (n.d.). *Dr. David C. Pollock — 1939–2004*. Chicago, IL: Author. Retrieved from www.interactionintl.org/whoisdavepollock.asp

Iyer, Pico. (2000). *The global soul: Jet lag, shopping malls, and the search for home.* New York: Vintage.

Kübler-Ross, Elizabeth, & Kessler, David. (2005). *On grief and grieving: Finding the meaning of grief through the five stages of loss.* New York: Scribner.

Lindsey, Ursula. (1994). Nostalgia. In Karen C. McCluskey (Ed.), *Notes from a traveling childhood: Readings for internationally mobile parents and children.* Washington, DC: Foreign Service Youth Foundation.

Mansfield, Katherine. (2010, September). "Caring for the children in unplanned relocations," by Rebecca Powell (Sidebar quote). *Among Worlds, 12*(3), 4.

McCaig, Norma. (2008, March). *Encouraging resilience in the global nomad child.* Presented at Families in Global Transition Conference, Houston, TX.

Mills, Karen M. (1993). *Americans overseas in U.S. census, 1930 census* (Technical Paper No. 62). Washington, DC: U.S. Census Bureau.

Milne, A. A. (1994). *The complete tales of Winnie-the-Pooh.* New York: Dutton's Childrens Books.

Morteimer, Malia. (2010). *Adult third culture kids: Common themes, relational struggles and therapeutic experiences* (Doctoral dissertation). Marital and Family Therapy Program, California School of Professional Psychology, Alliant International University, San Diego.

Nouwen, Henri. (n.d.). Retrieved from BrainyQuote.com website at www.brainyquote.com/quotes/authors/h/henri_nouwen.html

Okun, Barbara F., & Rappaport, Louis J. (1980). *Working with families: An introduction to family therapy.* North Scituate, MA: Duxbury Press.

Ota, Doug. (2009, March). *Writing your own story.* Presented at Families in Global Transition Conference, Houston, TX.

Pascoe, Robin. (2006). *Raising global nomads: Parenting abroad in an on-demand world.* Vancouver, Canada: Expatriate Press.

Pipher, Mary. (2002). *The middle of everywhere: Helping refugees enter the American community.* Orlando, FL: Mariner Books.

Pollock, David C., & Van Reken, Ruth E. (2009). *Third culture kids: Growing up among worlds* (Rev. ed.). Boston: Nicholas Brealey.

Potter, Constance. (2010, Fall). U.S. census schedules for Americans living overseas, 1900 to 1930. *Prologue Magazine, 42*(3). Retrieved from www.archives.gov/publications/prologue/2010/fall/overseas.html

Powell, John J. (1969). *Why am I afraid to tell you who I am? Insights into personal growth.* Allen, TX: Thomas More.

Purnell, Elsie. (2004). MKs and marriage: Observations on choices they make. In L. Andrews (Ed.), *The family in mission* (pp. 145–153). Palmer Lake, CO: Missionary Training Institute.

Quick, Tina. (2010). *The global nomad's guide to university transition.* Great Britain: Summertime.

Samuels, Allison. (2003, October 13). The Kobe Bryant you don't know. *Newsweek Magazine.*

Sandoz, Josh. (2009). *International therapist directory.* Retrieved from http://internationaltherapistdirectory.com

Sawhney, Nitin. (2006). The same song. On *Namesake* (DVD). Retrieved from www.metrolyrics.com

Schaetti, Barbara. (1996). Phoenix rising: A question of cultural identity. In C. S. Smith (Ed.), *Strangers at home: Essays on the effects of living overseas and coming "home" to a strange land* (pp. 177–188). Bayside, NY: Aletheia.

Schillinger, Liesl. (2008, April 6). American children. *The New York Times*. Retrieved from www.nytimes.com/2008/04/06/books/review/Schillinger3-t.html?pagewanted=all

Shallcross, Lynne. (2012). A loss like no other. *Counseling Today, 54*(12), 26–31.

Tennyson, Alfred Lord. (n.d.). Retrieved from BrainyQuote.com website at www.brainyquote.com/quotes/authors/a/alfred_lord_tennyson.html

United States Government Accountability Office. (2004). *2010 census: Counting Americans overseas as part of the decennial census would not be cost-effective.* Washington, DC: Author. Retrieved from www.gao.gov/new.items/d041077t.pdf

Useem, Ruth. (1973). Third culture factors in educational change. In C. Brembeck & W. Hiler (Eds.), *Cultural challenges to education: The influence of cultural factors in school learning* (pp. 121–138). Lexington, MA: D.C. Heath.

Useem, Ruth H. (1993, January). Third culture kids: Focus of major study. *Newslinks, Newspaper of the International School Services, 12*(3), 1.

Van Reken, Ruth. (2012). *Letters never sent.* Great Britain: Summertime.

Van Reken, Ruth. (n.d.). *Cross cultural kids blog.* Retrieved from http://blog.crossculturalkid.org/?page_id=24

Van Reken, Ruth. E., & Bethel, Paulette. M. (2005). Third culture kids: Prototypes for understanding other cross-cultural kids. *Intercultural Management Quarterly, 6*(4), 3, 8–9.

Wallin, David J. (2007). *Attachment in psychotherapy.* New York: Guilford Press.

Ward, Ted. (1989). The MK's advantage: Three cultural contexts. In P. Echerd & A. Arathoon (Eds.), *Understanding and nurturing the missionary family* (pp. 49–61). Pasadena, CA: William Carey Library.

Weaver, Gary. (2011, October 14). *Growing up cross-culturally: New paradigms for research*. Keynote address presented at Cross Cultural Symposium, Indianapolis, IN.

Weaver, Gary R. (1986). Understanding and coping with cross-cultural adjustment stress. In R. M. Paige (Ed.), *Cross-cultural orientation: New conceptualizations and applications*. Lanham, MD: University Press of America.

Wennersten, John. (2008). *Leaving America: The new expatriate generation*. Westport, CT: Praeger.

Wertsch, Mary Edwards. (1991). *Military brats: Legacies of childhood inside the Fortress*. Bayside, NY: Aletheia.

Westwood, Duncan. (1998). *Expatriate journeying: A holistic perspective on the care and development of overseas personnel* (Doctoral dissertation). The Union Institute, Cincinnati, OH.

# Appendices

# Appendix A

# The Powerful Impact of Systems

# on the Globally Mobile

*by*

## *Lois J. Bushong & Ruth E. Van Reken*

---

### Note to Therapists

While I know that therapists are very aware of systems, I (Lois) developed these models with Ruth Van Reken when we were asked to do a talk on the power of the organizational system for TCKs as discussed in Chapter 6. I have found since then that it has been very helpful to *show* these to my TCK clients when talking about the impact on them and their family of the organization for which their parents worked when they went overseas. I have found these same charts and illustrations can help describe family systems to others as well, but our primary examples will relate to the organizational systems TCKs have known. Since we feel your clients will be able to read this and learn from it, we have written it "to the TCK"; however, we hope you will also gain insight about using what you know about systems theory with your clients. Please note that "you" refers to the TCK, but in a broader sense, "you" can be anyone reading this information.

You have permission to copy this appendix for an individual client, but not for further publication. To make it easier for your clients to access, it is available for download from my website: **www.quietstreamscounseling.com**

---

# The Powerful Impact of Systems

# on the Globally Mobile

*by*

## *Lois J. Bushong & Ruth E. Van Reken*

During the years we have both lived and worked with globally mobile families and individuals—first in our personal lives, then Lois as a therapist and Ruth in listening to countless people tell her their stories informally—we have realized one thing: there are very powerful messages that come from the family and organizational systems in which we all grow up, live, and work which can profoundly shape our lives. For those in the military the message may be something like "Duty over desire." Religious missions may say, "If you have enough faith, you shouldn't feel overwhelmed with sadness when separated from friends and family." The implication in both of these messages is that the purpose for each system is so important, it is *not okay* to worry about your *personal feelings* as you live out this calling. In the end, the message in our heads is similar to a message children raised in dysfunctional family systems also hear: "Don't think; don't feel; don't talk."

On the other hand, the messages can be positive ones: "You showed incredible courage when terrorists attacked the embassy. That brought honor not only to you, but also to your country." These messages give a new confidence about ourselves in such times.

One problem in dealing with this reality, however, is that the idea of systems is a rather nebulous concept. How can some non-personal entity such as "the military," or "my mission agency," or "the foreign service," or "the company," or even a non-governmental agency (NGO) such as UNICEF have power over you or me when I can't even name any one person who is "the system" or is a face for "the system"?

Sometimes it gets more complicated when we feel we are wrestling with some sort of negative emotion or belief, but the people we know who are associated with our family or organizational system are such nice people (even those we love dearly), we can't believe anything negative could come from them. Or we "understand" why things are or were, so we rationalize that we *shouldn't* feel so badly—yet we do. The messages all get twisted and we can't figure out the source of the message. So how do we begin to sort this out?

## Beginning with the Basics

The truth is, whatever your story—whether you've stayed in one place all your life or moved to a new place every two years for as long as you remember—wherever you have lived, however you have processed the events of your life, one thing is sure: You have grown up in various systems. All of us come from a family and each family—from the healthiest, happiest ones in the world to the most dysfunctional—is some sort of system. There are written and unwritten rules and expectations for how this particular family works. Each member has a particular role that is unlike the others.

There are other systems at play in each of our lives: school, university, career, even the local and national culture around us. While moving into a new system as an adult can be either disconcerting or invigorating for adults, children in particular are shaped by all of these systems that surround them as they grow up because each system tells children in one way or another how they are "supposed" to be.

Those of us who have grown up globally as *third culture kids (TCKs)* often have another powerful system which has influenced our lives—the organizational system in which we grew up because of our parents' career choice. Whether it was the military, a large international corporation, the Foreign Service, or religious missions, each of them can be as powerful a cultural influence as the culture of any country where we have lived. All of them have clear rules and expectations for how all ages, including children, will or won't behave and what privileges they do or don't have. Like any system in which we are raised, they are a piece of how we are shaped and, in many cases, part of our sense of identity. How many times have you or someone you know said something like, "I'm a military brat" or "I'm a Shell Oil kid" or even "He's a missionary kid"?

Systems can be wonderful things, or dreadful. Often they are a bit of both. For many TCKs—maybe even you—the messages that come from these systems can be powerful for spurring you on. Or, these messages can create invisible ties holding you back without your conscious awareness.

Since systems are so important in our lives, we hope the following ideas will help you better understand what a system is and answer other questions about systems, especially if this is a new concept for you or you have no previous training in systems theory.

- What is a system?

- What is the purpose of a system?

- How do the means and methods relate to the purpose or goal of the system?

- What is a healthy system? How does an individual function within a healthy system?

- What is an unhealthy or broken system? How does it affect the functioning of the individual?

- How do sick systems develop? How do they affect the individuals in them?

- How does all of this relate to you (or your clients)?

Everything described here about systems can be applied to any other types of system, but for our purposes we will use examples from the TCK experience to make clear why these organizational systems can have particular power in a TCK's life.

## What is a System?

In his book, *Structural Family Therapy,* Dr. Carter C. Umbarger, Director of the Family Institute of Cambridge, basically defines a system as a group of objects, people, principles, or units combined to form a whole to move or work together. A system includes unspoken and spoken expectations and dynamics. In any system, "each sub-unit is impacted by the rules of the sub-units above it, while other sub-units in the same system may not share the exact same rules or expectations" (Umbarger, 1983, p. 8).

### How hierarchy works in a system

To better understand what Umbarger means, let's take a look at the following chart at a pretend military system to see how all units and subsystems basically work.

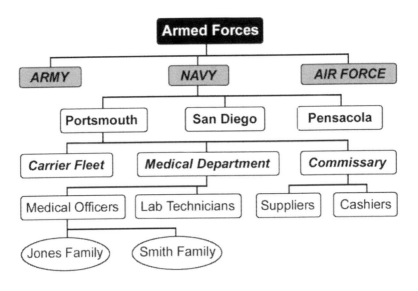

**Figure 1: Example of an Organizational System**

At the top is the overarching unit or system to which all other sub-units belong—the Armed Forces. Whatever the Commander-in-Chief of the Armed Forces decrees is law for every person in every branch of the service all the way down to the bottom. It doesn't matter whether you are in the Army, Navy, or Air Force.

However, if the top General in the Army makes a rule, those in the Navy and Air Force are not obliged to obey that command. They are in the same overall system, but in different sub-units. And so it goes on as you follow the hierarchy of this system all the way down to the individual families where the same principle of hierarchy applies. If the Smith parents say that 10 p.m. is curfew for their kids, all the Smith kids have to be in at 10 p.m. If you are a Jones kid, however, you can stay out as long as your parents agree.

Understanding hierarchy helps us see how it is that you and another person may have both been TCKs in a particular sector such as military or missions and had quite different experiences. Sometimes it can be something as simple as what type of family you had or what department your parents worked for in that system compared to your friend that can make all the difference in how you both experienced what would appear to be essentially the same circumstances. If you grew up in the Smith home with tight rules for most every event in your daily schedule, you might have grown up feeling you had little choice for controlling your own life while the Jones kids seemed to thrive with making adventurous choices in their lives. Folks looking on may say, "But both grew up in the military. Why do they see life so differently?" and not realize how different your family systems were inside the structure of the bigger system.

### *How a system affects an individual's behavior*

It's also important to remember that a system is *more then the sum of its parts*. In other words, how people behave within a system might be quite different from how they might act when completely alone in a non-systemic context. This is part of the confusion we can feel when we really like someone on a personal level but don't understand how they operate in their systemic roles.

The best example of this is the children's story *The Emperor's New Clothes*, written by Hans Christian Anderson (1837, see references). In this story, two rogue tailors came to the Emperor and explained that they had a way he could know whether or not his subjects were loyal to him. They promised to weave an outfit out of magical thread. Those who were loyal would be able to see the thread. Those who were disloyal would not.

Of course, the king's attendants who watched the tailors do their imaginary cutting and sewing each day couldn't see a thing, but no one dared say so for fear of being labeled "disloyal." They didn't want to lose either their positions or their heads. Finally the promised day came when the tailors scheduled a parade so the Emperor could wear his new clothes and discover who were or were not his loyal subjects. As the Emperor paraded down the streets, all the people along the roadside praised the beauty of these imaginary garments.

Finally, a child spoke up. "But, Mommy, the Emperor doesn't have any clothes on." At that point, the story goes: "Did you ever hear such innocent prattle?" said its father [presuming he was now in trouble because of his child!]. And one person whispered to another what the child had said, "He hasn't got anything on. A child says he hasn't got anything on."

"But he hasn't got anything on!" the whole town cried out at last. The Emperor shivered, for he suspected they were right. But he thought, "This procession has got to go on." So he walked more proudly than ever, as his noblemen held high the train that wasn't there at all.

Obviously, all along, each person looking at the invisible suit should have said, "How stupid. Look at those crazy tailors. There's nothing there." But what happened when every individual heard someone else talk about the beautiful suit? They began to doubt their own perceptions because others were affirming a different reality.

This is what we mean by "a system is more than the sum of its parts." In the end, the fear of each individual—including the Emperor—to stand up to the "system message" resulted in the parade of a naked emperor. Such is the power of a system.

Seeing this can lend understanding of why parents—or even you as a teen or young person—may have made choices that now seem puzzling. When you look at Figure 1, you will recognize the influences of the system. This is why the messages of the organizational system affect family dynamics; parents who want to keep their jobs usually have to acquiesce to the system's way of doing things—even when they would personally disagree or take a different action in another context.

## The Purpose of a System

The idea that "no person is an island" is more than a catchy phrase; it is reality. We are made as relational beings and when we attempt to live a life that is not relational, things can derail in our lives. Systems help us live relationally in meaningful ways. They are necessary for any group of people to live and work together—be they family, co-workers, church members, schoolmates, or neighbors in the community. We all need certain structures around us that make life predictable and safe. When we have them, we find a sense of belonging. In clearly defined systems, we know who is "us" or who is "them," depending on who is living in awareness with and keeping the written and unwritten codes and expectations of the system.

## The Messages of a System

The messages of a system are basically the expectations for conduct or a way of thinking. These messages may be in written form, such as the policies of the organization or company which state "Everyone who works here will . . . ." or "The following will not be tolerated . . . ."

Most system messages, however, are unwritten, but they are "the messages in your head." So if you want to know what some of your system messages might be, whether from your family or from an organization, ask yourself this question: "Whose voice is the one I hear in my head?" If you grew up being taught to always listen to those in authority over you (parents, boss, God, president, commander-in-chief), it is difficult to suddenly not listen to that voice. Why? Maybe you don't know the sound of your own voice yet! You may have no confidence in your voice or decisions because you were taught that your decisions or thoughts were all wrong if they deviated from what the system message was. If for any reason the message is "don't think; don't feel; don't talk," then you learned to just shut up and do what "that voice" in your head was telling you to do and simply push on through whatever needed to be accomplished without assessing the <u>need</u> to do it or the <u>rightness</u> or <u>wrongness</u> of doing it. If that is the way you grew up, you probably still do not stop to figure out if something is right or if it is what is best for you. Goodness knows, it was unfathomable to even think of launching out in a new direction altogether!

Of course, the flip side of those types of messages can also be the positive messages we receive when we behave or think in ways that are consistent with our system's purposes or values. We can then have a deep pride in being part of something bigger than ourselves. Every human being needs to have a sense of significance, and often the messages of our systems can instill a sense that our lives can and are making a difference. Sometimes that is right in the family as we take pride in the work our parents are doing, sometimes it is in being part of an even greater whole. And when the members of a group share the same values and codes of conduct, that sense of belonging grows for each person in it.


## Why Organizational Systems are Particularly Significant for TCKs

It would be natural to wonder, "So I grew up in one of the organizational systems you mentioned above, but why is that any bigger deal for me than for other children around the world whose parents worked for organizations or corporations in their local community?"

When an organization or corporation sends families overseas, it functions in the role of a parent over the family. In many cases, decisions are made by the sending agency or corporation about the most fundamental issues affecting a family's life, such as choosing which area of which country the family lives and where the children go to school. Maybe the organization or company told your parents they had a choice, but the reality was that the agency would only pay for, or encourage, a particular type of schooling.

Compare that dynamic to former eras when parents traditionally climbed their career ladder while staying in the same geographical area. If a parent worked for a local bank in the first half of the 20th century, it had no branches in foreign lands (maybe not even in another state, and often not even other parts of that state). That parent could have begun to work there as a teller and risen to become the president one day, but the family could have lived in the same house or community for the children's entire childhood. What went on at work wouldn't directly affect the family, outside of perhaps a parent coming home a bit grouchy after a bad day! The children would have gone to school in the local community or neighborhood with other children who were pretty much living the same sort of life. Their parents would have worked a variety of stable, necessary jobs—at the local factory, in the stores and groceries, or as a professional such as a doctor or dentist or nurse. Most of the children would have known what the other children's father (and mother) did for a living because the families would have had necessary interaction through purchases or needed services. The children would have been friends from childhood or elementary school until university. The parents would have made the ultimate decisions that directly affected their family's life and choices—what groups each family member would join, where to swim in the summer, what neighborhood to live in, what school to attend, and even which friends were approved.

Now, just because a company or organization has power to make decisions that affect your life doesn't mean it's a bad system. Not at all. Remember individuals can gain from systems too and there can be wonderfully healthy systems. When parents joined these corporations or organizations, there was a good reason. They may have joined for better pay or to live for purposes they believed were greater than individual comfort. There can be many perks as well. There was the adventure of seeing the world, perhaps at the company's expense. It may have been a way to better use their talents or training. In some cases, it was at the request of someone in that company because of what the person could contribute. For most, joining the system made life interesting. If it was a healthy system, the parents and family had as much choice as possible, even as they helped fulfill that group's purpose. But the point is simply that for good or bad, companies and agencies that send families overseas have more influence on decisions that affect the family than was or is the case in more monocultural situations.

That's why you (as a TCK) need to look at all the systems you grew up in, including this organizational one, as you seek to understand your own life story better. Some people love and treasure the experience of being part of a particular system; for others, there is a lot of pain. For many, it can be a mixed bag—some great things from being associated with this group are cherished, but some experiences may need to be sorted out or worked through.

So let's look at the difference between healthy and unhealthy, and even sick, systems before we look further at how they affect your identity. Finally, we will end with how to learn good ways of viewing system messages and how a person can decide which systems' messages they may want to keep and how to release those that they would like to release.

## The Life Cycle of a Healthy System

### *How healthy systems form*

Every system starts for a reason. In other words, there is some *purpose* that motivates a person or group to start it. For example, people get married because they love each other and want to stay together. They may also want to raise a family and feel this is the best way. The organizational systems many TCKs grew up in also began for good reasons: "We need to protect our country/Share our faith/Maintain good relationships with others/Provide for our family's needs/Feed the poor."

After a person or group decides what they want to do, they have to decide how they want to do it. In other words, they have to consider by what *means* they can practically accomplish these goals. "We need to have a baby if we want to have a family." "We need a strong military structure." "We must form an organization to send missionaries." "We have to set up an embassy in Timbukto." "We will start a company to make and sell computers." "We can form a non-governmental organization that can teach better farming and harvesting methods in developing countries."

Once the original group members have defined their goal and the basic means by which they will reach it, they have to decide on the specific *methods* they will use to get there. The country that wants to maintain good relations with Timbukto by setting up an embassy realizes that they will have to choose an ambassador. But, guess what? The ambassador will need logistical support to be able to live and work there. Soon deputies, attachés, secretaries, and consular officers must all be put in place. Of course, that raises the issue of how to care for the families of these employees and diplomatic officers. What kind of housing will they need? Where will the children go to school? Someone has to begin investigating those possibilities, perhaps building new homes and schools if needed, so that the diplomatic effort can be successful. The same type of thinking or strategizing would be needed for each of the other examples listed.

When the means (e.g. setting up an embassy in Timbuktu) and methods are decided upon (such as what types of personnel will be needed, where they will live, how they will school their children), those in charge can start the processes of reaching the original goal. In the example, that means hiring an ambassador, getting a contractor to build the embassy, and finding out what is or isn't available for the children's schooling.

Figure 2 shows how these factors—purpose, means, methods—work together in the life cycle of a healthy system.

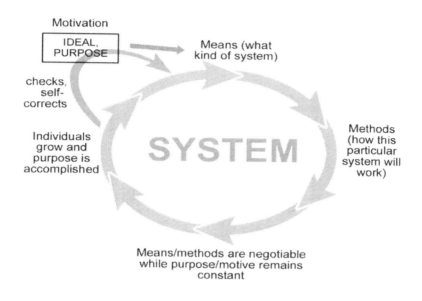

**Figure 2: Life Cycle of a Healthy System**

In a healthy system, the purpose (for example, maintaining good relationships with another country) remains a constant, but the means and methods by which that goal can be accomplished are not fixed in stone. Maybe in time the ambassador might be replaced by an attaché. The local international school first chosen may not be satisfying to parents, so some teachers may be dispatched to begin a small school within the embassy itself. In other words, as times or needs change, new methods or approaches can be substituted for old ones. The system is dynamic—changing methods and means with the changing needs.

*Characteristics of a healthy system*

We can judge the state of a system by noticing the characteristics that define it and how it affects those who live and work within it. We will liken a system to a box which is holding the individual inside. In our diagrams, we will show the characteristics of the system on the outside of the box and the characteristics of a person in such a system on the person inside. As you look at each type of system you can begin to consider which diagram best describes your own experience (or your client's)in the different systems in which you (or the client) grew up and lived or still live.

*The structure of a healthy system*

A healthy system is one where the following characteristics describe what this box looks like (Figure 3):

- basic principles
- respect for individuals
- appropriate boundaries
- open at the top

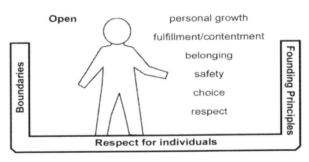

Offers stability while promoting growth and change

## Figure 3: The Healthy System

SIDE 1: *Founding Principles* form the first side of our strong, sturdy box. These principles are what might be called the *core values* by which this system will operate. For a family, such things might include "speak the truth in love." For a business, it might include "use only the best material," or "treat our employees fairly," or "make a profit." These are non-negotiable principles, the ones which underlie all future decisions and practices.

SIDE 2: *Respect for Individuals* is the foundational side of this system box. A healthy system is one where individuals can be creative or are free to ask questions. In a family, siblings are not compared, but all are encouraged to explore their own particular gifts within the context of their particular personalities. In an organization, CEOs understand that employees are not the means to the end but that in allowing them to develop their skills within the basic values of this group, not only will the goals of the organization or corporation be met, but the individuals will grow and ultimately contribute even more. *In a healthy system, there is acknowledgment that there are different ways people operate even while honoring the foundational principles.*

SIDE 3: *Appropriate Boundaries* form the third side of the box. Every healthy family, group, organization, or corporation must have appropriate boundaries for the individuals within their system. In a healthy system, boundaries are clear for what is appropriate and non-appropriate behavior in this environment. For a family, it might be something such as "we love to have fun together, but mean teasing isn't fun or acceptable." For a corporation, "we encourage creative ideas, but you must check with your supervisor before changing procedures in your department." Boundaries are important for people to function peacefully with one another.

TOP: *Open lid.* The sides of the box give strength and protect the contents within. The top is open. People have true choice. That means individuals have space to grow while remaining within the security and support of the system. While the sides offer protection, they are neither claustrophobic nor confining.

## The Person within a Healthy System

One way to see if a particular system is healthy is to look at those living or working within it. Are they thriving? The person within a healthy system:

- experiences freedom for personal growth
- is fulfilled or contented
- has a sense of belonging
- feels a sense of safety to share feelings, needs, ideas, and concerns
- enjoys freedom to make individual choices
- is respected by others in the organization

Individuals are free to move in and out of the system without the need for a crisis in order to escape. For example, when a child marries and leaves the day-by-day interactions of the nuclear family, the parents can affirm this new freedom and also welcome back their child (and in-laws!) when they return for holiday celebrations or other gatherings. There is free movement. In an organization, people may leave for a better position elsewhere without being regarded as pariahs in their original group. A healthy system is also open within the systemic structure itself. People can maintain an air of openness in their interactions with one another and try out new ideas without fear of shame. Deep within the system, there is an atmosphere that offers stability while promoting growth and change. Each person inside feels safe, secure, and respected as an individual.

## How Unhealthy Systems Form

So what takes a system from being healthy to unhealthy? Figure 4 shows how an unhealthy system forms. Often it evolves so slowly that no one notices it is happening until it may be almost too late.

The unhealthy system (Figure 4) begins the same way a healthy system does. Again, there is a reason for it. An individual or group pursues a vision of what needs to be done. The means to accomplish this vision are once more defined. Methods develop to make the means possible. All of this is the same but then the subtle changes come.

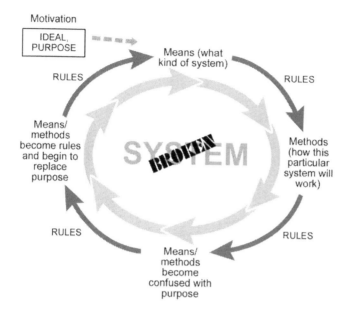

## Figure 4: Life Cycle Of An Unhealthy System

### Confusing means and methods with original purpose

A system starts to become unhealthy when the means and methods designed to accomplish the original vision become equated with the vision itself. In Ruth's first book, *Letters Never Sent* (2012), she wrote of her sadness the first night in boarding school at age six. Soon after its publication, a recruiter for a mission organization told Ruth he would never give her book to any prospective missionaries because then they would not send their children to boarding school and "missions will cease to exist." In an era when many other possibilities exist for how children can be educated overseas, this person had mixed up an earlier method of educating children in missions with the primary reason for missions.

*Maintenance of the means and methods per se begins to replace their original purpose*

Not only did this person tell Ruth why he feared giving her book to those considering missions, but also his mission had a rule that all parents must send their children to boarding school at age six. What was once *one* way of educating children had now become *the only* way and replaced the original reason for the method altogether. It didn't seem to matter that there were other good ways now to educate children. For this mission system, the method had become synonymous with such things as proving a parent's faith was enough to put God higher than their children and so on. Once any method used to accomplish the end becomes equated with the end itself, a system is broken. Soon, maintaining the system itself begins to become a motivating factor all on its own. Often more time and energy is put into maintaining the means or the methods than in working to accomplish the purpose—so much so in some unhealthy systems that many of those in the system are no longer sure what the purpose is.

## Characteristics of an Unhealthy System

### *The structure of an unhealthy system*

Having looked at healthy systemst, what does an unhealthy system look like? How do we know it is unhealthy if we see it or work in it or live in it?

Once again, using a box to represent a person in an unhealthy system, Figure 5 demonstrates the identifying characteristics of an unhealthy system.

- Absolute rules
- Disrespect for individual
- Power
- Top is closed

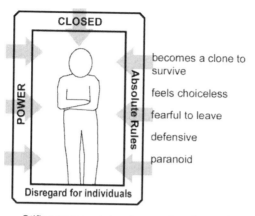

Stifles personal development and growth

## Figure 5: The Person in the Unhealthy System

SIDE 1: *Absolute Rules* replace *Foundational Principles.* For example: An NGO group working with AIDS education in a refugee camp began with the principle that their field workers must know the local language. How else could they teach and interact with the refugees if they couldn't communicate? Because of that, the organization made a policy that *all* new recruits must go to language school for six months. When an adult TCK arrived who had grown up in the area and already spoke the language, they insisted she attend language school with everyone else, despite her repeated protestations. "It's how we do it here," was their only reply. A great principle had turned into a rigid rule.

SIDE 2: *Disrespect for Individuals* replaces *Respect for Individuals.* In an unhealthy system, "one size fits all" thinking is common: "If we let one recruit skip language school, the next one will want to do the same. Soon, no one will want to go and how can they be effective in the work if they can't speak the language?" A fear of "what will happen to our system?" creeps in. Soon, maintaining the system becomes more important than each individual's needs or potential.

SIDE 3: *Power Reigns* where *Appropriate Boundaries* stood before. For those who do not speak the language used by refugees at the camp, the message "you cannot begin your job at camp until you go to language school" is a healthy boundary serving to protect those who have never worked in that country or language before. For the young woman who already spoke the language, it becomes a power issue when it becomes an absolute rule with no exceptions. To challenge this rule would mean to challenge the authority of the organization.

TOP: *Closed lid* replaces *Open lid* at the top. The system is no longer a healthy place to grow. New thoughts are unwelcome. Questions to authorities are seen as rebellion. Unhealthy systems are easy to join, but difficult to exit. Some people have physically attempted to leave particular broken systems, only to "hear" reverberating messages in their brains of being "wrong" or "out of step" because they were breaking the unwritten rules which remained deep within their psyche. The tangled messages of the broken system are difficult to escape.

## The Person in an Unhealthy System

As we see in Figure 5, these are the characteristics of the person in an unhealthy system:

- becomes a clone to survive
- feels choiceless
- reacts defensively
- is fearful of leaving
- may border on or become paranoid

Because the top is closed, individuals begin to feel blocked on every side. Each idea for how to make changes leads to an invisible glass ceiling. Those with the most creative ideas may soon be seen as "troublemakers." Becoming a clone seems to be the best way to survive. Their mantra becomes, "Just be quiet and do what 'they' say."

Often, people in such a system have a victim mentality because they feel choiceless—not only choiceless within the system, but virtually choiceless to leave the system. Some, like those who acquiesced to the falsehood of the tailors weaving the Emperor's clothes, may fear the fault lies with them and if they leave, their family, coworkers, government, or even God will look down on them. Many become defensive, argumentative, or very philosophical. Some resort to humor in order to keep others at a distance. In the end, some develop a strong sense of paranoia and a strong distrust of everyone.

## How Does an Unhealthy System Resolve?

When the means and methods start to become confused with the original motivating factor, organizational systems and those who work in them face a crisis. Figure 6 shows the two basic outcomes that happen to unhealthy systems at this point.

One potential outcome is that those in charge take a moment to say: "Wait a minute. Let's try to figure out the difference between the means and methods we have chosen and our original reason for existence."

At this point, the system may begin to self-correct. Perhaps an organizational consultant will come in to help or perhaps insight will come from those within the organization. Either way, someone will come along who says, "Wait a minute. If this recruit already knows the language, then to let her begin working with the local people immediately is not negating our fundamental principle. The fact is, if we are looking for communicators, she will likely do a better job than those we send to language school!"

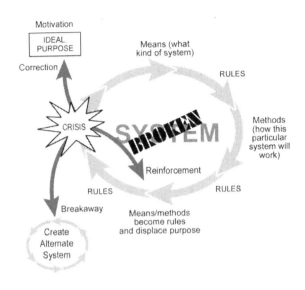

## Figure 6: Lifecycle of an Unhealthy System

We know of leaders who came into mission organizations like the one above that still required children to go to boarding school at age six and said, "Wait a minute. Boarding schools were a method to try and give our kids a good education. There are lots of ways for that now." In such a systemic correction, new choices are offered, new policies are put in place, and the system refocuses on the reason it began in the first place. Individuals can once more find freedom to grow and make choices, they are respected, they can question, they can share ideas, and all is well.

If this correction does not happen, however, then one of two things usually happens. Some people will break away, and start an alternative system to accomplish the original goal. This may be a good—and indeed, necessary—choice. Often they find new joy and purpose.

However, beware of this type of new system! We have also seen people create another closed system because, at times, they wind up forming an anti-identity both individually and in their new system rather than freely pursing who they are or the original purpose for the system.

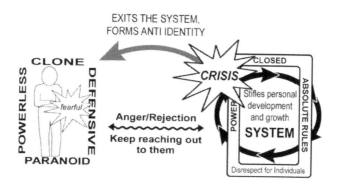

## Figure 7: Leaving an Unhealthy System

The other thing that happens is that people stay. It is those who don't leave, however, and refuse to understand the difference between *how* they are seeking to achieve their goal vs. *why* they are doing using those means who wind up in a very unhealthy system. <u>Maintaining</u> the <u>system</u> <u>becomes</u> the <u>purpose</u> rather than the original purpose or vision. Ultimately, the real danger is that the system will move from simply unhealthy to truly sick.

## How a Sick System Develops

A sick system begins as a healthy system: a strong motivational purpose followed by the means and methods to achieve the original goal. It can morph into an unhealthy system. However, if the leaders choose not to correct it back to a healthy state, it becomes more and more rigid and closes in on itself like the spiraling circle in Figure 8. The "top dogs" control, with increasingly stringent rules, how this community will operate. No one can question their power or authority without severe consequences. The system is the main and only thing to preserve, no matter the cost.

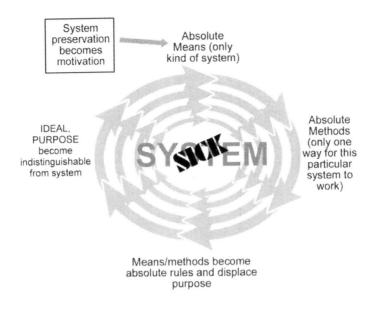

System preservation becomes motivation

Absolute Means (only kind of system)

IDEAL, PURPOSE become indistinguishable from system

Absolute Methods (only one way for this particular system to work)

SYSTEM / SICK

Means/methods become absolute rules and displace purpose

## Figure 8: Life Cycle of a Sick System

How does an unhealthy system differ from a sick one? A good example of this is the story of Jim Jones, the man who convinced over 900 of his followers to drink Kool-Aid® laced with cyanides and sedatives in the settlement he had started in Guyana. Jones began his group as an attempt to deal with racism and to help the poor. But as he gained power, he became more and more dictatorial. When being investigated for tax evasion, he fled, convincing hundreds of people to accompany him, to Guyana. In 1978 Congressman, Leo Ryan, headed a team which went to Guyana to investigate the reports that some were being held against their wills, in addition to reports of physical abuse. In the end, Mr. Ryan and several others were killed as they tried to take with them 20 cult members who desired to leave Jonestown. After that, Jim Jones forced his people to drink the Kool-Aid and over 900 men, women, and children died in that one day. That was, indeed, a sick system.

## Characteristics of a Sick System

So let's take a look at how we can know if a system is merely unhealthy or actually sick.

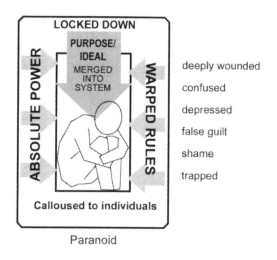

**Figure 9: The Sick System**

SIDE 1: *Warped Rules* now reign. If we look at the story of Jim Jones, his order that all who followed him must drink poisoned Kool-Aid was definitely a warped rule. Yet again, the power of the system was so great that, despite the number of followers who could have said "No" and likely killed Mr. Jones if they desired, hundreds went along to their own ultimate detriment. While this may seem extreme, there are some situations where rules seem to be there just for the sake of having them so that people who are in positions of political, religious, financial, or legal authority can demonstrate their authority and power over others.

SIDE 2: *Callousness toward the Individual* becomes the hallmark of a sick system. Jim Jones didn't care what happened to the individuals he forced to drink the poisoned Kool-Aid or the pain their deaths would cause the families. All he cared about was that they obeyed him.

What about those in power who don't care what their edicts and judgments or greed do to those under them? Such is the outstanding characteristic of a sick system.

SIDE 3: *Absolute Power* takes over. No matter what the rule is, or what terrible effect it will have on the person, unquestioning and total obedience is required. Any who disagree or do not conform are dismissed and ostracized, or, in the worst cases, killed. The few who tried to escape Jones' edict were shot as they ran away.

TOP: *Locked Down* describes this world. It is now "duct-taped shut." There is no room for people to grow and think new thoughts. The system has to lock down in order to prevent anyone else outside from becoming aware of what is taking place within this sick system and prevent those in the sick system from becoming aware of another way to live. The entire system is permeated through and through with the strong stench of paranoia which paralyzes everyone within it.

### The Person in a Sick System

Individuals in this system:

- suffer deep wounds
- become confused
- give in to depression
- feel anxious
- are trapped

They are wounded to the point that their core self is almost extinguished. They don't seem to know who they are anymore or what they like because they are now brainwashed. Confusion about their self-worth reigns. Depression and high anxiety are rampant. There is "false guilt" which is a guilt that is not merited but is taken on oneself. Some would call that "shame"—that sense that "something is wrong with me because I can't be as good as I 'should' be" or "I am wanting things I 'shouldn't' want if I were just a better person." These deep feelings of shame lie beneath the surface, and ultimately, individuals are trapped in a world of hopelessness. People within the system become more fearful to state their feelings for fear of the wrath of the leadership. Ultimately, they realize that they are not allowed to think, feel or talk lest they be banned. They feel (and often are) completely trapped and, often, suicidal.

We need to make one other note here: There can be a sick subsystem within a healthy system. A typical example of this would be a sick or abusive family unit working in a healthy organizational system. It can be a silent cancer but it may be one reason for some of the differences in how various people respond within the same overall sponsoring organizational system.

As we have tried to delineate what a system is as well as the purpose for any type of system and looked at what healthy, unhealthy, and sick systems might look like from the outside, we hope you have been taking some time to consider the impact of various systems on your own life. Now we will look at how different personalities can relate quite differently to any system—even ones that are essentially healthy.

## Finding Identity within the System

The next thing to consider is how the system and its messages can further shape a person's view of self, not so much because the system itself is healthy or unhealthy, but in terms of how the person's own personality relates to the system.

Many TCKs struggle to find a clear sense of personal identity when the usual markers of place, community, culture, and sometimes even family are constantly changing; however, the one thing that stays constant is the system. But there can be a bit of a catch here too. Every system has messages of what is expected and what is "right" and what is not.

That's fine, but sometimes you're a person who is, by personality or gifting, unable to fit into the system of your childhood as well as another, even a sibling or parent. Maybe you are incredibly creative and never think in straight rows or boxes, but you grew up in a system like the military, or some missions, or even a fairly rigid family system where the rules for how life operated were pretty clearly defined. When you deviated from those written and unwritten rules by thinking or acting a different way, the message was pretty clear: "This is NOT how you're supposed to be or act."

Maybe you happen to love straight lines and organized boxes and would have loved being in an environment where you had a clear structure telling how and when to do life. Instead, it happens your family or organizational system seemed incredibly chaotic and it drove you nuts. "Why can't someone figure out how to run this show properly?" you may have often wondered.

## Different Ways People Relate to a System

The truth is that how you relate to any particular system in terms of who you are yourself can make a big difference in how you begin to see and identify yourself. Look at this simple diagram for four ways in which people relate to a system.

| Doesn't fit the system<br>Tries to fit the system | Doesn't fit the system<br>Doesn't know they don't fit |
|---|---|
| Fits the system<br>No problem going along<br>with the system | Doesn't fit the system<br>Spends entire life proving<br>they are not the system |

### Figure 10: Identity in Relationship to the System

### *Doesn't fit the system, tries to fit the system*

When you don't internally fit the system, but believe this is what you "should" be, you keep trying to squash who you really are into your perception of who "they" say you should be. When it doesn't work, you feel shame. "What is wrong with me?" is the question that spins round and round.

For Ruth, it happened because she had a mind that thought in questions but in the well-defined system of boarding school in first and second grade, hands raised high with new questions didn't seem to be the teacher's favorite show. Ruth soon got the message that it was "wrong" or "faithless" to question so much, but her brain didn't stop working that way and so the shame of not being "right" began.

### Fits the system with no problems

Perfect! You can go along with the system and still be true to who you are inside. Other kids at Ruth's school never seemed to have any questions. They went along with what was said and how things were done—and it seemed they were truly fine.

### Doesn't fit the system, but doesn't seem to know it

You might not fit the system, but you can live in and under it, still doing your own thing, and be true to who you are anyhow. Maybe you were one of those kids who just never quite got with the program at home or school, but you were a bit oblivious to it. You loved to be in your room playing with your Legos® and cars. You might not have fit the system so well, but you were busy expressing your identity from an internal place rather than trying to fit to some external message about who you "should" be. And, more than likely, such positive independence continues to this day.

### Doesn't fit the system and tries to prove it

If you happen to be one of these people, you might not realize that in the very effort to be free from a system you despise at some level, you are actually still a prisoner to it. It continues to define you, even if only in the negative, for there may be things you secretly would like to be or do in that system, but you dare not lest you be swallowed back into it. Instead of going on to find out who you are or become independent, you spend a life proving who you are not—and that is not true freedom.

We have one other thing to say in summary. Given that we are all in many systems at the same time, it is very possible that a person can be in an "I fit" box in their family system but not in their organizational or school system or vice versa. It is important that each person has at least one place of belonging. But if it happens that you look at these boxes and there is no place where you feel you fit, then a deeper look at the health of your systems might be a very important thing to do as you continue to sort out your basic sense of identity.

## Viewing the Systems in Your Life

You've learned about systems. You've had a chance to consider yours. Were most of yours pretty healthy? Unhealthy? Were there or are there any that you would call sick? Which person in the system boxes did you relate to most—the one in the healthy system (Figure 3), the one in the unhealthy system (Figure 5), or the one in the sick system box (Figure 9)?

If you're feeling like the person in the unhealthy box or the sick box, you realize that the messages in your head say you are stuck, that there really isn't much you can do about this. All you know is that if you try to go a different way than the unhealthy system tells you is "right," you'll be in trouble. Maybe you already tried it, either physically or in some other action, and someone or some group got upset. "No, you can't leave. This is the right way. Besides, if you really loved us, you would never dream of doing this." Or "If you take that other job and move away, you'll take my grandkids from me. How could you?" And so you gave in. You learned as a child to just follow the commands of the system and forget your own dreams and what may be best for you. But you still feel trapped.

Or you may feel as if you have escaped. You are living a very different lifestyle than your parents or organizational system would say is "right." You have screamed loudly, "I'm not like you. I don't want to be you. I'll be anything but you." But still, deep down there is no peace because you have also lost some good things in taking this stance. In spite of your hard shell, you feel sadness. You know deep down that besides hurting others, the place of loneliness you refuse to show to the world never goes away. You are stuck as well.

But some of you may still not think this information has much to do with your story. You might be like Freddie who grew up with a very controlling father who was a lieutenant general in the military. The military dictated where they would live, where they would shop, which doctors they would use if they wanted their medical services covered, which schools they would attend and when they would return home to see their extended family. His father dictated who they would have as friends, what sports he would play, what music he would listen to in his room, how they would address their father, topics they were free to discuss, how they felt about religion, and on and on. Some rules were good as they needed rules to function effectively as a military and as a family. But in Freddie's family the kids were not free to display any type of individuality for fear of the shaming, anger, and sarcastic humor they would receive from their father.

Now that Freddie was a man, he could easily recite "the family rules." But when asked if this is what he believed or what his father believed, he would quickly respond with "Why of course, this is what I believe." When pressed about why, it eventually became apparent he did so because this is what his father had told him he should believe if he was smart. He was still getting his identity from the system, not from who he was inside.

Ironically, for all of these situations—the people who don't think they can get out of the messages or power of the system that might not be helpful, the person who has totally rejected the system in every overt way, or those who don't consciously understand how totally the system they grew up in still controls them—the truth is, it is often far easier to let someone else or the system make all of your decisions for what you will or will not be or do than to figure out what is best for you. That is hard work.

Why? Because the messages in our head become a part of us and it gets difficult to sort out the reason we follow that voice. Is it our voice or the voice of the unhealthy system? And if it is the voice of the unhealthy system, we have been trained to follow it for the well-being of the system and of ourselves. We have learned that if we want to thrive in life, we must follow the system because we cannot achieve life by living on our own without the system.

We want to end with the story of one woman who was courageous enough to wrestle with the hard stuff and find her way out of a system she knew was killing her emotionally, psychologically, and even spiritually. She emerged, not with an anti-identity, but as a whole person who could use pieces of her past that had served her well while adding new pieces and participating in joy-giving experiences she never before knew she could have.

## Finding the Way Out

This is a true story. Rosalinda gave permission to share it with only her name changed.

Rosalinda grew up as a missionary kid and loved her life of global mobility. As an adult, she went back into missions with the same agency that had sent her parents. There are, most likely, two reasons for this decision. She loved to travel, but the stated reason was "God has called me." The deeper truth, however, behind that conscious statement was the lurking system message that going overseas with a mission agency (like her parents had done) was the only true way to serve God. Of course, if you had asked that question outright to the adult missionaries she knew as a child, all of them would have been quick to say, "Of course not. You can serve God anywhere." But the truth is she had heard them give their "testimonies" through many years and somehow, those who could name how many of their children had, in fact, gone back into missions had a few more "oooh's" and "aaah's" after they finished. She knew they were the superstar missionaries.

But the rules of her particular mission system became more and more rigid. It wasn't what she remembered from her childhood at all. Finally, Rosalinda felt she had no option but to leave if she planned to survive emotionally. For her, this was as traumatic an event as other clients have expressed when trying to make a break with a dysfunctional nuclear family or a cult-like system.

When she first met with Rosalinda, Lois heard a lot of anger and hurt, cloaked in somewhat cynical comments, but there was one piece she couldn't quite work out. Previously, many MKs she had counseled who seemed to feel angry at their past had also totally given up their faith. As Lois listened to Rosalinda, she didn't hear the same flat-out denial of faith, but neither did she hear the usual spiritual jargon many from this background frequently used to justify or cover their pain. Finally, Lois asked Rosalinda where God did or didn't come into her story at this point. Rosalinda became silent for a few seconds and then said, "I don't know."

The next week, Rosalinda returned with a simple drawing in hand with three boxes, one representing her mission system, the others representing herself and God (see Figure 11).

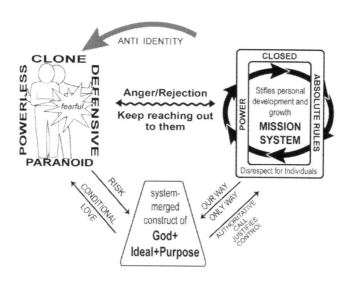

### Figure 11: The Locked Box

*Note: It was from this first hand drawn sketch that we began to work with these ideas in deeper ways to develop this model. All diagrams have been professionally drawn by Barbara Knuckles for this book.*

Rosalinda began to explain her little diagram. "This is where the mission is and I am over here. There is a lot of anger and rejection going in both directions between us. I will die if I stay in it, yet it has always been my family and I am angry at their rejection when I tried to explain what I needed and they, I'm sure, feel angry towards me for having rejected them. Yet, oddly, those feelings of anger and rejection also keep us connected to each other. But God is down here (and she pointed to the bottom of the diagram). I would like to come back to God, but if I do, then I believe I will have to go back to them and I can't go back to them so I can't go back to God either. I feel totally trapped."

Aha!! The clouds began to lift for Lois. "So why do you think coming back to God will force you to go back to them?"

"Because it feels as if they are the same thing. God and the system are one."

Obviously, this was a pretty major awareness—both for Rosalinda and for Lois. The tragedy for her was that her sense of connection with God had always been strong but now she felt she must keep God at arms' length just as she was doing with the mission because if she returned to God, she believed she would instantly be sent back to the system. Either she thought if she went back to God, he would send her back into the system or the system represented God to her (the system and God were one).

The next weeks of therapy involved examining the feelings that had resulted from being trapped in this belief of God and the system being one. Lois tried to help Rosalinda find ways to un-enmesh herself from these messages she had internalized so deeply and to begin to look at three distinct entities— herself, God, and her mission system. Rosalinda had God and the mission linked together into one heavy chain. Were missions and God the same? What was her identity outside of being a missionary kid? Only when she was able to see that the system was not the same as God OR her could she begin her personal and spiritual journey in newer and healthier places. The beauty was that in the end, Rosalinda realized she could dare to explore her faith once more because, in returning to God, she didn't have to return to her former system—they were not the same. And this is what it looked like for her in the end.

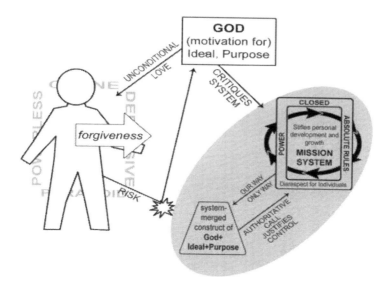

**Figure 12: The Way Out**

By the time she finished therapy, Rosalinda had discovered a new sense of personal identity and gifts that her system didn't deem as "spiritual." But, because God and the system were no longer one, she could dare to develop and exercise those gifts and maintain her faith because it was no longer an either/or choice as it had been before. She also discovered as she grew in positive ways in that new sense of identity that she could relate in fresh ways with those who were part of her old system now that they could no longer define her.

## Concluding Thoughts

Each person has a unique relationship with every system of which they are a part. Your story is probably different from those told in these pages. But you have messages in your mind that come from your various systems. Perhaps for a banker's child you "heard" that the only true success in life is measured by your bank account, but you would rather do your artwork and live on a different financial margin than to work your way up the banking system. You may have grown up moving every two years with parents in the foreign service or military and heard about how exciting and wonderful these opportunities were, but secretly you are tired. You just want to settle down in one place and no one seems to understand why you aren't sitting for the foreign service exams so you can globe-trot "because you'd be so good at it and it is so natural."

As Lois teaches graduate counseling students in a local university, she frequently asks them, "What is the systemic diagnosis of your client?" This is also a key question to consider if you are an ATCK: "How did the system I grew up in shape me—in good ways, in other ways? What are the messages that ring in my head of the 'shoulds' and 'oughts' of my life?"

So often, we are caught in a dilemma. If I venture outside of the system, I will die. If I stay in the system, it will be emotional suicide. The escape out of the trap is long, but it is there. As you slowly develop your own decision-making skills, trust yourself first in the small things before you try the big things, and begin to check out the credibility of the voices you hear in your head.

This is where a good therapist can help sort out what is you and what is not you. You need to begin to understand what messages are indeed true and dependable, and which ones are false. Additionally, a small group of mentally healthy, patient, gentle friends can encourage you in this walk to freedom and self-confidence. For the journey, you will need to take along your own determination to find yourself and not let your past define you today.

And that's why we've written this. Both of us know this journey. Both of us affirm the globally mobile life we have lived. We have also not only been stuck ourselves at points along the way, but we have seen others stuck too because they couldn't separate themselves from their system or from the messages that have run their lives. It matters to us to try to help you find out a bit more about your own journey because we do believe that the truth sets us free. And as you gain new freedom, may you pop right out of whichever box you saw yourself and run with patience and great joy the race that is the life before you.

# References

Anderson, Hans Christian. (1837). *The emperor's new clothes*. Retrieved from www.andersen.sdu.dk/vaerk/hersholt/TheEmperorsNewClothes_e. html

Pipher, Mary. (2003). *The middle of everywhere: The world's refugees come to our town*. Orlando, FL: Mariner Books.

Pollock, David C., & Van Reken, Ruth. (2009). *Third culture kids: Growing up among worlds* (rev). London/Boston: Nicholas Brealey Publishers.

Townsend, John & Cloud, Henry. (2003). *How people grow: What the bible reveals about personal growth*. Grand Rapids, MI: Zondervan Publishers.

Umbarger, Carter C. (1983). *Structural family therapy*. New York: Grune and Stratton.

Van Reken, Ruth, Wickstrom, David, & van Dalen, Emily. (2004). "Adult MKs Returning as Missionaries: Going Home?" Chapter 15. In Andrews, Leslie (Ed.) *The family in mission: Understanding and caring for those who serve*. Palmer Lake, CO: Mission Training International.

# Appendix B

# Emotionally Focused Therapy (EFT) Techniques for the Globally Mobile

*by*

## *Pamela S. Davis, Ph.D., and Keith J. Edwards, Ph.D.*

Allison is a successful, 27-year-old event planner who grew up in Zimbabwe and Tanzania but has been living in the U.S. since finishing high school. She attended college in the Midwest, graduated at the top of her class, and has attempted to "settle" into American life. Still, Allison says she doesn't really feel at home in the U.S. Some of her most difficult memories revolve around family sojourns to the U.S. while she was growing up. She lived in the U.S. and attended public schools during her fourth grade, eighth grade, and part of her eleventh grade years. With a wavering voice and tears in her eyes, Allison remarks to her counselor, "For as long as I live, I don't think I'll ever understand Americans. Sometimes I think I *hate* Americans. This country just isn't home to me."

For people like Allison, the process of reentry and acculturation to the passport country is considered to be one of the most difficult aspects of growing up abroad. Children often find repatriation even more challenging than their parents do, because core parts of their identity have been formed during their developmental years overseas. Add to that the frequent cultural transitions that create multiple experiences of loss for most expatriate families. As a result, two challenges that Third Culture Kids (TCKs) encounter include difficulty with cultural identity integration and unresolved grief. Counselors who work with the TCK population need effective strategies to help clients in these two important areas. Because the challenges that TCKs encounter take place in the context of relationships marked by emotionally intense experiences, Emotion Focused Therapy (EFT), which uses a process-experiential therapeutic approach, can be a useful model for counseling TCKs.

## Process-Experiential or Emotion-Focused Therapy

In the book, *Learning Emotion-Focused Therapy: The Process-Experiential Approach to Change* (2004), the authors suggest that intense emotions are activated during the making and breaking of attachment bonds. Emotions are also activated by experiences of challenge or threat to one's personal identity. Considering the multiple losses that TCKs face, as well as the challenge of creating a personal cultural identity after growing up abroad, EFT seems particularly well-suited to this population.

However, it is important to remember that the attachment and identity challenges TCKs face, while emotionally intense, do not always become problematic. In fact, many TCKs emerge from their childhood of cross-cultural living with a healthy identity, a rich history of secure attachments, and a resilience that is more robust than their monocultural peers. They experience what has come to be known in the positive psychology literature as *stress-induced growth*. What creates the difference? Why do some TCKs experience growth after multiple losses, emerging with a healthy cultural identity and secure attachments, while others struggle?

An important component of resilience during times of stress is healthy emotion regulation and processing. Parents and other caregivers, including counselors, play a crucial role in helping TCKs experience healthy emotions during stressful experiences. By tuning in to the child's needs, expressing empathy, and intentionally engaging in the child's world, caregivers can help children be aware of and tolerate their emotions, put their feelings into words, and recognize their needs. This then facilitates healthy, adaptive behaviors.

Considering the multiple transitions experienced by TCKs, the primary challenge is coping with losses of relationships and familiar environments. The primary emotion in such situations would be sadness, with a need for soothing and encouragement. Adaptive behaviors would include saying goodbye in a healthy way, creating memorials for their significant attachments, and grieving losses. TCKs may also feel angry at having to go through painful, stressful experiences that they have little or no control over. Some TCKs may bury these angry feelings, while others may choose to act out inappropriately. The challenge for parents and caregivers in these situations is to provide validation and empathic understanding of the anger while managing the child's verbal and behavioral expressions.

Identity problems are more difficult for caregivers to help TCKs manage, because they are not as noticeable as transition challenges. Often the emotional strain of TCK identity confusion does not become apparent until the person is in severe emotional or behavioral distress. EFT techniques are designed to help clients process their emotional experiences, validate their needs, and resolve unfinished business. As a result, clients create new personal meaning about their experiences and construct a new narrative about their self-identity.

EFT is an empirically supported therapeutic approach that uses empathy-based relating and active experiential techniques to help clients make meaning of their experiences. This approach is informed by current models of attachment and social-affective neuroscience (see Elliott & Greenberg, 2007). EFT suggests that the way we process emotion impacts the way we attach to others, the way we behave, and the way we create meaning about our experiences. The EFT model identifies three stages of therapy: emotion awareness, emotion regulation, and emotion transformation with problem resolution (see Greenberg, 2002).

### *Emotion awareness*

The first stage of EFT involves assisting clients to become more aware of their emotions. Emotion awareness tasks are aimed at increasing clients' abilities to access, experience, and verbalize their emotions. This allows them to make sense of their experience and helps them to integrate the experience as part of the rich, narrative story of their life. Emotional awareness is not merely *talking about* feelings; awareness involves re-experiencing the feelings with self-reflection and narration. The core process in EFT is for clients to re-experience their emotions as they tell their stories in the presence of an attuned, empathic counselor. This re-experiencing in-the-present allows clients to come to a new understanding of their emotions, perceptions, physical reactions, and behaviors as related to past conflicts, trauma, or unfinished business.

When using an EFT framework, counselors should be listening for client *markers*. Markers are in-session statements or behaviors that indicate the client is ready to work on a particular problem. Each marker is linked to an EFT task that is designed to resolve a particular problem.

The first of these tasks is termed ***Empathic Exploration***. Empathic Exploration is the core processing task in EFT, from which other markers emerge. The marker for Empathic Exploration occurs when the client relates an experience that was difficult, troubling, or puzzling to him or her. It is important for the counselor to be empathically attuned as clients talk about their experiences, so that the counselor can immediately facilitate deeper exploration. The goal of Empathic Exploration is to bring out into the open whatever may be at the edge of a client's awareness. During Empathic Exploration, counselors attempt to promote understanding, provide validation, and communicate acceptance to the client.

One way that counselors facilitate deeper Empathic Exploration is through the use of ***Empathic Understanding***. TCKs need to be able to understand their experiences in a safe, therapeutic relationship. The foundation of a safe relationship allows TCKs to approach painful and difficult emotional memories that may, for a variety of reasons, have been avoided or kept out of awareness.

A second way that counselors can deepen Empathic Exploration is through ***Empathic Validation***. The marker that a client can benefit from empathic validation is that a client expresses personal vulnerability or shares a painful emotion related to his or her view of self. In validating a client's experiences, the counselor implicitly communicates, "You make sense to me." When a counselor uses empathic validation, clients become more confident about their own level of emotional awareness and are increasingly willing to continue exploring their emotional experiences and behaviors. For example, when working with an adult TCK whose family had to flee the country very quickly following a terrorist attack, a counselor may respond, "Your family left so quickly, there wasn't time to say goodbye, and no one seemed to know how hard it was for you. You had such great friends there and leaving them was really hard." Empathic validations are especially effective when helping clients confront emotions they find unacceptable, confusing, or disorienting.

Some TKCs who present with significant spiritual struggles may benefit from having empathy and validation for their spiritual struggles. This validation may be particularly helpful for children of missionaries, who are often raised in a religious subculture that emphasizes sin. Thus, a TCK who is dealing with unresolved anger towards their missionary parent may believe that expressing anger toward that parent is "sinful." It can be effective to empathize with and validate both the client's anger and the spiritual struggle over expressing that anger. In these situations, a counselor's empathic validation can strengthen the client's ability to tolerate deeper emotional engagement and to become more open to exploring other experiences.

A third intervention that facilitates Empathic Exploration is the use of **Evocative Questions.** Evocative questions are open questions designed to evoke deeper exploration of what is happening internally, in the present moment, for the client. Evocative questions can help clients differentiate between external events and their internal responses to those events. For example, the counselor may ask, "What's happening right now, as you say that?" It is important for counselors to remember that EFT is an evocative therapy that can trigger difficult emotional memories. It is essential that as clients approach painful experiences, they be given tools to regulate their level of emotional arousal. Keep in mind that EFT is not merely about catharsis. The goal of emotional processing is to *gain access to, understand, and resolve problems that persist in the TCK's present-day experience.*

### Emotion regulation

Following emotion awareness, the second stage of therapy is emotion regulation. This stage involves assisting clients to experience their emotions at an appropriate level of arousal, so that they are better able to reflect upon and integrate their emotional experiences. Emotions that are under-regulated can overwhelm the client and inhibit the client's ability to cope. Emotions that are over-regulated or avoided can limit the client's ability to resolve these experiences. TCKs avoid painful and difficult emotions for a reason: Their feelings are distressing, hard to regulate, and difficult to resolve alone. Many times TCKs who over-regulate their emotions do so because they fear that the emotions may actually overwhelm them and they want to avoid under-regulation at all costs.

There are a variety of ways that counselors can help TCKs approach and regulate painful emotions. For example, counselors can assist clients to tolerate difficult emotions by teaching and practicing self-soothing skills (e.g., deep breathing, muscle relaxation, mindfulness, contemplative prayer/meditation), both during and between counseling sessions. Counselors can also encourage TCK clients to adopt a safe, "working-distance" from their experience, perhaps encouraging them to view the experience as if they are in an airplane at 10,000 feet and looking down. Also, it is helpful for the counselor to validate the difficulty of experiencing painful emotions and to affirm the client's efforts to regulate their emotions and self-soothe (even if those efforts are not successful).

TCKs who have trauma and abuse histories are especially at-risk for becoming emotionally flooded, and so these techniques for emotion regulation may be especially applicable to TCKs with trauma history. It is now well-established that for traumatic memories to be transformed, they need to be activated and experientially accessed. However, counselors want to keep in mind that for the processing of traumatic emotions to be effective, the level of emotional arousal needs to be at a moderate and manageable level, until distress subsides. When clients effectively learn emotional regulation, they are ready to move on to the next stage and transform, or resolve, their emotional experiences.

### *Emotion transformation and problem resolution*

The third stage of EFT is emotion transformation and problem resolution. Although the EFT framework suggests many helpful techniques for this stage of therapy, there are three tasks that seem particularly suited for work with TCK clients: Meaning Protest, Empty Chair to Resolve Unfinished Business, and Two-Chair for Critical Splits.

## Meaning protest

Remember that EFT counselors listen for *markers* that indicate a client is ready to work on a particular problem. The marker that indicates a client is ready for the *Meaning Protest* task is when he or she shares a difficult or traumatic experience that violates cherished beliefs. The TCK might describe some loss, crisis, or trauma that violates what they always believed to be true. For example, one adult TCK whose parents were missionaries in Europe was raped at age 16, while at a mall with friends. For her, this experience was a direct violation of what she was taught about what it means to trust God for care and protection. This created a challenge for her to make sense of difficult life experiences. Other TCKs who are wrestling with Meaning Protest may experience a crisis of faith in their religious world view that is upsetting to them and puts them at odds with their parents and their religious community. They may struggle with resentment toward parents and God for being taken to difficult environments because of their parents' sense of calling to work cross-culturally. If the TCK has suffered abuse or neglect in the country where they grew up, the crises of faith and trust can be overwhelming.

When an EFT counselor hears a crisis-of-meaning marker in a client's story, the Meaning Protest process begins by the counselor calling attention to the cherished belief that the client holds and then helping the client to identify their emotional responses to the challenging event. This is followed by a time of reflecting with the client how the cherished belief came about. The client can then explore and evaluate whether the cherished belief is true and whether it is valuable to continue holding onto that belief. During this process, the counselor remains attuned to the client and empathically reflects any alternate, emerging ideas about the client's cherished beliefs. The Meaning Protest task concludes as the client and counselor explore what the consequences of revising the cherished belief might be and identifying any actions that might need to be enacted. For the TCK mentioned earlier who was raped at age 16, her Meaning Protest work involved clarifying that although she held a cherished belief that God would protect her and her family since they were missionaries, God never actually promised her such safety. Instead, He promised to never leave her and to help her through all situations. For this client, she could see that her cherished belief that God would always protect her was not true and was hindering her getting on with her life.

## Empty chair technique for unfinished business

Another EFT technique that is particularly useful when working with TCK clients is that of the *Empty Chair* technique for helping to resolve unfinished business. A primary source of unfinished business for TCKs is unresolved grief. Unresolved grief for the TCK can be multi-faceted. The cross-cultural experiences that many TCKs feel especially proud of also are associated with multiple, repeated losses.

The same life of exciting travel that gives them friends on every continent also precipitates many painful losses. They build solid friendships that are torn apart by furloughs, re-assignment, graduation, or an unexpected crisis. Frequently, the time to leave a country occurs without any attempt to say goodbye to special people or special places, and so the TCK leaves the host country with a great deal of unfinished business. Sometimes parents may inadvertently throw out possessions that are important to the child simply because there is not enough room in the luggage. In such cases, the child is left not only with the loss but unresolved resentment toward the parents. At other times, a natural disaster or terrorist incident necessitates the TCK leaving the country immediately, without a chance for needed emotional closure. Other examples of unfinished business, resulting in unresolved grief among TCKs, include painful emotional experiences with boarding school or agency personnel in the country that was left behind and emotional abuse emanating from the host culture—such as touching, crowding, staring, laughing, and teasing brought on by the TCK's ethnic differences from the national population.

Considering these experiences from an EFT framework, it is important to remember that one of the ways people handle emotionally overwhelming experiences is to deny or block the expression of their needs and feelings. However, these unexpressed feelings and unmet needs remain in the person's emotional memory scheme. Whenever that emotion scheme is evoked, even years later in a seemingly unrelated situation, the memories and related painful feelings are often experienced again. Feelings of resentment and hurt are the most common markers of this type of unfinished business, and these markers signal to the counselor that using the Empty Chair technique may be beneficial.

The Empty Chair dialogue begins with the client evoking a memory of a person or place with whom they have unfinished business. Counselors may assist clients by instructing them to involve as many of their senses as possible as they bring the imagined person into the room. What was the imagined other wearing? Did they smell a particular way? What were the atmosphere and the decor in the room? Next, the counselor facilitates the client speaking to the imagined other, expressing any unresolved feelings. It is important for the client to name specific situations and then connect those situations to any emotions such as sadness, fear, or anger that the situation may have elicited. Thus, the Empty Chair technique, which is a part of the Emotion Resolution stage of therapy, builds upon the foundational work accomplished during the first two stages of Emotion Awareness and Emotion Regulation.

The turning point in Empty Chair work comes when the client is able to identify, validate, and finally express unmet needs. Sometimes, only partial resolution emerges. In these situations, the client may be able to identify that her needs were unmet and express those needs to the person in the empty chair. Often, even this partial resolution brings about better understanding and acceptance of the situation and people involved. Full resolution comes when the client can affirm her own unmet needs and resolve those feelings by imagining and enacting alternative behaviors. For example, using an Empty Chair dialogue, a client may be able to move beyond what actually happened at the time in order to express sadness, say goodbye, forgive others, or hold others accountable.

For TCKs, using the Empty Chair technique may involve visualizing a friend from childhood sitting in the chair and expressing feelings that were left unsaid when the TCK left the country years ago. It may involve expressing angry feelings toward a teacher or boarding house parent at the overseas school that the TCK attended, while visualizing the offending person in the empty chair. It may involve resolving unfinished business with the TCK's parents, since some TCK issues center around unresolved grief and unmet needs engendered by the parents' decision to work overseas.

It is important to emphasize the here-and-now principles of the model. The *Empty Chair* technique is guided by in-the-present statements and markers of unfinished business. The technique does not attempt to delve into the past looking for unfinished business. The marker alerts the EFT counselor that the past is continuing to influence the client's present because of unresolved issues. The *Empty Chair* task focuses on the here-and-now experiencing of feelings in order to promote resolution and create new emotional meaning.

As applied to the specific TCK experience, this technique is useful because it helps TCKs to re-experience their feelings in the present moment, rather than intellectualizing what should have been felt in the past or what should be felt presently. Some TCKs are hesitant to acknowledge painful feelings about living overseas, because they are afraid that admitting any pain may negate the many joys of their overseas experience. Thus, they become reluctant to acknowledge pain of any kind regarding their experiences. Their avoidance of difficult emotions prevents resolution of the experience by blocking their ability to make meaning. For other TCKs, acknowledging these feelings may be painful or scary because they have received a subtle (or sometimes not so subtle) message from an authority figure suggesting that it is not acceptable to express their grief. This is an especially potent message in the military and missionary communities.

As noted earlier, establishing a positive therapeutic relationship through Empathic Exploration and Emotion Regulation is foundational to implementing the Empty Chair technique. When counselors offer unconditional acceptance, empathy, validation, and genuine presence, TCKs will be more apt to face the painful, anxiety-producing aspects of their experiences. A positive therapeutic relationship increases the likelihood that the TCK will participate in the Empty Chair dialogue. Although the Empty Chair technique is powerful, some clients are initially reluctant to engage in the process. This may be especially true when working with adolescents or young adult TCKs, who may feel embarrassed or self-conscious when the Empty Chair technique is proposed. In these situations, counselors can alter the task slightly by asking the client to write a letter to the person first, before using the actual dialogue.

## Two-chair dialogue for conflict splits

A final technique of EFT that is useful when working with TCKs is the *Two-Chair Dialogue*. The Two-Chair Dialogue in EFT is typically used when a client expresses some type of internal conflict or split. The classic marker for this task is when the client describes conflict between two parts of the self, stating that this internal conflict is producing emotional distress. Thus, the Two-Chair Dialogue may be very useful for helping TCKs resolve identity conflicts and confusion.

Inherent in the experience of nearly all TCKs is confusion regarding cultural identity and belonging. For most people, personal identity involves identification with a home country—yet the concept of home can be ambiguous and indefinable to TCKs. On one hand, home is the passport country; the place where their parents were raised and where their relatives live. On the other hand, home is the country or countries (or places) where they spent their formative years: where they grew up, went to school, and made their best friends.

This frequent mobility between cultures produces a significant challenge when considered in light of Erikson's psychosocial stages of development. Often, as TCKs begin to approach the stage of development referred to by Erikson as "Identity versus Identity Diffusion," they are required to leave one country and culture and move to a different country. Some TCKs move multiple times during their adolescence. One way that counselors can assist TCK clients to formulate a more solid cultural identity is by utilizing the Two-Chair Dialogue of EFT.

A marker that a client may benefit from a Two-Chair Dialogue is when he expresses to the counselor that he has separate and distinct parts of himself that seem rooted in distinct cultures, and these parts seem to be in conflict or confusing to him. In this case, exploring and clarifying the distinct cultural parts the client experiences must precede the Two-Chair task. Once the identification of these separate parts has occurred and some tension point is clarified, the dialogue can begin. The classic Two-Chair task typically begins with the most critical, judgmental voice speaking to the other. The goal of the task is to soften the critic, identify the needs of the critic and the self, and then facilitate integration of the two parts.

For TCKs who are experiencing cultural identity "splits," the counselor and client need to collaborate in determining which self-part speaks first. Typically, it is helpful to begin with the part that is most critical of the other part. Remember Allison, the TCK client presented at the beginning of the chapter who expressed disdain for Americans after growing up in Africa? In this case, the counselor might ask her to begin with a clear sense of her African identity. She would be encouraged in the Two-Chair Dialogue to express criticism, disdain, and any sense of cultural superiority or incompatibility with her American identity. The counselor might also prompt her to argue for competing advantages and disadvantages of the African and American cultures. As the dialogue ensues, the counselor will need to listen carefully for where there might be tension between cultural parts, and focus on those areas.

At certain points during the dialogue, particularly when powerfully evocative statements are made, the counselor might ask Allison to shift chairs (voices/identities), and speak from the other voice (cultural identity). The key question asked when the client switches chairs is, "How do you feel when you hear her say that?" The intent is to evoke the deeper meanings being experienced during the dialogue, allow both parts to express unmet needs to the other, and bring about integration between the two parts.

## Conclusion

The EFT model is a well-established therapy framework that emphasizes in-the-moment, experiential transformation of emotionally charged memories that are unresolved. In their unresolved state, emotion schemes continue to impact clients either by inhibiting them as they attempt to block painful memories or by disrupting them when they become emotionally overwhelmed. EFT is based on the current understanding of emotion as it relates to the two most important tasks in child development—attachment bonding and identity formation. The chair work tasks discussed in this chapter are the most well-known tasks in the EFT model. Their use must be embedded in the EFT three-phase model of (1) *Emotion Awareness*, (2) *Emotion Regulation*, and (3) *Emotion Resolution*. Emotionally evocative techniques can be very powerful and helpful, but they can also be harmful. Emotional expression is only a means to the end of deeper processing and transformation of experiential memories. Experiential work with emotionally evocative memories must be grounded in adequate theory, sound clinical and empirical research, and a well-specified therapy process. EFT appears robust on all of these accounts.

Work with TCKs using the EFT model should always begin with the *Empathic Exploration* task. Exploring relationships and identities in a safe, empathic, validating environment can bring much relief and healing resolution for TCKs. During *Empathic Exploration*, the counselor is also establishing a collaborative relationship with the client that is a necessary foundation from which to launch the more evocative tasks described above. *Meaning Protest* is actually a special form of *Empathic Exploration* in which a TCK's difficult history can be explored in light of his or her worldview and cherished beliefs. For TCKs whose experiences have alienated them from the worldview of their families, *Meaning Protest* is an essential process for them to come to terms with their pain and their own worldview beliefs.

Many TCKs readily express awareness of their ambivalent, two-culture self, and for this reason they may respond more favorably to participating in a *Two-Chair* dialogue than they would to participating in an *Empty Chair* dialogue. Unresolved grief tends to be more of a hidden issue for TCKs. They may be more likely to openly acknowledge their multiple cultural identities. From this perspective, counselors utilizing these techniques with TCKs may be wise to begin with a *Two-Chair* dialogue for cultural identity integration and later introduce an *Empty Chair* technique for resolution of grief. The EFT model provides guidance for the counselor regarding which intervention to use by identifying problematic markers.

As counselors, it is wise to remember that although TCKs face unique challenges, there are also numerous benefits that occur as a result of being raised cross-culturally. Many parents of TCKs—whether they are military personnel, missionaries, government workers, or businessmen working overseas—wrestle with ambivalent feelings regarding raising their children overseas because of the challenges that are inherent in such an experience. There are no clear-cut responses to such difficult questions, no easily defined rights and wrongs.

Perhaps we would do better to reflect on the notion of *dialectic tension* (Elliott, Watson, Goldman, & Greenberg, 2004). As we come to understand the dynamic energy of dialectic tensions, we can more readily embrace both the good and the bad, the pain and the joy surrounding the TCK experience. It is when TCKs are able to experience both sides of the tension that true healing begins. It is for this reason that EFT techniques such *as Empathic Exploration, Meaning Protest, Empty Chair*, and the *Two-Chair* dialogue can be beneficial when used with a TCK population. In these techniques, change occurs because emotions are re-experienced in a way that facilitates the creation of a new, integrated meaning.

---

*The ideas in this chapter have been expanded and adapted from the following classic works on Emotion-Focused Therapy:*

Elliott, R., & Greenberg, L. S. (2007). The essence of process-experiential/ emotion-focused therapy. *American Journal of Psychotherapy, 61*(3), 241–54.

Elliott, R., Watson, J. C., Goldman, R., & Greenberg, L. (2004). *Learning emotion-focused therapy: The process-experiential approach to change.* Washington, DC: American Psychological Association.

Greenberg, L.S. (2002). *Emotion-focused therapy: Coaching clients to work through their feelings.* Washington, DC: American Psychological Association.

Pam Davis is an Assistant Professor at the Wheaton College Graduate School, where she teaches in the M.A. program in Clinical Mental Health Counseling. She has an M.A. in Counseling Ministries and a Ph.D. in Counselor Education and Supervision. Pam spent 22 years as a missionary in Thailand, serving first as a teacher of missionaries' kids and later as a professional counselor for missionary families. Although currently living in Wheaton, Illinois, she remains actively involved in missionary issues through both research and direct services to missionaries and their families.

Keith Edwards is currently Professor of Psychology at Rosemead School of Psychology, Biola University. He holds an M.A. and Ph.D. in quantitative methods and a Ph.D. in clinical psychology. Dr. Edwards is a licensed clinical psychologist, specializing in marriage therapy. He has taught family life and mental health seminars and provided therapy to missionary families and member care workers in Europe, Africa, Asia, Mexico, and South America as a staff associate of the Narramore Christian Foundation in Arcadia, California. He lives in Hacienda Heights, California, with his wife, Ginny, who is a retired elementary school teacher. The Edwards have been married since 1966 and have 3 married children and six grandchildren.

# Appendix C

# The TCK Wall of Fame

If I were to establish my own "Wall of Fame" of those individuals who have contributed to the field of Third Culture Kids since Dr. Ruth Useem, it would include the following individuals. These are my heroes and I encourage you to get to know them and their writings. They have much to teach all of us about this field. I want to give you a glimpse into how they fit in this movement and their reasons for their passion for understanding and helping TCKs. Each one of them has an inspiring story.

## David Pollock

During the early 1960's, Dave Pollock, a young college student in Houghton, New York, became interested in working with TCKs. But it was not until 1975 when he and his wife, Betty Lou, along with their four children, moved to the beautiful Rift Valley in Kenya, Africa that his research career really started. Among their many responsibilities with the mission agency for which they worked was serving as dorm parents for adolescent boys at Rift Valley Academy (RVA), a boarding school for missionary kids. This experience at RVA gave Dave the solid foundation for his future passion as the ambassador for Third Culture Kids around the world. He spent hours listening to the stories told by missionary kids, of the joys and challenges of their world.

Upon his return to the United States in the mid-1980s, Dave founded the organization Interaction International whose mission was "to provide and contribute to an ongoing flow of care that meets the needs of Third Culture Kids (TCKs) and internationally mobile families." Through Interaction International he expanded his work beyond missionary families to include Foreign Service, military, and international business families. He traveled to many countries and groups, speaking to TCKs, parents, schools, organizational leaders, and caregivers about the "flow of care" for the TCK from childhood into their adult years. Dave was recognized as the authority or spokesman on the topic of TCKs. He spent many long hours traveling literally around the world and listening to TCKs of all ages, all sectors, and varied careers and statuses. TCKs would frequently feel they were completely understood by this man with a well-groomed, white beard who would be quick to shed a tear or two as he sat and listened. (www.interactionintl.org/whoisdavepollock.asp)

In 1984, Dave co-directed the first International Conference for Missionary Kids (ICMK) held in the Philippines. This event was important, not only because it was the first large conference centered on the new topic of Third Culture Kids, but because of the friendship that was formed at that conference between Dave Pollock and Ruth Van Reken. Ruth would later take up Dave's passion and run with it after his untimely death in 2004 while speaking in Vienna, Austria, on his favorite topic of Third Culture Kids.

## Ruth Van Reken

Ruth Van Reken is one of those individuals who gives and gives and gives, not even thinking of setting limits on her devotion of time and energy to others. Even though Ruth lives only a few miles from my home and office, I rarely see her. Why? She is constantly traveling to talk to and about TCKs. If she isn't on the road or in the air or at a conference, she always has company either staying a few days in their "home away from home," chatting over a meal, or a dropping in for a cup of coffee. She stays up until the late hours of the night listening to their stories and then goes down to her basement office to answer the emails of TCKs who pour out their hearts to her via the Internet. She gets up the next morning to do it all over again. Time after time, Ruth reaches out to TCKs to listen, encourage, nudge, teach, and cheer them on. If their problems are beyond her, she sends them to me for counseling! Even at times, she pays out of her own pocket for their therapy. Ruth is a "nurturing mother" to hundreds. And her husband, David, is the quiet, calming, reassuring voice in the shadows supporting his wife. Ruth has seen the need and uses her resources and skills to fill that need. Even though she is not a therapist, she does an exceptional job of doing what she can to come alongside the TCK.

The field continues to grow and develop as new ideas come to the forefront. Ruth Van Reken is one of the few pioneers who is still with us today. Her brain never stops, even though her counterparts are no longer around to brainstorm with her. She surrounds herself with young graduate students, thinkers, philosophers, researchers, and anyone who wants to contribute to the discussion. Out of this interaction she has launched into some new and exciting concepts. She also serves as the chief encourager of those writing on the topic of TCKs and attempts to match workers in the field with writers and editors and to bring people together in myriad ways to further the education about and for TCKs, their families, their counselors, and their friends.

## Norma McCaig

Norma McCaig was a TCK who grew up in the Philippines, Sri Lanka, and India because her father was an international business executive. Because she sensed that her experiences as a "corporate kid" were similar to TCKs and those of other sectors, she attended the second International Conference on Missionary Kids (ICMK) held in Quito, Ecuador in 1987. Norma was the only non-mission representative in the conference. She wanted to explore her ideas with this group gathered in Ecuador as she grappled with what exactly constituted a global nomad. Norma and Ruth spent hours talking and were amazed at the connections between their worlds even though they had not grown up in the same part of the world or come from the same sector.

The following year, 1988, Norma founded Global Nomads International (GNI) and was the first to offer a conference for all global nomads from all sectors. It was dubbed "a gathering of old friends meeting for the first time." Ruth was one of the presenters at this first conference of global nomads in Washington, DC, that year. Norma is also credited for coining the terms "cultural chameleon" and "hidden immigrant."

I first met Norma at a Families in Global Transition (FIGT) conference in Indianapolis, Indiana. I sat in her workshop and listened to this very friendly, redheaded, intelligent woman share her knowledge and enthusiasm for Global Nomads. She encouraged me to use my own experience as a Global Nomad to help others during their times of transition. Her enthusiasm was contagious.

During the last years of her life when she was dealing with cancer, she would talk about her dream to have just another conference for Global Nomads. Her passion was to continue to develop the literature and to continue to organize groups of Global Nomads on university campuses. Like her friend, Dave Pollock, Norma died during the prime of her life.

## Elsie Purnell

A number of years ago I met a very compassionate lady who had worked for many years in the missions community primarily in Thailand. Elsie Purnell was one of the first people I met who was actively involved in helping TCKs make the transition from living outside their passport country to life in a world that was supposed to be their home country. Elsie was a quiet and very nurturing person. When she found out that I was a TCK, she instantly took an interest in me as a person and then in my career as a counselor.

Elsie had eight support groups for adult TCKs from Santa Barbara to San Diego, all in southern California. Although she never passed up an opportunity to talk with TCKs of whatever age and wherever she met them, she did not base any of her groups on college students. She felt they weren't old enough to really process their experiences. The age she preferred to have in her groups was 35 and older; some were in their 60s.

She formed support groups that would continue to meet without her—this was never her goal—and help one another. The support groups were for ATCKs to meet, discuss issues, and be a help to each other. Occasionally, if she couldn't be there for some reason, one of the group might try to facilitate the meeting based on what Elsie had planned. But these were one-off events. However, they didn't run for long without her and ceased to exist after she could no longer meet with them. She was indispensable to the groups because of her empathy, her varied experiences, and her ability to connect with TCKs. She showed videos that TCKs felt reflected their experience and introduced and chose readings that would create insightful and lively discussion.

She gleaned much knowledge from what she learned from these "kids." Her own experience with her own TCK children, observations, extensive reading of the literature regarding TCKs, and discussions with groups such as the one where I met her at a Missions and Mental Health Conference, gave her a wealth of wisdom. Sadly, Elsie died after a long struggle with cancer.

## Robin Pascoe

Robin Pascoe is another one who, even though she is not a trained therapist, has for many years filled the vacuum in the field of helping TCKs, particularly the parents of TCKs. Robin accompanied her husband, Rodney, a diplomat from Ottawa, Canada, to many postings in Asia with their two young children. Robin, a journalist, quickly learned that she could not get a job in the countries where they were stationed. She thus began to write about their experiences as a family. She wrote several books on the subject of raising a family while living an international life.

I remember well the first time that I met Robin. I was attending a Families in Global Transition Conference, and was trying to figure out which session I would attend as none of the sessions offered that particular hour seemed to be of special interest to me. I was outside the door to Robin's session on a "Moveable Marriage." I heard laughter coming from the room, so I stuck my head in the door and saw that the room was packed and thought, "Hmm, she must be a good speaker. I guess I will stay, even though I am single and this topic doesn't apply to me." I squeezed my way through the maze of chairs and tables to the only remaining seat, front and center. This woman with wild curly hair, a dry sense of humor, and a talk filled with blunt statements drew me in right from the start. I found myself laughing and crying at her stories. I identified with her style of presentation and most of all with what she was saying. She was talking about my life as a Third Culture Kid and what I had experienced and was continuing to experience. Robin was accurately dubbed "The Expat Expert." Robin knew the TCK. And as a journalist, she knew how to describe that life.

A number of years later, Robin published the book *Raising Global Nomads: Parenting Abroad in an On-Demand World* in 2006. I had the honor of writing a chapter for that book on "Keeping Your Family in Good Mental Health." Robin, one of the pioneers in this field and now retired, still has a big heart for helping families adjust to global living.

She ends her book on Global Nomads with the following statement:

> Nurturing young people is never more critical than when you are living abroad. Help your children to become sturdy, to take sustenance in the roots of your family and the experiences you share. Assist them as they negotiate the inevitable obstacles that block their paths, but make them do the heavy lifting. Then you can stand back and watch your children thrive, secure in the knowledge that you have done your very best in raising your global nomad." (Pascoe, 2006, p. 205)

Robin saw a need to help the family through her books, blog, and a wealth of resources on her website. She has given the counseling community a wealth of information.

## Families in Global Transition (FIGT)

The next big piece in the history of the TCK world took place in 1998 in Indianapolis, Indiana, with the formation of Families in Global Transition (FIGT). Four women from the Association of International Women sat around Ruth Van Reken's kitchen table to brainstorm how they could bring together those from various sectors (missions, military, educational, diplomatic, corporate) to learn from one another about the internationally mobile *family*. Their mission was "to bring together those living this global lifestyle with those working with them, and create a dialog that would be good for all." They were four housewives on a mission—with no money. They had lived the experience and wanted to help others to do it better.

On May 16, 1998, they had their first conference with Dave Pollock as their plenary speaker in a meeting room at Eli Lilly, a local pharmaceutical company. The night before the conference, Ruth invited all of the attendees to her home to meet Dave Pollock. This was the first time I met Dave and Ruth. My life and career were to be forever impacted that next day as I listened to Dave give the "The TCK Profile." This was also the weekend when I struck up a long-lasting friendship with Ruth Van Reken, Dave Pollock, and Matt Neigh who worked alongside Dave in Interaction International.

At the second FIGT conference, a Board of Directors was formed to lead this new organization. President Beverly Roman chaired this new Board consisting of Matthew Neigh, Sally Lipscomb, Paulette Bethel, Ruth Van Reken, Lois Bushong, Barbara Schaetti, and Samuel Britten.

**Beverly Roman,** an author of several books on helping the family make effective transitions around the world and the founder of BR Anchor Publishing, took FIGT, a "mom and pop" organization, and used her watchful eye over the little details and her nurturing to turn it into a professional organization with structure.

Families in Global Transition conferences continue to be the "think tank" for empowering families as they move throughout the world. The FIGT website states,

> FIGT has, for over ten years, led the worldwide community in empowering families and those who serve them in global transition. FIGT is the premier advocate and educational resource for families, organizations and service providers. We build our global community by bringing together corporate, diplomatic, academic, the arts, military, missionary, and NGO sectors to share and develop leading edge research and concepts that address international relocation issues. (www.figt.org)

As the organization has continued to grow and ultimately become recognized as the conference of choice for those organizations and individuals interested in helping families make a good international transition, it has attracted more and more psychologists, mental health therapists, and coaches. The FIGT annual conference is a gathering of adult TCKs, researchers, parents of TCKs, human resources directors of international agencies, educators, and mental health providers

Most recently, **Dr. Ann Baker Cattrell,** a researcher from San Diego University in California, and **Dr. Rebecca Powell,** Director of Religious Education for the U.S. Army, organized the FIGT Research Network. A number of graduate students have been very active in this group of researchers on families in transition. As a former FIGT Board member, Dr. Duncan Westwood, stated, "FIGT is where research comes to life."

## Sam Britten

In 2001 I heard Samuel Britten, a TCK who grew up in the military, give an interesting talk titled "My Home is My Backpack." His session was packed with many TCKs in the audience who were grappling with the question, "Where is home?" Sam developed the first TCK website (TCK World) which at that time was the only website for TCKs and was very popular. Sam, as a founding board member, was instrumental in helping FIGT with the myriad of legal documents that were needed for establishing a new not-for-profit organization.

During his session, he handed out a chart on which he had compared each of four major sectors (Corporate, Foreign Service, Military and Missionary). I found Sam's chart intriguing as it compared the degree of mobility, interaction with locals, educational options, and the level of attachment to their immediate world for TCKs from each of the four major sectors. Sam is one of those individuals with a brilliant mind and many skills in the legal and technical world.

## Doug Ota & Barbara Schaetti

There are many fine counselors with great insight into the lives of their students who are working with young TCKs in international schools, American schools, and boarding schools. One example of these counselors is Dr. Doug Ota. Doug and several co-workers founded the "Transitions Program Team" now called "Safe Harbour" at the American School of The Hague located in the Netherlands. Dr. Barbara Schaetti served as their trainer and consultant. Doug is an adult CCK and Barbara is an adult TCK. The program they developed is one of the premiere programs to be found in the International Schools. Doug still works in the international school scene, not as a counselor in the school itself, but as a consultant in helping others set up their own transition programs. This handsome, young man with a brilliant mind is a great example of a counselor who understands the challenges and the makeup of the CCK. (www.dougota.nl)

Barbara also continues to work with international schools, consulting primarily on integrated approaches for addressing developmental intercultural competence. Through both virtual and in-person services, she is using her skills to help people and organizations develop leadership from the "inside out." Her business is based out of Seattle, Washington. (www.transition-dynamics.com)

## Becky Grappo

I have had the joy of meeting several consultants in the international school systems such as Rebecca (Becky) Grappo. Becky started out working as an Education and Youth Officer for the U.S. Department of State from 2002 to 2006. There her role was to be the advocate for and serve as a guide for Foreign Service families as they navigated their way through various assignments around the world. Becky left the State Department in 2006 and founded RNG International Educational Consultants. She still works mainly with expats and international students and does a marvelous job of matching up the educational needs of students with the right schools and universities. One of the things that impressed me with Becky was when she sees a student struggling emotionally she works hard to match them up with a professional counselor who can help that young person. Becky has a heart for TCKs. Yet, as we talked several months ago, the resounding question she asked was "Where are the counselors who are trained in working with TCKs?"

## Tina Quick

A new player in the field of working primarily with TCKs is Tina Quick, the author of *The Global Nomad's Guide to University Transition* published in 2010. Tina was raised in a military family and then, as an adult, she followed her husband's career to four continents with their three daughters.

When I asked her why she wrote a book on TCKs, her response was:

> I wrote the book because I kept running into TCKs from all the places we lived overseas. In discussions with them and their other TCK friends, I began hearing the same, familiar, but sad stories over and over again. I kept listening to TCKs talk about feelings of alienation, isolation, and depression. I just thought, "It doesn't have to be this way." If these students knew a few things about themselves

and their life experiences, they would have a much smoother adjustment. So I wrote the book to tell them about it. (Personal email on February 29, 2012)

Tina is not a therapist, but is a nurse who is a good listener due to her medical training. As a result, she has had many college-aged TCKs share their stories with her. Often she is asked to share some pointers with university counselors on how to better their services to the international student. She takes that opportunity to do some training on what a TCK is and how they can tailor their therapy to meet the needs of that student population.

## Josh Sandoz

In August of 2009, Josh Sandoz, a TCK and therapist, launched the International Therapist Directory website in hopes of connecting TCKs with counselors who do understand the world of the TCK. In his first blog, he gives us a glimpse into why he is passionate about his website.

> The emails came in from women and men of all ages, individuals concerned either for their own sake or for a son or daughter who were [sic] struggling and wanting to meet with a therapist who really "gets it" with respect to the cultural and lifestyle components of living an internationally mobile life. Those who wrote were having a hard time finding a therapist in their location who claimed to have these familiarities, and as I joined them in their search, I too found the hunt to be both painstaking and difficult. Something needed to be done. (http://.internationaltherapistdirectory.com)

As one of those few therapists who was constantly answering the same types of emails as Josh—and searching for that therapist for someone in a faraway state who understood the world of the TCK or someone who may not be a TCK but had spent their entire adult life traveling the world—I am so happy to see 36 countries listed so far on Josh's website. Currently, the number of therapists in a country can vary from one to 85 (U.S.). This is encouraging, but we need so many more therapists who are trained in this field. Josh is a fellow TCK and therapist who shares my passion of making available more well-trained mental health therapists who understand the uniqueness, the challenges, and the beauty of this international heritage.

# Resources

## Creative Arts

*Reflection Photos* by Anne P. Copeland: www.interchangeinstitute.org

Artwork on TCK life by Beth Eisinger: www.thefinetoothedcomb.etsy.com

*A.H. Dance Company* by Alaine Handa: www.ahdancecompany.com

*Handbook of Art Therapy, 2nd Edition,* edited by Cathy A. Malchiodi (2012). New York: The Guilford Press.

## Books

*The Family in Mission: Understanding and Caring for Those Who Serve*, edited by Leslie A. Andrews (2004). Palmer Lake, CO: Missionary Training Institute.

*Writing out of Limbo: International Childhoods, Global Nomads and Third Culture Kids,* edited by Gene Bell-Villada and Nina Sichel (2012). Newcastle Upon Tyne, UK: Cambridge Scholars.

*Raising Resilient MKs,* edited by Joyce M. Bowers (1998). Colorado Springs, CO: Association of Christian Schools International.

*Mixed Heritage: Your Source for Books for Children and Teens about Persons and Families of Mixed Racial, Ethnic, and/or Religious Heritage*, by Catherine Blakemore (2012). Albany, WI: Adams-Pomeroy Press.

*Global Baby,* by Anne Copeland (2004). Brookline, MA: The Interchange Institute.

*Unrooted Childhoods: Memoirs of Growing up Global,* edited by Faith Eidse and Nina Sichel (2004). Yarmouth, ME: Intercultural Press.

*The Global Soul: Jet Lag, Shopping Malls, and the Search for Home,* by Pico Iyer (2000). New York: Vintage Books.

*You Know You're An MK When . . .,* by Andy Kerr and Deborah Kerr (1999). Self-Published: mk@cheerful.com

*Notes from a Traveling Childhood: Readings for International Mobile Parents and Children,* edited by Karen Curnow McCluskey (1994). Washington, DC: Foreign Youth Service Foundation.

*Raising Global Nomads: Parenting Abroad in an On-Demand World,* by Robin Pascoe (2006). Vancouver, Canada: Expatriate Press.

*Expat Teens Talk: Peers, Parents and Professionals Offer Support, Advice and Solutions in Response to Expat Life Challenges as Shared by Expat Teens,* by Lisa Pittman and Diana Smit (2012). Great Britain: Summertime.

*Third Culture Kids: Growing Up among Worlds,* by David C. Pollack and Ruth E. Van Reken (2009). Boston: Nicholas Brealey.

*The Global Nomad's Guide to University Transition,* by Tina Quick (2010). Great Britain: Summertime.

*Strangers at Home,* by Carolyn Smith (1996). Bayside, NY: Aletheia.

*Letters Never Sent: A Global Nomad's Journey from Hurt to Healing,* by Ruth Van Reken (2012). Great Britain: Summertime.

*Military Brats: Legacies of Childhood inside the Fortress,* by Mary Edwards Wertsch (1991). Bayside, NY: Aletheia.

## Children's Books

*We Are Moving,* by Rachel Biale (1996). Berkeley, CA: Tricycle Press.

*Moving House,* by Anne Civardi and Stephen Cartwright (1985). Tulsa, OK: EDC.

*Sammy's Next Move: Sammy the Snail Is a Traveling Snail Who Lives in Different Countries,* by Helen Maffini (2011). CreateSpace Independent Publishing.

*Footsteps Around the World: Relocation Tips for Teens,* by Beverly Roman (1999). Wilmington, NC: BR Anchor.

*Let's Move Overseas: The International Edition of Let's Make a Move,* by Beverly Roman (1999). Wilmington, NC: BR Anchor.

*Let's Move Together,* by Carol Schubeck (1998). Orange, CA: Suitcase Press.

*When Abroad Do as the Local Children Do,* by Hilly Van Swol-Ulbrich and Bettina Kaltenhauser (2002). The Netherlands: X-Pat Media.

*The Kids' Guide to Living Abroad,* by Martine Zoer (2007). Washington, DC: Foreign Service Youth Foundation.

## Digital Magazines for TCKs

*Denizen* magazine: www.denizenmag.com

## International Counselors

American Association for Marriage & Family Therapy (AAMFT): www.aamft.org

American Counseling Association: www.counseling.org

American Psychological Association (APA): www.apa.org

EMDR International Association (EMDRIA): www.emdria.org

International Therapists Directory: www.internationaltherapists.com

# Movies

*All God's Children* (2008). Directed by Scott Solary and Luci Westphal.

*Amreeka* (2009). Produced by First Generation Films, Directed by Cherien Dabis.

*Bend It Like Beckham* (2002). Produced by Kintop Pictures, Directed by Gurinder Chadha.

*Brats: Our Journey Home* (2005). Produced by Beth Goodwin and Donna Musil, Directed by Donna Musil.

*Edge of America* (2003). Produced by Showtime Networks, Directed by Chris Eyre.

*Home Again: A Documentary about Missionary Kids* (In production). Directed by Julie Englander.

*Les Passagers: A TCK Story* (In production). Directed by Aga Magdolen.

*Mean Girls* (2004). Produced by Paramount Pictures, Directed by Mark Waters.

*Neither Here Nor There* (2011). Produced and Directed by Ema Ryan Yamazaki.

*Somewhere Between* (2011). Produced by Long Shot Factory, Directed by Linda Goldstein Knowlton.

*The Great Santini* (1979). Produced by Bing Crosby Productions, Directed by Lewis John Carlino.

*The Interpreter* (2005). Produced by Universal Pictures, Directed by Sydney Pollack.

*The Karate Kid* (1984). Produced by Columbia Pictures Corporation, Directed by John G. Avildsen.

*The Namesake* (2006). Produced by Fox Searchlight Pictures, Directed by Mira Nair.

*The Road Home* (2010). Produced and Directed by Rahul Gandotra.

# Organizations

Families in Global Transition: www.figt.org

Military Child Education Coalition: www.militarychild.org

Mu Kappa: www.mukappa.org

Society for Intercultural Education, Training and Research (SIETAR): http://sietarusa.org/

# About the Author

**Lois J. Bushong,** M.S. is a counselor at and owner of Quiet Streams Counseling in Fishers, Indiana; adjunct professor at Indiana Wesleyan University in the Graduate Counseling Department; published author; and international speaker. She has a Masters of Arts in Religion from the Anderson School of Theology; a Masters of Science in Community Counseling from Georgia State University; and is a graduate of Richmont Graduate University (formerly Psychological Studies Institute) in Atlanta, Georgia. Lois is licensed in the state of Indiana in Marriage and Family Therapy and is a Clinical Member and Approved Supervisor of the American Association for Marriage and Family Therapy (AAMFT) and a member of the American Counseling Association (ACA).

Lois is a Third Culture Kid who grew up in Latin America. As a child, she had to learn the customs and culture of her parents' home culture like any foreigner who has come to live in the United States. After her parents repatriated to the United States, Lois returned to Latin America and worked with an international agency for ten years. Upon her return to the United States, she worked with an international agency before she returned to graduate school to be able to effectively counsel individuals, couples, and families.

Lois' clients include internationals, Third Culture Kids, multicultural couples, and those who have not traveled outside of the state. Lois frequently uses her fluency in Spanish in counseling with a growing number of Hispanics who have migrated to central Indiana.

When Lois is not working, she enjoys reading biographies, watching a good mystery movie, listening to "oldies" music, and being an avid sports fanatic.

If you would like to contact Lois Bushong, please use the following:

ljbushong@gmail.com

www.quietstreamscounseling.com

*"Restoring Souls....Empowering Dreams....Reviving Inner Strength"*

t want to want a normal settled extensive life
Didn't anyone edit this book?! So many errors.

48271430R00166

Made in the USA
Middletown, DE
14 September 2017